PRIN̶̶̶̶̶̶̶̶̶̶̶̶̶̶̶̶̶UNTS

Principles of Accounts

R. MOODY
B.A.(Econ), F.C.A.

HULTON EDUCATIONAL PUBLICATIONS

© 1974

R. Moody

ISBN 0 7175 0683 5

First published 1974 by
Hulton Educational Publications Ltd.,
Raans Road, Amersham, Bucks

Made and printed in Great Britain by
William Clowes & Sons, Limited
London, Beccles and Colchester

Contents

Introduction

The Reasons for Keeping Books

The recording of business transactions which can be expressed in terms of a monetary unit is known as book-keeping. The aim of this book is not only to show as clearly as possible how these transactions are entered in the books of a business, but also to underline the theory that lies behind these entries. In a number of instances the book-keeper will have to make his own decisions regarding the recording of specific items and unless the principles are known it would be impossible to accomplish this.

It must be borne in mind that book-keeping systems are not rigid, once the principles are known they can be adapted to suit the needs of the business proprietor. The costs involved in keeping books can be excessive if the information produced is too little or too much for the proprietor's needs. A simple set of books may be all that is required for a sole trader operating a small retail shop, whereas a large company employing thousands of workers and manufacturing a wide variety of products will require a very sophisticated system which will incorporate controls over all items of income and expenditure. Similarly, the books of account may be modified to incorporate the additional information.

However, no matter how big or small the enterprise is, the recording of transactions is vital to the businessman. Even in the smallest of businesses there are numerous changes taking place hourly and it is impossible to retain a clear picture of the overall effect of these movements unless they are committed to paper. For his own information the owner will want to know what assets it possesses at any given time, e.g. an inventory of the business machines and fixtures, the amount owed to the business by debtors, i.e. the names of the customers and the individual amounts due. Similarly, with the business's liabilities he must know how much it owes to outsiders, if this is not known the business could incur large debts which it could not repay within a stipulated time.

The main purpose of being in business is to make a profit and obviously the accurate determination of this figure is essential. Not only is the final figure important but also how it is made up. The major part of the profit is derived from sales, but against these must be set off the cost of goods sold and the various operating expenses; by a comprehensive comparison of these items with past results the owner can see where inefficiencies have occurred—sales falling off, certain expenses rising—and by knowing this information can take steps to maximise his profit in the future. Thus historical figures can be of use to guide the future.

Not only are records important to the owner of a business, but also to third parties who have dealings with it. Persons lending money or supplying goods on credit must be assured that their risk is kept to a minimum, that is, that the security for the amount owed is adequate. Documentary evidence in the nature of well-kept books and accounts will furnish this proof. This is especially true if an approach is made to a bank for a loan or overdraft. If the business is that of a sole trader or partnership the profits are the basis on which income tax is payable The Inland Revenue will require proof of the profit figure put forward by the owners, otherwise the amount may be rejected and an estimated higher figure may be substituted, and thus the owner may pay an increased amount of tax.

In the final event of a business being sold, the prospective purchaser will want to know the current value of the concern, its total assets less its liabilities, and also its profit record over the preceding few years to enable him to determine if the benefit of acquiring the business justifies the price being charged.

In the case of limited companies, books and records must be kept, these requirements being stated in Acts of Parliament. The same applies to partnerships under the Partnership Act of 1890 (though these could be amended by a specific Partnership Agreement). However, even if there is no legal obligation to keep proper books of account, it can be seen from the foregoing that it is in the owner's interests that an adequate system of book-keeping is installed.

The Concepts and Conventions

Because book-keeping is not a natural science it is governed by a number of rules and customs, these are known as concepts and conventions. The purpose of these is to attempt to bring as much objectivity as possible in book-keeping. The reason for objectivity is that greater reliance may be placed on the final results and records and statements may be compared not only with past results but also with statements from other businesses. If every accountant produced accounts according to his own rules, third parties would not be able to judge whether the results were accurate or just an optimistic opinion.

The basic concepts are outlined below, but further descriptions appear in chapters particularly relevant to each.

1 The Monetary Measurement Concept

Entries in the books of a business are restricted to those transactions which can be measured in terms of money, e.g. a payment for a motor vehicle. Other facts which are just as important have to be omitted, the state of health of the owner, or the near expiration of the lease of rented premises. The effect of this is that the accounts never can tell the whole story, and when interpreting accounts or obtaining the whole picture it is necessary to go beyond the figures in the books (see Chapter 19).

2 The Double-entry Concept

All entries are made on the basis of an exchange. For every outgoing there is a benefit, i.e. in the sale of goods though stock is depleted, cash is increased, for the payment of wages the benefit of the workers' labour is received. Every transaction involves two factors, and these are both recorded in the books of account (see Chapter 1).

3 The Business Entity Concept

Only business transactions are entered in the books of account, the business is treated as an entity completely divorced from the owner. This may be difficult to visualise in the case of the sole trader who owns and runs the business without any outside help, but all private expenses and income must be ignored in the books. The owner does have an account in the firm's books (capital account) and this represents his share of the business assets after claims by third parties (see Chapter 3).

4 The Cost Concept

In order that a degree of objectivity is achieved, all transactions entered in the books are recorded at the cost paid or the value received. This does not always reflect the true worth, particularly of assets over a period of time, and in certain conditions adjustments may be made. For example, where stock can be replaced at a value lower than that which was paid for it in the first instance, the market value may be substituted (see Chapter 10).

5 *The Going Concern Concept*

Because different values would apply to the same asset under varying circumstances, the value taken for book-keeping purposes is its worth to the business assuming the business has an infinite life. For example, a piece of machinery may have little or no value if sold on the open market, but its value to the firm may be incalculable. The value to be taken in the accounts would be its cost to the business subject to any necessary adjustments (see Chapters 8 and 9).

6 *The Accrual Concept*

It is not necessarily correct that cash paid and received during a particular period of time represents the true income and expenditure for that duration. In order to obtain true information it is essential that all transactions are accounted for. Electricity bills are rendered in arrear although the benefits of heating and lighting have been received prior to the receipt of the invoice. On the other hand, rent may be paid several months in advance. It is essential that only the benefits actually received must be shown in the accounts, adjustments being made for the payments in advance or in arrear (see Chapter 7).

7 *The Consistency Convention*

Where there is a choice of applications of treatment, the book-keeper should be consistent in his usage. For example, where depreciation is written off assets (see Chapter 8) a choice of methods is available. Once the choice has been made it should be adhered to for as long as possible otherwise the results shown in the accounts would not be comparable over a period of years and reliance could not be placed on the final results.

8 *The Materiality Convention*

A book-keeping system should be designed to give correct and sufficient information to justify the cost of installing it. If an adjustment to the original entries would necessitate a great deal of expense to obtain a figure which is almost negligible and would not distort the accounts to any degree if it was omitted altogether, then that adjustment would not be made. Although the cost of unused stationery may be adjusted for in the cost of stationery purchased during a particular period, it would be almost impossible to value the unused proportion of value in, say, issued ball-point pens or packets of paper clips which have been opened. What represents materiality will vary from firm to firm. A large undertaking with sales of millions of pounds will be able to ignore items which would drastically affect a business whose sales amount to several thousands of pounds.

9 *The Conservatism Convention*

This states that a book-keeper or accountant must not anticipate future profits. Thus stock is always entered at the lower of cost or replacement price, never at selling price, even though the sale may be assured. On the other hand if a loss is foreseeable or anticipated it is accepted that a prudent man would provide against that loss. Examples of this convention is to make a provision for doubtful debts where the amount of debtors at the end of an accounting period is large, or any debtor suspect. Where orders for goods have been placed by customers, the sale should not be recorded until the goods have been despatched, or the title to the goods belongs to the customer.

The Scope and Nature of this Book

This book is intended for students preparing for the General Certificate of Education at "O" level and other similar examinations. The nature of these examinations is changing, more emphasis being placed on theory than was previously considered necessary. This book attempts to describe the mechanical aspect of book-keeping entries with an explanation of accounting thought which lies behind them.

It is hoped that a student who has read and worked through the exercises in the text will have gained sufficient knowledge to answer either a mechanical or essay question on each topic.

The sequence of chapters is arranged so that whilst a student starts at original entries in the books of a firm, within a short period of time he should be in a position to prepare a simple set of final accounts. From this point more complex year-end adjustments are explained. The control aspect of accounting is then considered and the presentation of final accounts in modern form described.

Particular systems are then dealt with, partnership accounts, incomplete records, branch accounts, etc. It must be emphasised that in order to completely understand these systems a student must have acquired a knowledge of the basic material outlined in the first nine chapters. The book ends with a chapter on company accounts.

1 The Ledger and the Double-entry Concept

The ledger is the basic book in which all accounting entries are made. In theory every financial transaction could be entered directly into this book, but in practice certain groups of items are collected in subsidiary books of account and the total entered in the ledger (see Chapter 6). However, until the double-entry principle is fully understood it is best to regard every item as being entered (or posted) in the ledger.

In its simplest form each page of the ledger is divided into two equal identical parts, viz.

DATE	DETAILS	REF.	F.	AMOUNT	DATE	DETAILS	REF.	F.	AMOUNT

The left-hand side of the ledger is known as the debit, the right-hand side the credit. The columns are used for the date of the transaction, a brief description, a reference (so that in case of a query the original document covering the transaction can be located), a folio reference (intimating the corresponding entry), and the amount to be recorded.

The pages of the ledger are divided up into a series of "accounts". These accounts are merely collection centres, recording all items which refer to a particular series of transactions. Thus a trader by looking at the account for fixtures and fittings will be able to see the total amount for this asset and its composition, or by looking at the sales account see what sales have been achieved in a given period.

For the sake of convenience accounts are grouped under three major headings. (i) Real accounts referring to dealings in property, i.e. land, buildings, machinery, fixtures, vehicles etc. (ii) Nominal accounts relating to expenses or income (the names of things), i.e. wages, salaries, rent, rates etc. (iii) Personal accounts (the names of people) referring to debtors, persons owing the firm money, and creditors, persons to whom the firm owes money.

Where the number of accounts is great, or the transactions numerous, the ledger itself may be split into several groups, the private ledger listing real accounts and those relating to the owner, the nominal ledger containing nominal accounts, the debtors' and creditors' ledgers. The ledger rulings may also be modified so as to be able to provide additional information to the participants in the firm. It must be emphasised that accounting or accounting records are not a rigid application, each firm will devise its own system provided that the entries conform to the concepts and conventions and the amount of information required. In the case of a small enterprise certain groups of similar transactions may be grouped together, e.g. rent and rates account or printing, postage, and stationery account.

Because of the unique relationship between the owner and the business, two accounts are included in the ledger. The first is the capital account which consists of the indebtedness of the business to the owner, that is, a business liability. The amount involved is the initial money or goods supplied by the owner plus any profits made by the business (for the benefit of the owner) less drawings. Drawings consist of any cash or goods withdrawn from the business for the owner's own use, or any private expenses paid out of the business's funds. These items are collected in a separate drawings account which is periodically transferred to the capital account.

Every transaction will affect two accounts. When the owner starts the business with cash the two accounts involved are cash and capital. Thus, the business has an asset of funds, but has an equal amount of liabilities, viz. capital. The initial difficulty is the appropriate side of each account to enter the transaction. Although no comprehensive list can be given to encompass all transactions the following table should be a general guide.

DEBITS	CREDITS
Acquisition of assets	Reduction of assets
Reduction of liabilities	Acquisition of liabilities
Expenses	Gains
Receipts of cash	Payments of cash
Purchases	Sales
Losses	

7

Examples of transactions illustrating the double-entry principle are:

	Account to be Debited £	Credited £
(a) The owner pays in £500 to start the business	Cash 500	Capital 500
(b) The business buys a cash register for £90	Fixtures 90	Cash 90
(c) The business pays £200 for goods to sell	Purchases 200	Cash 200
(d) The business sells some of these goods for £175 cash	Cash 175	Sales 175
(e) The business sells the remainder of the goods for £75 on credit to Green	Green 75	Sales 75
(f) The business buys £100 of goods for resale from Brown on credit	Purchases 100	Brown 100

It will be seen from items (c) to (f) above that the purchase and sale of goods necessitate two accounts in the ledger even though the transactions relate to the same commodity. However, it must be realised that the purchase of the goods represents the cost price of them, whereas in the sales account the selling price is recorded. In items (e) and (f) no cash is involved. Instead a debtor—Green— and a creditor—Brown— are involved. These are illustrations of personal accounts. When Green pays for the goods he has bought the entries are a debit to cash account and a credit to his personal account which will then be cleared.

Ledger Accounts—Worked Example

			£
Jan.	1	J. Able starts a business as a greengrocer with cash	800
	2	Paid rent for 3 months	250
	3	Bought goods for resale paying cash	200
	6	Paid wages of shop assistant	20
	6	Week's cash sales	350
	8	Bought goods on credit from J. Baker	120
	9	Bought stationery for cash	10
	10	Withdrew cash for own use	50
	13	Paid wages of shop assistant	20
	13	Cash sales for week	180
	13	Paid J. Baker	120
	15	Bought goods for resale, paying in cash	300
	16	Paid for electric fire	45
	17	Withdrew cash for own use	40
	20	Paid wages of shop assistant	20
	20	Cash sales for week	425

CASH (1)

			£					£
Jan. 1	Capital	2	800	Jan. 2	Rent	3	250
6	Sales	6	350	3	Purchases	4	200
13	Sales	6	180	6	Wages	5	20
20	Sales	6	425	9	Stationery	8	10
				10	Drawings	9	50
				13	Wages	5	20
					J. Baker	7	120
				15	Purchases	4	300
				16	Fixtures	10	45
				17	Drawings	9	40
				20	Wages	5	20

CAPITAL (2)

			£				£
				Jan. 1	Cash	1	800

RENT (3)

			£				£
Jan. 2	Cash	1	250				

PURCHASES (4)

			£				£
Jan. 3	Cash	1	200				
8	J. Baker	7	120				
15	Cash	1	300				

WAGES (5)

			£				£
Jan. 6	Cash	1	20				
13	Cash	1	20				
20	Cash	1	20				

SALES (6)

			£				£
				Jan. 6	Cash	1	350
				13	Cash	1	180
				20	Cash	1	425

J. BAKER (7)

			£				£
Jan. 13	Cash	1	120	Jan. 8	Purchases	4	120

STATIONERY (8)

			£				£
Jan. 9	Cash	1	10				

DRAWINGS (9)

			£				£
Jan. 10	Cash	1	50				
17	Cash	1	40				

FIXTURES (10)

			£				£
Jan. 16	Cash	1	45				

Because the solution shows ledger extracts, each account has been numbered, whereas in practice each account will be entered on a different page in the ledger. This is necessary for completion of the folio column for cross reference purposes. The correct description for each entry is of the utmost importance. In, for example, the opening entry of cash introduced on January 1 the trader must enter it as a debit in the cash account (the acquisition of a business asset), but in order to determine in the future to what this cash relates, the word capital is written in the description column, and the opposite entry appears in ledger account 2 (entered in the folio column). The credit entry is entered in the capital account (the acquisition of a liability) and the origin of this amount was cash which was entered in ledger account 1.

The cash account shows the individual receipts and payments and the description of each transaction. If the trader wishes to know the amount of wages paid during a particular period he will look in account number 5 and find all items relating to this particular type of expenditure. If the ledger is entered promptly, the trader will not only have an up-to-date picture of every type of transaction, but can also refer back to any previous period. He can compare for instance the amount of sales or expenses which took place in a comparative period the previous year with current transactions and discover whether the business efficiency is improving or receding. Exercises dealing with the opening and recording of ledger accounts often appear to students to be long and tedious. In practice once all the accounts have been opened the book-keeper enters transactions on a daily or weekly basis, whereas the student not only has to open the ledger accounts, but also enters up to a month's transactions at the same time. Nevertheless, ledger exercises are very necessary in that the student becomes familiar with debits and credits and should eventually reach the stage where the double-entry concept is thoroughly understood and the recording of entries becomes second nature. Another feature of this type of exercise is that it should inculcate neatness, description and legibility into the student's work which are the basis for all future work.

EXERCISES

1.1
Name the accounts to be debited and credited in each of the following transactions:

	Account to be	
	Debited	*Credited*
(i) J. Robinson starts a retail business with cash of £500		
(ii) The business pays £100 for shop fixtures		
(iii) Rent of £30 is paid for premises		
(iv) Goods for resale to the value of £300 are acquired on credit from W. Jones		
(v) Cash sales are made amounting to £60		
(vi) Wages of £25 are paid		
(vii) J. Robinson takes out £30 for his own use		
(viii) Goods are sold to E. Smith for £120 credit		
(ix) J. Robinson brings in his motor car valued at £750 for business use		
(x) The business pays £10 for stationery		

11

1.2

Write up the ledger accounts in respect of the following transactions:

Jan. 1   F. Green commenced business with cash of £750
     2   Bought goods for resale from B. Sykes on credit for £400
     3   Paid cash for stationery £10
     4   Sold goods for cash amounting to £100
     5   Sold goods to A. Fagin amounting to £200 (on credit)
     6   Paid wages £40
        F. Green withdrew £30 for his own use
        Paid B. Sykes the amount due to him
     8   A. Fagin paid the amount due from him
     9   Sold goods for cash £150
   10   Paid £100 for goods for resale
   11   Paid £25 rent
   12   Sold goods on credit to A. Dodger £90
   13   Paid wages £40
        Sold goods for cash £85

1.3

Write up the ledger accounts for the following transactions:

July 1   J. Brunel commenced business as a furniture remover, bringing in
        cash amounting to £300, and a motor vehicle valued at £1,000
     2   Paid for advertising £20
        Bought petrol and oil for £10 cash
     3   Received £75 for delivering goods
     4   Received £120 for delivering goods
     5   Paid for vehicle repairs £25
     6   Received £80 for delivering goods
     8   Bought new set of tyres £75 on credit from E. Steptow
        Received £60 for delivering goods
     9   Paid £140 for office safe
   10   Received £30 for delivering goods
   11   Paid £10 for stationery
   13   Paid £10 parking fine
        Paid £50 wages
        Received £75 for delivering goods

1.4

State whether you would expect the balances on the following accounts to be debit or credit:

1. Drawings
2. Rent received
3. Carriage on goods bought for resale
4. Bank charges
5. Capital
6. Carriage on goods sold
7. Commission received

8. Insurance
9. Sales
10. Creditors—(amounts owing for goods bought)
11. Debtors—(amounts owing for goods sold)
12. Shop fixtures

1.5
Complete the ledger accounts for the following transactions:

J. Smith commenced business with a bank balance of £675 on 1st May.
During the first weeks of trading the following transactions took place.

May	1	Bought goods for resale paying by cheque £250
		Bought packing materials paying by cheque £12
	2	Sold goods for cash £60
	3	Sold goods for cash £75
	4	Paid rent for shop by cash £25
	5	Bought shop fittings paying by cheque £80
	6	Paid wages in cash £30
		Sold goods for cash £50
	7	Mr. Smith withdrew cash for own use £25
		Paid £75 cash into the bank
	8	Sold goods on credit to F. Jones for £80
		Sold goods for cash £50
	9	Purchased goods for resale paying by cheque £100
	10	Paid advertising charges by cash £15
	11	Sold goods for cash £60
	13	Paid wages in cash £30
		Mr. Smith withdrew cash for own use £25
		Paid into bank all but £15 of the cash

2 The Trial Balance and Revenue Accounts

Balancing Ledger Accounts

The main purpose of book-keeping is to provide a constant stream of information to the owner of a business. The basic entries, as explained in Chapter 1, are recorded in ledger accounts, but as the number of entries increases the accounts become overloaded and important facts become hidden or are difficult to obtain.

In the case of the cash account it is essential that the businessman knows the source of money received and how it has been spent, but of equal importance is how much money is available at any time. Similarly, if he sells goods on credit to a customer he will want to know what goods he has sent (in order to assess the importance of the customer), which goods have been paid for (to check the regularity of payment), and also the amount still owed.

In order to obtain these amounts, i.e. the cash in hand and the total amount due, the accounts must be "balanced". To carry out this procedure it is necessary to determine which side of the account totals the larger amount. Using the cash account constructed in the preceding chapter it can be seen that the debits total £1,755 whilst the credits amount to £1,075, i.e. the debits exceed the credits by £680. The word "balance" is entered in the description column under the last entry on the side having the smaller total amount. Total lines are then drawn under the lowest entry on the account and also directly opposite.

The highest figure (i.e. £1,755) is entered on both sides, but as the credit side does not total this amount the difference of £680 must be entered against the description "balance" thus ensuring that both debit and credit columns agree. In order to complete the double entry the figure of £680 must be entered below the total line on the opposite side to the original entry and the word "balance" written in the description column. This figure represents the cash in hand when the account was balanced. The fact that the account is now renewed with a starting figure of £680 debit summarises the original entries where it was discovered that the total debits exceeded the total credits by this amount.

The cash account will now look like:

Cash Account

		£				£
Jan. 1 Capital	2	800	Jan. 2 Rent	3	250
6 Sales	6	350	3 Purchases	4	200
13 Sales	6	180	6 Wages	5	20
20 Sales	6	425	9 Stationery	8	10
			10 Drawings	9	50
			13 Wages	5	20
			J. Baker	7	120
			15 Purchases	4	300
			16 Fixtures	10	45
			17 Drawings	9	40
			20 Wages	4	20
			Balance	C/D	680
		£1,755			£1,755
Jan. 20 Balance	B/D	680			

There are four points to bear in mind when balancing accounts.

1. The total amounts must be on the same horizontal line.
2. The total must be entered on the line immediately below the lowest entry in the account in order that no additional entries can be made after the account is balanced. It is usual for a line to be drawn through the "details" column on the side which has the fewest entries for the same reason.
3. The double-entry principle is fulfilled in that two entries are made, debit and credit, one above the total and one on the opposite side of the account below the total.
4. The description of the balance refers to the figure below the total. In the above example it will be a debit balance. This is because originally the debit entries exceeded the credit entries.

In some cases the account can be balanced and closed at the same time. This particularly applies to personal accounts, viz:

G. SMITH

		£			£
Feb. 1 Sales	6	100	Feb. 10 Cash	1	325
2 Sales	6	150			
3 Sales	6	75			
		£325			£325

15

It can be seen from the above account that G. Smith bought three separate deliveries of goods from the business, but paid in full for them on 10th February. The account balances without any adjustment so is merely totalled and "closed off".

There is no compulsion to balance the accounts at set times, it is purely a matter of convenience. The cash and bank accounts may be balanced daily, weekly or monthly depending on the number of entries made. Personal accounts may only be balanced when payments are made or received, whilst nominal accounts may be balanced yearly.

The Trial Balance

Due to the numerous entries that have to be recorded in a book-keeping system it is advisable that periodic checks are made on the mathematical accuracy of the entries (or in accounting terms "postings"). For this purpose a TRIAL BALANCE is taken out.

Because book-keeping is based on the double-entry principle, each transaction being recorded as a debit and as a credit, it follows that the total debits must equal the total credits, or that the debit balances equal the credit balances. If a summary is drawn up listing all the accounts in the ledger together with the balances contained in each, the totals must agree. If not, then an entry must have been incorrectly recorded or omitted.

It must be emphasized that the trial balance is not in itself part of the double entry, it is merely a separate check on the recording of transactions within the system. Furthermore, it is not set out in ledger form but with two columns on the right-hand side of the paper, one showing debits and the other showing credits.

Using the figures in Chapter 1 an example of a trial balance would be:

Trial Balance as at 20th January

		(*Debit*) £	(*Credit*) £
Cash	1	680	
Capital	2		800
Rent	3	250	
Purchases	4	620	
Wages	5	60	
Sales	6		955
J. Baker	7	—	—
Stationery	8	10	
Drawings	9	90	
Fixtures	10	45	
		£1,755	£1,755

The trial balance will only show that certain types of error have been avoided. These errors are:

1. Where the double entry has not been completed for any one transaction, e.g. the debit has been entered but the credit has been omitted.
2. Where a particular balance has not been entered below the total line.
3. Where additions have been wrongly calculated in individual accounts.
4. Where totals have been incorrectly brought forward.
5. Where figures have been transposed in part of the double entry, e.g. a debit of £791 entered as £971 on the credit side.

It must not be assumed that because a trial balance "balances" the books of account are correct. The trial balance only proves that where a transaction has been recorded the double-entry principle has been correctly applied, and that additions and balances are mathematically true. Individual accounts may be wrong because an item has been posted to the wrong account, or a transaction may have been entirely omitted from the books.

Errors which are not shown by a trial balance comprise:

1. *Errors of Omission*—where the original transaction is not entered in the books. If a purchase invoice has been mislaid, the debit entry in the purchases account would not be entered, and also the credit entry in the suppliers' account would also be missing. Both accounts would therefore be understated.
2. *Errors of Original Entry*—where the original entry is incorrectly recorded. If a payment of £78 for wages is entered in the cash account as £87 this latter amount would be debited to wages account. Thus both entries are overstated by £9.
3. *Complete Reversal of Entry*—where each account involved has the entry recorded on the wrong side. For example, if rent has been received from a tenant the correct entries should be to debit cash account and credit rent received account. But if instead cash has been credited and rent paid account debited, the books would still balance.
4. *Compensating Errors*—where two errors cancel each other out. For example, where a credit balance has been overstated because of an addition error, but a debit balance has also been overstated by the same amount.
5. *Errors of Principle*—where the double entry has been applied, but one of the entries has been entered in the wrong type of account. For example, the purchase of a motor vehicle has been entered in the purchases account instead of in a separate asset account.

17

6. *Errors of Commission*—similar to an error of principle except that one entry has been made in the wrong account of a similar type. For example, where sales have been made on credit to a customer, the sales account has been correctly credited but the debit entry posted to C. Shaw Ltd. instead of C. Shaw & Sons.

Although the trial balance does not point out any of the above errors other checks will be described later in the book which will help to detect most of these discrepancies.

Revenue Accounts

At least once a year the businessman must prepare a set of final accounts. These consist of revenue accounts in order to determine the profit or loss for the period, and a balance sheet showing the financial position of the business at the end of the period.

The revenue accounts consist of two inter-related summary accounts named the trading account and the profit and loss account. The former determines the gross profit on trading, i.e. the difference between sales and cost of goods sold; the latter determines the net profit, i.e. the gross profit plus any other gains, less the expenses of running the business.

Revenue accounts comprise those ledger accounts relating to expenses, purchases and losses together with sales and gains. The remaining accounts, being assets and liabilities, are dealt with in the following chapter. A "rule of thumb" method to determine which debit accounts are expenses (revenue) and which are assets is to decide whether the benefit derived is past or still present. Payment for wages (expense) is for the workers' labour which has been completed almost as soon as the payment is made whereas a payment for a motor vehicle (asset) is a long-term benefit which at the date of the balance sheet is still in existence.

The revenue accounts are closed off by transferring the balance on them either to the trading account or profit and loss account, e.g.

Sales Account

		£				£
Dec. 31	Transfer trading a/c	5,500	Sept. 30	Amount	B/fwd	4,000
			Oct. 31	Sales	C/B	400
			Nov. 30	Sales	C/B	500
			Dec. 31	Sales	C/B	600
		£5,500				£5,500

It can be seen that the trading and profit and loss accounts are a continuation of the double-entry system. In the above example the sales account is debited with £5,500 and the trading account credited with the same amount.

If we assume, for the time being, that there is no closing stock of goods for resale, and using the trial balance previously computed in this chapter, the trading and profit and loss accounts will be constructed as follows:

Trading and Profit and Loss Accounts
Period 1st–20th January

		£			£
Purchases		620	Sales		955
Gross profit	C/D	335			
		955			955
Rent		250	Gross profit	B/D	335
Wages		60			
Stationery		10			
Net profit		15			
		£335			£335

The gross profit is entered as a debit in the trading account (being the balancing figure) and as a credit in the profit and loss account. The net profit is debited in the profit and loss account and credited to the owner's capital account as the business owes this amount to the owner, for it cannot keep this gain for itself.

Closing Stock

It is usual for an adjustment to be made in the trading account for opening and closing stocks, these being purchases of goods for resale which have not been disposed of at the close of business. The closing stock figure does not appear in the trial balance, but is incorporated in the final accounts, being debited to a stock account and credited to the trading account, though in practice it is more usual to deduct this figure from the purchases on the debit side. A deduction on one side of the account has the same effect as entering the item on the opposite side.

To illustrate this adjustment the entries are shown below.

19

Stock Account

Year 1		£
Dec. 31	Trading Account (closing stock)	2,000

Trading Account (Year 1)	
Purchases	10,000
Less Closing stock	2,000
Cost of goods sold	£8,000

The purchases in the trading account are a direct transfer from the purchases account. The closing stock is now incorporated in the ledger and appears as the opening stock for Year 2. Thus it will appear in the trial balance extracted at the end of Year 2 and will be transferred to the debit of the trading account.

To show the effect of this Year 2 is illustrated below:

Stock Account

Year 1		£	Year 2		£
Dec. 31	Trading account (closing stock)	2,000	Dec. 31	Trading account (opening stock)	2,000
Year 2					
Dec. 31	Trading account (closing stock)	3,500			

Trading Account (Year 2)	
	£
Opening stock	2,000
Purchases	22,000
	24,000
Less Closing stock	3,500
Cost of goods sold	£20,500

It can be seen that the stock account now contains once again only the closing stock at the end of the year. The figure of £20,500 for cost of goods sold is explained by the fact that the firm started off trading with goods valued at £2,000 and bought during the year a further £22,000 worth, making a total of £24,000 which it could sell. However, at the end of the year it still possessed £3,500 of these goods so that the cost of goods actually sold was £20,500.

The items debited to the trading account require further mention. These debits should consist of all expenses required to bring the goods to a saleable condition. This means that not only must the cost of goods themselves be entered, but also carriage paid in respect of purchases (carriage inwards) and warehouse wages. All other expenses, e.g. administrative and selling, must appear in the profit and loss account.

The Accounting Period

The periods covered by the final accounts should be of uniform duration, usually of one year. The net profit calculated forms the basis on which income tax is paid to the Inland Revenue by the owner each year. This income tax, although it may be paid through the business bank account, is the personal liability of the owner and should be charged to his drawings account. It is not a business expense.

Apart from the necessity of computing annual final accounts for income tax purposes, it is also helpful to the trader in enabling him to compare profits, income and expenditure if the periods are of equal length. He will be able to see at a glance which expenses have increased or decreased by examining several sets of accounts, whereas if the periods are of unequal duration this would be impossible.

For his own benefit interim final accounts may be prepared either monthly or quarterly. These would be particularly useful if the business was seasonal, for example, in a retail clothing shop where sales of summer and winter clothes are made. Apart from these two aspects of trading it will be found that certain months are less busy than other months, so that not only will the owner be able to compare similar periods, but will also be able to plan in advance his purchases, the necessity for hiring part-time staff, and the best time for clearance sales.

EXERCISES

2.1
    (a) Using the information in exercise 1–2 balance the accounts and extract a trial balance.
    (b) Using the information in exercise 1–3 balance the accounts and extract a trial balance.
    (c) Using the information in exercise 1–5 balance the accounts and extract a trial balance.

2.2
The following transactions are to be entered in the ledger for May. The accounts are to be balanced and a trial balance extracted.

    May 1   Started business with £1,000 in the bank and £75 cash in hand
               Paid rent by cheque £80

21

    2   Bought goods on credit from the following persons: A. Abel £125,
        B. Baker £250, C. Charles £175
    3   Sold goods on credit to V. Victor £200, W. Williams £120
    4   Bought motor van paying by cheque £600
    5   Sold goods for cash £80
    6   Paid wages in cash £50
    8   Paid motor expenses in cash £25
    9   Bought goods on credit from B. Baker £200
    10 Paid sundry expenses in cash £8
    11 Sold goods on credit to W. Williams £80
    12 Paid advertising expenses in cash £12
    13 Paid wages in cash £50
    15 Sold goods for cash £75
    16 Paid B. Baker by cheque the amount due to him
    17 W. Williams paid us £40 in cash
    20 Paid wages in cash £50
    22 Sold goods for cash £120
        Bought goods on credit from A. Abel £100
    23 Paid motor expenses in cash £25
    24 Paid A. Abel the amount due to him by cheque
    25 W. Williams paid us a further £40 in cash
        Paid sundry expenses in cash £15
    27 Paid wages in cash £50
    29 V. Victor paid us £200 by cheque
    30 Withdrew £80 for own use (in cash)
        Paid all but £60 of the cash into bank

2.3

Record the following details for the month of February, 19x9 and extract a trial
balance as at 28th February, 19x9.

    Feb. 1 Started business with £3,000 in the bank
          2 Bought goods on credit from R. Robin £250, T. Thrush £150
             Sold goods £60 for cash
          3 Sold goods on credit to L. Lark £80, S. Sparrow £120
          4 Paid sundry expenses £14 in cash
             Paid rent £25 in cash
          5 Sold goods on credit to S. Sparrow £90
          6 Paid wages in cash £20
          8 Sold goods for cash £80
          9 Bought goods on credit from T. Thrush £130
         10 Paid sundry expenses £20 in cash
         11 Bought goods for cash £50
         12 Sold goods to L. Lark £40
         13 Withdrew £50 cash from bank
             Paid wages in cash £30
         15 Paid T. Thrush £280 by cheque
         16 Sold goods for cash £60
         17 Paid sundry expenses £10 in cash

18 Received a cheque from L. Lark for the amount due
20 Paid wages £30 in cash
22 Sold goods on credit to L. Lark £50
23 Paid advertising expenses £18 in cash
25 Sold goods for cash £75
26 Bought goods on credit from R. Robin £250
27 Paid wages in cash £30
    Banked all but £20 of the remaining cash

2.4

From the following trial balance prepare a trading and profit and loss account for the year ended 31st July, 19x5.

Trial Balance as at 31st July, 19x5

	£	£
Sales		8,000
Purchases	4,000	
Carriage inwards	200	
Wages and salaries	1,000	
Heating and lighting	400	
Motor expenses	500	
Rent	400	
Rates	250	
Sundry expenses	120	
Carriage outwards	300	
Sundry assets	3,830	
Capital introduced		3,000
	£11,000	£11,000

2.5

From the following trial balance extracted on 31st May, 19x2, prepare a trading and profit and loss account for the year ended as on that date.

	£	£
Purchases	16,000	
Motor expenses	780	
Rent paid	800	
Rent received		200
Commission received		2,000
Salaries and wages	8,000	
Insurance	120	
Sundry expenses	200	
Sales		26,800
Sundry assets	5,100	
Capital introduced		2,000
	£31,000	£31,000
Closing stock valued at	£2,000	

2.6

From the following list of balances extracted at 30th April, 19x7, compute a trial balance and prepare a trading and profit and loss account for the year ended 30th April, 19x7.

	£
Sales	33,000
Wages and salaries	9,000
Rent paid	600
Rates	250
Insurance	175
Carriage inwards	375
Carriage outwards	500
Purchases	17,000
Sundry expenses	350
Lighting and heating	250
Advertising	70
Motor expenses	430
Commission received	2,000
Rent received	300
Sundry assets	7,300
Capital introduced	5,000
Drawings	4,000

The closing stock was valued at £2,500

3 The Balance Sheet

The balance sheet is a statement drawn up after the trading and profit and loss accounts have been completed. It consists of a summary of the balances remaining in the ledger after the revenue accounts have been closed off. In its conventional form the balance sheet is constructed in a similar form to a ledger account. On one side are listed all the types of assets the firm owns, and on the other side the firm's liabilities, i.e. those persons who have a claim on those assets.

There are three major differences between the balance sheet and the trading and profit and loss account.

1. The balance sheet (like the trial balance) is not part of the double-entry system. The items tabulated in the balance sheet represent the ledger accounts still in operation and which form the starting point for the following year's transactions.
2. It is customary to show the asset balances (which are debit balances in the ledger) on the right-hand side of the balance sheet, and the liabilities (credit balances) on the left-hand side. This method of presentation may be difficult to understand and cause confusion, but if it is realised that double-entry principles do not apply to the balance sheet then its construction can be varied at will.
3. The balance sheet shows the position of the business at a specific moment in time, whereas the trading and profit and loss accounts show a summary of transactions covering a particular period of time. The heading for the trading and profit and loss account should always state this period, e.g. "for the year ended 31st December, 19x1". The balance sheet should give the date of extractions, e.g. "at 31st December, 19x1". In this respect the profit and loss account can be likened to a movie film of events and the balance sheet to a still photograph of a particular situation.

When listing the assets and liabilities in a balance sheet a certain procedure has been adopted in practice, though in the case of sole traders no laws have been enacted to enforce this practice. The assets are divided into two main classes—fixed, and current assets. Fixed assets are those which generally have a long life, are of a more permanent nature, and are necessary for the long-term continuance of the business. Examples of these are property, equipment and vehicles. Current assets are those which have a relatively short life or are constantly changing their constitution and are necessary for the day to day trading of the business. Examples of current assets are stock, debtors, and cash. Although the totals of these individual assets may remain within specific limits the constituent parts are constantly changing. Stock is being sold and replenished, new debtors are being acquired, whilst old debtors are settling their accounts, and bank and cash balances are constantly changing.

Within each class individual types of assets are listed in a particular order. Fixed assets are recorded according to their length of life, e.g. firstly freehold land and buildings, secondly fixtures and fittings, thirdly plant and machinery, and fourthly motor vehicles. Current assets are recorded in order of least liquidity, i.e. starting with that asset which of the trading assets is the most difficult to convert to cash. The accepted order is stock, debtors, bank balance, and finally cash.

Liabilities are divided into three groups. Capital, which represents the firm's indebtedness to the owner. This liability is a permanent one as it will exist until the firm is closed down. Next are grouped long-term liabilities which are those debts which do not have to be paid within twelve months after the date of the balance sheet. Finally, current liabilities which represent the short-term debts of the business and consist of creditors and bank overdraft.

It is important that the sequence of listing the items in the balance sheet is adhered to, for it enables comparison, between one year and another, or between two firms, to be more easily accomplished. It is also important when assessing the strengths or weaknesses of the firm. This latter aspect will be dealt with in a later chapter, but for the moment it can be appreciated that to pay the current liabilities and meet day-to-day running expenses of the business the firm should have sufficient current assets, particularly debtors, bank, and cash. If it cannot provide sufficient funds to pay off its immediate debts it must sell some of its fixed assets. If it has to do this, the operating potential of the business contracts and therefore future profits will decline.

A typical balance sheet would be shown as on the opposite page.

Several items in this balance sheet require explanation.

The capital account is shown in some detail and reflects a summary of the ledger account. It starts off with the cash introduced or the balance brought forward from the previous year. The profit which the business

JOHN SMITH
Balance Sheet as at 31st December, 19x1

	£	£		£	£
Capital			Fixed assets		
Opening balance	5,000		Freehold property	2,000	
Profit for year	2,000		Fixtures and		
	7,000		fittings	500	
Less Drawings	1,500		Plant and		
			machinery	1,000	
		5,500	Motor vehicles	1,200	
					4,700
			Current assets		
Long-term liabilities			Stock	3,000	
Loan from W. Jones		2,000	Debtors	1,000	
Current liabilities			Bank	750	
Creditors		2,000	Cash	50	
					4,800
		£9,500			£9,500

has made (which belongs to the owner) is added. However, if the owner has drawn any amounts out of the business, the total must be deducted to give a true balance which the firm owes to him. In the ledger the balance on drawings account is transferred to the capital account to reconcile with the figure in the balance sheet.

If the business has suffered a loss, this would have been deducted from the opening balance as the loss has to be borne by the owner thus reducing the amount he is owed by the firm.

Individual debtors and creditors are not shown in the balance sheet, this is because only types of assets and liabilities are shown. The balance sheet shows an overall picture of the state of affairs existing at a particular time. If further information is required regarding an item, this will be contained in the ledger account. Details of each vehicle will be found in the motor vehicle account and individual debtors will be found in their separate accounts in the ledger.

In certain circumstances assets and liabilities may be difficult to allocate to a particular group. A car-sales business will have certain cars which it uses itself, but the majority of cars will be held for resale. In this case the former will be regarded as fixed assets whilst the latter will be classified as stock and therefore a current asset. A business that acquires shares may intend them to be a long-term investment (a fixed asset) or may have bought them because it has an over-sufficient bank balance and wants to earn interest and also speculate against inflation, but nevertheless, intends to sell them when the need arises. Thus the investment can be regarded as a current asset.

Long-term liabilities will eventually become current when they are nearing the date for repayment and will have to be shown as such in the balance sheet. It is very important that items appear in their right class otherwise the balance sheet will not show a true view of the financial position.

Although at this stage it is advisable to regard the balance sheet in the way described, alternative methods of presentation are common. Banking companies who are perhaps more interested in liquidity (to meet clients' cheques) list their assets in order of liquidity starting with cash and ending with freehold property. This is a complete reversal of the commercial and industrial presentation, but it illustrates the business governing the accounts and not being subject to them. The accounts should emphasise what is required by the business.

Balance sheets of foreign companies reverse the balance sheet listing the assets on the left and the liabilities on the right, but this practice has not been accepted in this country. The modern approach has swept away the account form of the balance sheet and presents it in vertical or narrative style, and this form will be discussed in Chapter 13.

The Business Entity Concept

The balance sheet illustrates the concept of a separate entity or being, where the firm has a life of its own. In law no distinction is made between a sole trader and his business. If a dispute arises, the owner has to take legal action, not the firm. If the firm becomes insolvent (i.e. unable to meet its debts), the firm's creditors have a claim on the private assets of the owner. This is unlike a limited company which does have a separate entity. The owner's assets which are used primarily for the business are to be segregated from his other personal assets and recorded in the business's books.

This means that though the balance sheet records the assets as belonging to the business, they do in fact belong to the owner. Some of the assets may be registered in the owner's name though the name of the business may be different. If in fact a sole trader trades under a name other than his own, it must be registered under the Registration of Business Names Act (1916).

Some assets may be used by the owner partly for business purposes and partly for private purposes. Examples of this is where the business

28

is a lock-up shop, the shop premises being on the street front, but private accommodation being located at the rear or above the shop. A car may be used for delivering goods, but also used for private jaunts at the weekend. If all expenses relating to these assets are paid by the business then a distinction must be made to show only the business proportion, the private part being transferred to drawings. The proportion is usually agreed by the Inspector of Taxes. An example of this would be:

Rent Account

	£		£
Total rent for year	1,200	Transfer drawings private proportion	550
		Transfer P & L a/c business proportion	650
	£1,200		£1,200

Careful scrutiny must also be made of payments out of the business bank or cash accounts to ensure that only business items are bought. If a record player is purchased by a greengrocery business it is evident that this is a personal acquisition of the owner rather than being of benefit to the business. The cost must therefore be charged (or debited) to drawings account.

It is claimed that book-keeping is an act of stewardship, for in regarding the business as a separate entity a record is kept, of assets, and claims on those assets. The balance sheet is a summary of that stewardship as it shows the assets which are used exclusively or to a greater degree by the business and are regarded as belonging to the business. The liabilities show the claims on those assets.

In the balance sheet illustrated in this chapter the assets total £9,500. Of this figure £2,000 is owed to creditors and a further £2,000 to W. Jones. This leaves £5,500 belonging to John Smith, the owner, and represents his stake in the business. This figure is known as the owner's equity and is equal to the net worth of the business. The latter represents the value an outsider would pay for the business, as it is the amount left after the business has paid off its debts to third parties.

Unfortunately, the balance sheet has its limitations. It can only show transactions which are measurable in terms of money. It does not show intangible items which may drastically affect the business. A small business is inevitably bound up with the owner; if his health is precarious, then the business is precarious. The balance sheets of two firms may be identical, but one firm may have greater prospects because of the business acumen of the owner. The imminent demolition of the business property may close the business down, or new legislation curtail future trading.

Even items which are measurable in terms of money may be misleading. Generally all items are recorded at cost so that comparisons can be made. This is only true if the measure of recording is a stable monetary unit. Unfortunately this is not true. Measures for weight and length remain the same irrespective of time, but the value of the pound varies from year to year. Thus, identical assets may be recorded at different prices, so that the balance sheet is a mixture of "old" pounds and "new" pounds. It may appear that the quantity of stock has increased during a particular period, whereas the quantity has remained constant, but the price at which it was purchased has increased.

Capital and Revenue Expenditure

Up to now capital has been taken to mean the amount introduced into the business by the owner. However, capital can also mean the expenditure on fixed assets as opposed to revenue expenditure which relates to expenses. It is most important to be able to differentiate between the two classes of expenditure. If a capital item is regarded as revenue, it will eventually be transferred to the profit and loss account and the profits will be understated. Conversely, if a revenue item is posted to a capital account, the profit will be overstated. In both cases the balance sheet will be incorrect. In the first both the capital account and fixed assets will be reduced; in the second, both will be increased.

The acquisition of fixed assets will obviously be a capital item, but the difficulty is calculating the cost of the asset. It may not consist solely of the cost of the asset obtained, but in addition the charges connected with bringing the asset to the business premises and the costs of installing it. Some large items of machinery need to be embedded in concrete, whilst others may require a complex system of wiring. All costs associated with the asset up to the moment of operating can be regarded as capital.

Another difficulty exists when improvements are carried out to an existing asset to either increase its operation efficiency or reduce the costs of operation. Any expenditure incurred in improving an existing asset is capital. Repairs to an asset which are necessary to bring it up to its original condition are, however, treated as revenue. Extreme caution is required when a faulty part is replaced with a modified version which improves on the original performance of the asset. In this case the expenditure is part capital, part revenue, and an arbitrary allocation of the payment made, the usual basis being to find out the cost of replacing the faulty part with a similar one and treating this cost as revenue and debiting the excess amount to capital.

Other items may, at first glance, be taken as revenue items, but which are in fact capital. Newspaper advertising either for staff or trading is revenue, but an advertising sign, being of a more permanent nature, is capital. Legal fees are more complex. If fees are paid for collecting debts or drawing up employees' service agreements, they are concerned with the day to day running of the business and they are revenue. If they are paid in respect of the purchase of a fixed asset, they should be capitalised and added to the cost of the asset.

In other cases the distinction between capital and revenue is even more obscure. If a business purchases a plot of land in order to build a factory, not only must the cost of the land be capitalised, but also the cost of preparing the land for development, e.g. the demolition of existing premises. If the business uses its own labour to build the factory, the wages paid to the employees engaged in the work should be capitalised as well as the cost of the materials used, viz:

A business trading as builders' contractors acquires property to be used as its own offices and then decides to improve it; given the information below:

Cost of property	£3,000
Legal costs re transfer of freehold	£500
Materials used in building extension	£1,000
Wages of men engaged in work	£1,200
Administration charges re above extension	£150

the ledger account would show:

Freehold Property Account

	£			£
Jan. 1 Cash—Cost of property	3,000	Jan. 31 Balance C/D		5,850
Legal cost	500			
31 Transfer–Purchases	1,000			
–Wages	1,200			
–Administration expenses	150			
	£5,850			£5,850
Jan. 31 Balance B/D	£5,850			

The cost of the original property and the legal fees can be charged directly to the account. Materials will have originally been debited to

purchases account as these are used in the ordinary course of trading, so
that the cost of materials used in the improvement must be transferred
from the revenue account to the asset account. This also applies to the
wages and administration expenses. The total value of the freehold
property therefore totals £5,850.

Worked Example of Final Accounts

From the following trial balance of B. Small as on 30th June, 19x4,
draw up a trading and profit and loss account for the year ended
30th June, 19x4, and a balance sheet as at that date.

	£	£
Sales		35,000
Purchases	17,642	
Salaries and wages	5,745	
Packing and postage	392	
Rent	1,000	
Rates	550	
Insurance	273	
Carriage inward	843	
Carriage outwards	1,251	
Motor expenses	2,337	
Sundry expenses	493	
Commission received		1,500
Debtors	4,000	
Stock as at 1st July, 19x3	6,462	
Creditors		2,500
Buildings	4,000	
Machinery	2,000	
Motor vehicles	3,200	
Loan from D. Butcher		6,000
Capital		11,588
Drawings	3,000	
Cash in hand	600	
Cash in bank	2,800	
	£56,588	£56,588

The closing stock was valued at £7,488.

B. SMALL
Trading and Profit and Loss Account
Year ended 30th June, 19x4

	£		£
Opening stock	6,462	Sales	35,000
Purchases	17,642		
	24,104		
Less Closing stock	7,488		
	16,616		
Carriage inwards	843		
Cost of goods sold	17,459		
Gross profit	17,541		
	£35,000		£35,000
Salaries and wages	5,745	Gross profit	17,541
Packing and postage	392	Commission received	1,500
Rent	1,000		
Rates	550		
Insurance	273		
Carriage outwards	1,251		
Motor expenses	2,337		
Sundry expenses	493		
Net profit	7,000		
	£19,041		£19,041

Balance Sheet as at 30th June, 19x4

	£	£		£	£
Capital account			Fixed assets		
Balance at 1.7.x3	11,588		Buildings	4,000	
Add Profit for year	7,000		Machinery	2,000	
	18,588		Motor vehicles	3,200	
Less Drawings	3,000				9,200
		15,588	Current assets		
Loan D. Butcher		6,000	Stock	7,488	
Current liabilities			Debtors	4,000	
Creditors		2,500	Balance at bank	2,800	
			Cash in hand	600	
					14,888
		£24,088			£24,088

33

PRINCIPLES OF ACCOUNTS

EXERCISES

3.1
B. Jones extracted the following trial balance on 31st December, 19x1, after the first year's trading. You are required to prepare a trading and profit and loss account for the year, and a balance sheet as at 31st December, 19x1.

	£	£
Purchases	12,600	
Sales		20,000
Salaries and wages	4,000	
Sundry expenses	750	
Rates	300	
Carriage inwards	150	
Carriage outwards	200	
Bank	1,000	
Debtors	1,500	
Creditors		1,000
Premises	3,000	
Motor vehicles	2,000	
Fixtures and fittings	500	
Drawings	2,000	
Capital introduced		7,000
	£28,000	£28,000

The closing stock of goods has been valued at £3,000

3.2
From the following trial balance of P. Smith draw up a trading and profit and loss account for the year ended 30th June, 19x3, and a balance sheet as at that date.

	£	£
Purchases	17,450	
Bank overdraft		2,000
Debtors	2,000	
Sundry expenses	300	
Rates	475	
Fixtures and fittings	500	
Motor vehicles	1,000	
Salaries and wages	6,250	
Drawings	1,000	
Creditors		1,000
Sales		24,850
Capital introduced		2,350
Rent	725	
Insurance	500	
	£30,200	£30,200

The closing stock is valued at £7,500

34

3.3

From the following trial balance of M. Williams draw up a trading and profit and loss account for the year ended 30th September, 19x7, and a balance sheet as at that date.

	£	£
Purchases	8,430	
Sales		12,000
Postages and telephone	275	
Motor expenses	490	
Salaries and wages	3,700	
Sundry expenses	240	
Rent	800	
Rates	360	
Carriage inwards	450	
Carriage outwards	680	
Insurance	640	
Balance at bank	2,000	
Loan from J. Swift		2,000
Stock at 1st Oct., 19x6	4,800	
Debtors	2,000	
Creditors		1,740
Motor vehicles	2,400	
Fixtures and fittings	750	
Drawings	3,000	
Capital—balance 1st Oct., 19x6		15,275
	£31,015	£31,015

Closing stock was valued at £6,000

3.4

The following list of balances was extracted from the books of G. Green at 31st March, 19x2. Prepare a trading and profit and loss account for the year ended 31st March, 19x2, and a balance sheet as at that date.

	£
Salaries and wages	12,300
Premises	8,000
Creditors	4,000
Carriage outwards	800
Purchases	36,310
Postages and telephone	790
Fixtures and fittings	1,300
Carriage inwards	600
Sales	58,000
Motor expenses	1,530
Bank overdraft	2,000
Stock as at 1st April, 19x1	14,000
Debtors	3,000
Sundry expenses	750

	£
Rates	1,200
Loan from W. White	4,000
Capital as at 1st April, 19x1	20,680
Drawings	4,000
Insurance	900
Motor vehicles	3,200

The closing stock was valued at £12,000

3.5
State whether the following items are capital or revenue expenditure and explain the reasons for your decisions.

(a) Cost of re-siting machinery to obtain greater operating efficiency.
(b) Delivery charges for purchase of new motor vehicle.
(c) Renewal of office radiator because of damage to the old one.
(d) Legal costs incurred in suing a supplier for breach of contract.
(e) Replacing worn-out tyres on a vehicle with a better type of tyre, e.g. radial instead of cross-ply.
(f) Cost of painting name of business and trademark on delivery vans.
(g) Cost of insulating roof and walls of existing offices.
(h) Cost of replacing cinder drive with one of concrete.
(i) Money paid to an employee in lieu of notice.
(j) Cost of hiring a motor van.

3.6
M. W. Duffield gives you the following figures and asks you to prepare from his balance sheet as at 30th June, 19x4:

Motor van £785, sundry creditors £2,073, stock £3,065, land and buildings £2,850, sundry debtors £2,500, cash at bank £647, loan from B. Just £5,000, fixtures and fittings £685, cash in hand £30. He does not know the balance on his capital account.

3.7
Mr. Livingstone gives you the following items which represent balances at the end of his first year's trading. He requires a balance sheet constructed in good style. He commenced trading on 1st January, 19x8:

Cash in hand £85, bank overdraft £1,250, motor vehicles £2,400, creditors £1,890, premises £6,000, loan from N. East £3,000, debtors £1,500, office furniture £675, stock £4,200.

Mr. Livingstone tells you that he introduced capital of £6,000 and has withdrawn £1,290 for his own use.

4 The Division of the Ledger—Cash Book and Petty Cash Book

When a business operates at a low level or where there are relatively few transactions, all entries can be entered in the ledger by one book-keeper. As the business grows the number of transactions increase and it becomes more difficult for one person to cope with all the work involved. Even if more book-keepers are employed the problem remains, for they will not all be able to use the ledger at the same time.

The answer to this dilemma is to divide the ledger into a number of separate sections so that several persons can work simultaneously entering and posting transactions. The consequences of doing this are that the work can be completed in less time and each individual can specialise in a particular aspect of book-keeping. This in turn should lead to greater efficiency and accuracy. A form of internal control can be introduced which will deter error, fraud, or theft if duties are so allocated that there is a check carried out by one person on another person's work. If one book-keeper is responsible for recording and posting credit sales whilst another records and posts cash received, should one transaction be incorrectly recorded or omitted the error should be discovered. Each debtor's account must eventually balance, so that if cash received is not recorded in the ledger, the account would show a debt owing. The person recording the cash cannot cancel the original sales invoice as it exceeds his duty.

The number of entries recorded in each account will vary considerably. Rent, rates, and insurance accounts will have very few items whereas cash, bank, sales, and purchases accounts will have numerous entries. This is because all transactions have to be paid for eventually, and if a business is conducted on credit, for every entry in each debtor's account there must be a reciprocal entry in the sales account. Unless some means can be devised to minimise the number of postings the business would have to keep acquiring new ledgers to replace those that have been completed. Besides reducing the entries in overcrowded ledger accounts work would become more efficient in that less time is taken to post entries.

Another important feature of dividing the ledger into separate sections is that should any errors be discovered when a trial balance is extracted, those errors can be located in a particular section. Each section, though distinct, is linked to the whole system. A shorter time is taken to ascertain the fault because of the fewer items that need to be checked. This aspect of accounting is known as Control Accounting and is dealt with in Chapter 12.

The features described above are dealt with as follows:

1. Extracting the cash and bank accounts from the ledger and combining them both in a separate book known as the Cash Book.
2. Isolating still further the smaller cash payments and entering these in a Petty Cash Book.
3. Removing all personal accounts from the main (or general) ledger, and keeping them in separate Debtors and Creditors Ledgers (see Chapter 12).
4. Summarising similar transactions in memorandum books, termed Day Books or Journals. This particularly applies to credit sales and purchases (see Chapter 6).

The "Two-column" Cash Book

It must be remembered that the cash book is an extension of the ledger, as it consists solely of the two accounts—cash and bank—combined in a separate book. Any transactions which have to be entered in the cash book form part of the double-entry concept. A debit entry in the cash book must be posted to the credit side of an account remaining in the ledger, and vice versa.

The reason for combining cash and bank is merely a matter of convenience. There is a relationship between both accounts in that they both deal with receipts and payments of money. It is important for a businessman to have in a convenient form information dealing with both aspects especially where both accounts are used for the same type of transaction, e.g. sales, where monies are received for cash sales and from debtors for credit sales. Because of the importance of the availability of money it may be necessary to balance these two accounts more frequently than other ledger accounts, and to have these balances side by side is of an advantage.

The design of the cash book is basically the same as an ordinary account except that it has two debit amount columns and two credit amount columns, one representing cash, the other representing bank.

To illustrate the entries in the cash book an example is given below, first showing the ledger accounts as if no cash book is in operation:

Cash Account

19x5			£	19x5			£
Jan. 1	Balance	B/D	40	Jan. 1	Purchases	11	40
2	Cash sales	12	80		Sundry exps.	15	10
3	Cash sales	12	40	3	Advertising	16	5
6	Cash sales	12	90	6	Wages	13	60
					Bank	9	100
					Balance	C/D	35
			£250				£250
Jan. 6	Balance	B/D	35				

Bank Account

19x5			£	19x5			£
Jan. 1	Balance	B/D	1,280	Jan. 2	L. Connery	19	100
3	J. Robinson	17	125		S. Oliver	20	50
4	Capital	1	500	3	Motor van	3	650
6	J. Andrews	18	80	6	Balance	C/D	1,285
	Cash	8	100				
			£2,085				£2,085
Jan. 6	Balance	B/D	1,285				

Cash Book

19x5			Cash £	Bank £	19x5			Cash £	Bank £
Jan. 1	Opening balances	B/D	40	1,280	Jan. 1	Purchases	11	40	
2	Cash sales	12	80			Sundry exps.	15	10	
3	J. Robinson	17		125	2	L. Connery	19		100
	Cash sales	12	40			S. Oliver	20		50
4	Capital	1		500	3	Motor van	3		650
	Cash sales	12	90			Advertising	16	5	
6	J. Andrews	18		80	6	Wages	13	60	
	Cash	¢		100		Bank	¢	100	
						Balance	C/D	35	1,285
			£250	£2,085				£250	£2,085
Jan. 6	Balances	B/D	35	1,285					

It can be seen from the entries in the ledger accounts that £100 cash has been paid into the bank, and the account references have been noted. In the cash book no reference has been made, the entries are marked ¢ which denotes a contra-item. The cash book is regarded as being a combined account distinguishing between cash and bank. A payment from cash into bank, or a cheque that is cashed, means that both entries appear in the same account and there is no entry in relation to either transaction in the main body of the ledger. Where cash is received and banked immediately it can be entered directly in the bank column. Where a cheque is cashed for a specific purpose, e.g. payment of wages, there is also no need to put a contra-item in the cash column.

The "Three-column" Cash Book

The three-column cash book is an extension of the two-column cash book. The third column is regarded as memorandum only and contains amounts of cash discount allowed or received.

In most trades a custom has evolved that a certain amount of time may elapse before invoices are due for payment. This time lag between the delivery of goods and the receipt of money may involve the seller in a certain amount of difficulty as he will have had to pay for the goods in the first place. In order to speed up payment for the goods the seller may decide to accept a smaller amount so that he can make use of the money. The difference between the amount actually received and the amount of the debt is known as "Cash Discount". The amount of discount is usually expressed as a percentage of the gross amount and is noted on the invoice. To take advantage of the discount the creditor must pay within a specified period of time.

Cash discount benefits both the buyer and seller. The buyer because the goods cost less, and the seller because he receives payment quicker and can use the money in a profitable manner.

The allowance a businessman gives his debtor is known as "Discount Allowed" and is regarded as an expense. The amount is entered as a debit in a discount allowed account and will be transferred to the profit and loss account at the end of the financial year. The allowance he is given by his creditors is known as "Discount Received" and is regarded as a profit or gain. It will be entered as a credit in a discount received account which will be credited to the profit and loss account at the end of the financial year.

Examples of the entries are:

J. SMITH (Debtor)

			£					£
Jan.	Sales	18	100	Jan.	Cash	C/B		95
					Discount			
					allowed	16		5
			£100					£100

Discount allowed

			£
Jan.	J. Smith	20	5

S. JONES (Creditor)

			£				£
Jan.	Cash	C/B	185	Jan.	Purchases	17	200
	Discount						
	received	17	15				
			£200				£200

Discount Received Account

			£
		Jan.	S. Jones	21	15

If the discount was not entered in the personal accounts, it would appear as though there were still balances remaining in them. Despite the cash being less than the value of the debt it is nevertheless settled because of the discount.

It can be appreciated that if discounts relating to individual debtors and creditors are entered in the discount accounts these would become unmanageable. It would need tens if not hundreds of pages to contain all the entries. A means has to be devised to summarise these allowances so that postings can be made to the individual personal accounts but an aggregate figure entered in the discounts account. As discounts are directly related to times of payment it would seem logical to note the amount of discount together with the net amount of cash. Thus an extra column in the cash book would meet this requirement as shown overleaf.

The net amounts of money plus the discounts are posted to the relevant personal accounts in the ledger. In the case of B. Finch (ledger account No. 15) the account will be credited with £95 bank plus £5 discount.

The discount columns are not balanced, but totalled and the respective amounts entered in the discount accounts in the ledger. The discounts

CASH BOOK

			Discount allowed	Cash	Bank				Discount received	Cash	Bank
			£	£	£				£	£	£
Feb. 1	Balances	B/D		40	900	Feb. 1	J. Wren	18	15		185
2	Cash sales	13		60		3	Sundry exps.	15		10	
5	B. Finch	17	5		95	5	Wages	14		30	
8	C. Robin	21	25		250	8	W. Falcon	22	3		57
9	T. Thrush	23	8		120	12	Wages	14		30	
12	Cash sales	13		45		18	T. Sparrow	20	20		380
18	P. Raven	19	4		76	19	Wages	14		30	
19	Cash sales	13		75		23	Sundry exps.	15		20	
26	Cash sales	13		50		26	Wages	14		30	
							Balance	C/D		120	819
			24	42	270	1,441			25	38	270	1,441
Mar. 1	Balance	B/D		120	819						

allowed, £42, will be debited to the discounts allowed account in the ledger. At first sight this may seem to be incorrect as it already appears as a debit in the cash book. It must be remembered that the discount columns are memorandum only and not accounts. The individual items have been credited to their respective ledger accounts; therefore, to complete the double entry, the total must be debited.

Discounts Allowed Account

£

Feb. 26   Debtors   C/B   42

This is in line with the account previously illustrated in this chapter.
Similarly, with discounts received, the discount and cash paid will be debited to the individual creditor's account. The total of £38 will be credited to discounts received account.

Discounts Received Account

£

Feb. 26   Creditors   C/B   38

Cash discounts must be distinguished from trade discounts. The latter are allowances immediately deducted from the total cost of goods sold. It is not dependent on the time of payment. Trade discount is given when either goods are ordered in large (or bulk) amounts or as a special concession to dealers within a particular trade. The net amount (total price less trade discount) is entered in the books of account and may itself be the subject for cash discount.

The Petty Cash Book

Small cash payments may be omitted from the cash book and instead entered in a "Petty Cash Book". The object of this procedure is two-fold. Firstly, it enables another person to be engaged, enabling the senior book-keeper to concentrate on other more important tasks. Secondly, the petty cash book is so designed that certain types of trans-action can be posted in aggregate to the ledger, thereby lessening the overcrowding of accounts.

Generally a business will pay most of its debts by cheque leaving only the smaller items to be paid in cash. These items may be of a re-curring nature. For example, salesmen may have their travelling ex-penses reimbursed daily or weekly. If there are a number of salesmen, there will be innumerable entries in the travelling expenses account in the ledger. The credit side of the petty cash book is divided into several columns, each one dealing with a particular type of transaction. Each column can be totalled at predetermined periods and the total of each posted to the ledger account.

The responsibility for dealing with petty cash can be left to a junior employee as long as the money he controls is kept to a sufficient minimum amount. The amount that is paid out during a fixed period is then reimbursed out of cash from the cash book so that the original amount of petty cash is restored. This is known as the "Imprest" system.

	£
Petty cash at start of week	50
Total expenses paid	35
Balance of cash remaining	15
Cash required to restore original amount	35
Cash at start of following week	£50

The above represents a summary of the transactions for the first week's transactions. The advantage of the imprest system is that the person dealing with it should at all times be able to produce cash and/or receipts totalling £50. This provides a useful check on the petty cash.

In the example shown overleaf each expense column total is posted to the debit of the respective ledger account. The total column is re-quired to enable the account to be balanced and also to provide a check on the additions. In the illustration shown only four entries are made in the ledger though eleven transactions were effected. The reference (V. No.) refers to the receipt or voucher number verifying the payment. The number of columns and the description of each is a matter of convenience for each business.

Example of petty cash book:

PETTY CASH BOOK

Receipts	Ref.	Date	Particulars	V. no.	Total	Travel-ling	Post-age	Stationery	Sun-dries
					£	£	£	£	£
£50·00	C/B	Jan. 1	Cash	—					
			A. Smith	1	1	1			
			Postage	2	5		5		
		2	J. Jones	3	2	2			
			Stationery	4	3			3	
			Sundries	5	3				3
		3	A. Smith	6	2	2			
			J. Jones	7	3	3			
		4	Postage	8	5		5		
			Sundries	9	2				2
		5	J. Jones	10	3	3			
			Stationery	11	6			6	
					35	11	10	9	5
			Balance	C/D	15	L.18	L.20	L.17	L.21
£50·00					£50				
15·00	B/D	5	Balance						
35·00	C/B	5	Cash						

In practice all cash is banked immediately or within a very short time after its receipt. The entry can, therefore, be in the bank column of the cash book. All items except those relating to petty cash are paid by cheque. Cheques are cashed for the exact amounts for payments of total wages and reimbursement of petty cash imprests, so that these too can be entered directly into the bank column. The result is that the cash book becomes used solely for bank items and the recording of discounts. The resulting benefits are that less cash remains on the premises and losses are kept to a minimum. Also, more use can be made of the cash book.

The cash book can have numerous columns for debits and credits depending on the information required. It is of great help when accounts are sectionalised (see Chapter 12), e.g.:

CASH BOOK (Debit side)

Date	Description	Discount	Debtors	Cash sales	Sundries	Total

CASH BOOK (Credit side)

Date	Description	Discount	Creditors	Wages	Cash purchases	Sundries	Total

Note. The discounts are not included in the total column as this represents the actual amount deposited or withdrawn from the bank.

Documents Used

The documents used for entering amounts in the bank columns are, for debits, the bank paying-in book which will be stamped by the bank thus verifying the amount deposited. Credit items will be entered directly from the cheque book. Unless a receipt is specifically demanded, the Cheques Act 1957 provides that a paid cheque is a valid form of receipt. Ultimately bank transactions involving debtors and creditors will be verified by the balances in the personal accounts.

Cash payments should be supported by receipts from the payee. Where documentary evidence is difficult to obtain a voucher should be made out describing the purpose of the payment and signed by a senior employee authorising the payment. Cash receipts are more difficult to verify, e.g. cash sales. If the business has recording tills the till roll total would be evidence of monies received.

EXERCISES

4.1

Write up a two-column cash book from the following details and balance the cash book at the end of the month.

19x4

Aug.
 1   Started business with £80 in cash and £600 in the bank
 2   Paid rent by cash £30
 3   Paid D. Latham by cheque £80
 4   Bought motor van paying by cheque £450
 5   D. Johnston paid us by cheque £120
 7   Cash Sales £75
 9   Paid W. Fitzgerald by cheque £90
11   Cash sales paid direct to bank £50
15   B. Dooley lent us £300 paying by cheque
16   Paid £100 cash into the bank
19   Paid rates by cheque £15
22   Cash sales £45
26   Paid motor expenses by cheque £12
30   Withdrew £50 cash from the bank for business use
31   Paid wages in cash £80

4.2

Write up a two-column cash book from the following details and balance the cash book at the end of the month.

19x5

June 1 Balances brought forward cash £100, bank £800
     2 Paid D. Cromwell £85 by cheque
     3 Paid rent in cash £75
     4 Received cheque from D. Irwin £90
     5 Bought office furniture £42 by cheque
     6 Cash sales £45
     8 Paid D. Lawler by cheque £100
     9 Paid motor expenses in cash £30
    10 Received cheque from D. Murphy £70
    11 Withdrew £50 cash from bank for business purposes
    12 Paid advertising charges by cheque £15
    13 Cash sales paid directly into bank £85
    15 Bought goods paying by cheque £30
    16 Bought goods from B. Hegarty paying in cash £40
    17 Paid D. Cromwell £75 by cheque
    18 Received cheque from G. Bonnell £115
    19 Cash sales £95
    22 Bought packing materials £28 by cheque
    23 Paid cash for stationery £30
    24 Paid electricity account by cheque £18
    25 Cash sales paid directly into bank £120
    28 Withdrew cash from bank for own use £75
    30 Paid wages in cash £60

4.3

Write up a three-column cash book from the following details, balance off at the end of the week, and show the relevant discount accounts as they would appear in the ledger.

19x3

Jan. 1 Balances brought forward, cash in hand £80, bank overdraft £640
       Cash sales £68
       Received cheques from debtors: T. Franks £80 (discount allowed £10), F. James £45 (discount allowed £5)
    2 Paid by cheque the following accounts (less 5% discount): S. Olive £120, J. Thomas £160, R. Percy £60
       Cash sales £92
    3 F. Ball paid his account by cheque £500 (less 10% discount)
       Cash sales £40
    4 Paid insurance premium by cheque £76
    5 Received cheques from the following customers in settlement of their accounts (less 5% discount); W. Ray £80, J. Paul £400, A. David £300

6   Cash sales £120
Paid the following accounts deducting a $2\frac{1}{2}\%$ discount (by cheque):
V. Arthur £40, P. Brian £120
Drew cheque for wages £64
Paid £300 cash into bank

4.4

From the following details write up a three-column cash book, balance off at the end of the week, and show the relevant discount accounts as they would appear in the ledger.

19x7

July   1   Balances brought forward: cash in hand £35, cash at bank £375
Cash sales £98 paid direct into the bank
Paid general expenses £12 in cash

      7   The following customers paid their accounts by cheque less $7\frac{1}{2}\%$ discount: C. Avery £400, G. Davies £200, J. Harrison £600

      3   Cash sales £112
Paid motor expenses in cash £45
Paid the following accounts by cheque deducting 10% discount: O. Challenor £90, J. Hayes £250, M. Daniels £80

      4   Cash sales £69
R. Dickinson paid us £420 by cheque after deducting discount of £60

      5   Cash sales paid direct into the bank £73
Paid the following accounts by cheque after deducting a discount of 5%: J. Hill £100, B. Farmer £60, J. Brooks £80

      6   Drew cheque for wages £75
Paid £50 cash into bank

4.5

From the following details write up a three-column cash book, balance off at the end of the week, and show the relevant discount accounts as they would appear in the ledger.

19x1

May   1   Balances brought forward: cash in hand £60, bank overdraft £240
Paid for stationery by cheque £34
Cash sales £55

      2   Paid the following accounts by cheque, in each case deducting 5% discount: B. Allen £140, J. Duckworth £260, F. Higgins £120
Cash sales £73

      3   Paid travelling expenses in cash £5
Received cheques from the following debtors after deducting 10% discount from their accounts: J. Ellis £110, E. Jones £80, J. Hope £150
Paid T. Kilner by cheque £75
Cash sales £90 paid direct to bank

4 Paid £150 cash into bank
Received from J. Price cheque for £75, discount £15
Cash sales £37
5 Paid wages in cash £40
Received rent for sublease £20 in cash
6 Cash sales £49
Withdrew £90 for private use by cheque

4.6
Enter the following transactions in a petty cash book, having analysis columns for postages and stationery, travelling expenses, motor expenses, and sundries. The imprest amount is £50 and the amount spent is reimbursed at the beginning of each week.

19x1
Jan. 1 Opening balance £27
Received cash to make up the imprest
Paid J. Green travelling expenses £2, postages £3, petrol £2
2 Paid J. Brown travelling expenses £1, F. White travelling expenses £2, stationery £3, repairs to typewriter £4
3 Paid office cleaner £4, office tea etc. £1, telegrams £2
4 Paid J. Green travelling expenses £3, petrol £2, food for guard dog £2, parking fine £5
5 Paid F. White travelling expenses £3, car repairs £4, postages £2

4.7
Enter the following transactions in a petty cash book, having analysis columns for postages and stationery, travelling expenses, cleaning, sundries, and a ledger column.

19x3			£
Feb.	3	Received imprest from cashier	60
	5	Postage stamps	10
	6	Stationery	8
	7	Paid S. Harrison's account in purchase ledger	8
	9	Travelling expenses—F. Slaughter	4
	11	Window cleaning	12
	12	Paid M. Lennon's account in purchase ledger	10
	14	Subscription—trade journal	4
	17	Office cleaning	4
	18	Received on account from cashier	50
	20	Travelling expenses—S. Todd	20
	21	Payment to office cleaner	5
	23	Electric light bulbs	4
	24	Travelling expenses—F. Slaughter	2
	26	Tea, sugar, and milk	6
	28	Balance the petty cash book and show the reimbursement of the amount required to restore the imprest	

4.8

Enter the following transactions in a petty cash book, having analysis columns for postages and stationery, travelling expenses, motor expenses, and office expenses. The amount of the imprest is £50.

19x4

July	1	Received from cashier to make up the imprest £35
		Paid taxi fares £3, window cleaner £2
	2	Bought postage stamps £2, string £1
	3	Paid parcel post £2, petrol £3
	4	Bought stationery £5, travelling expenses £2
	5	Paid typewriter repairs £5, petrol £3
	6	Paid travelling expenses £3, office tea, milk etc. £2

Balance the book as on 6th July, carry down the balance and continue.

July	8	Received cash from cashier to make up the imprest
		Bought short-hand notebooks £5, postage stamps £2
	9	Paid railway fares £6, petrol £3
	10	Paid subscription to trade periodical £4
	11	Paid office cleaner £3, hotel charges £6
	12	Bought envelopes £2, light bulbs £2
	13	Paid travelling expenses £4, office tea, milk etc. £2

Balance the petty cash book and carry down the balance.

5 Bank Reconciliation Statements

Wherever possible it is beneficial to apply a check on book entries, particularly if the entries are "prime" entries. Prime entries are those that are original; that is, the first part of the double entry. Transactions recorded in the cash book are of this type as they form the basis of postings to the ledger accounts. The entries in the bank columns of the cash book can be verified as the bank must, in its own interest, keep a record of its clients' monies. A duplicate record is therefore available which is forwarded periodically to the business by the bank in the form of bank statements or bank pass sheets.

Unfortunately, the balance on the statement will rarely agree with the balance in the cash book. This is because items are not recorded in both sets of records at the same time. However, by comparing the entries in each, a reconciliation statement can be achieved by adjusting the items omitted from either or by correcting errors in recording.

The first stage in reconciling the balances is to ensure that the balance shown in the cash book is correct. Errors may occur in two ways. Initially items may be incorrectly recorded, for example, transposition of figures, a cheque for £79 entered as £97. By comparing corresponding entries in the two records these errors should be discovered, and where necessary the cash book should be amended to show the true amount. The second type of error is that of omission, entries appearing on the bank statement but not in the cash book. Transactions usually omitted are:

1. *Bank Charges.* This can comprise two items. (a) The fee the bank charges for looking after the client's money; it may be referred to as commission or charges. (b) Interest which is charged on overdrafts or loans. The charges are not generally notified directly to the client, but appear on the bank statement usually at the end of June and December. The business will therefore not have recorded the amount, but an entry will have to be made in the cash book to show a correct balance.
2. *Bank Interest Received.* Interest is only received on bank deposit

accounts and never on current accounts (except in the case of Trustee Savings Banks). A deposit account is one where money is deposited, but restrictions are placed on withdrawals. The normal business banking account is a current account where cheques can be drawn as required up to the amount of the funds available. As with bank charges the business is not informed of this interest except when the statement is received.

3. *Standing Orders.* These are amounts the business has asked the bank to pay on their behalf at stated intervals, thus relieving themselves of having to draw cheques. These amounts are usually for annual subscriptions or for continuing payments of a fixed amount, e.g. hire purchase instalments. It is possible that a standing order may be forgotten and not recorded in the cash book.

4. *Bank Transfers.* Certain receipts can be paid directly into the bank account by third parties. Interest on investments, particularly government stocks, e.g. National Development Bonds, can be sent to the bank instead of a cheque being sent to the investor. Anyone can instruct their bank to transfer some of their funds into the account of another person, and unless they notify that person of the transfer it will be unrecorded in the latter's cash book. A great many salaries are paid in this manner, but of course the recipient is notified of the details by the employer.

5. *Direct Debits.* These occur when the owner of the business gives permission for a creditor to charge amounts to the business bank account. This system is designed to be used when regular payments have to be made to a creditor though the amounts themselves may differ. The business must authorise its bank to accept direct debits. The creditor should advise the business of the amounts charged so that the latter can enter the transactions in his books, but occasionally these notifications are lost or not received.

6. *Returned Cheques.* When a customer pays by cheque this is recorded in the cash book and posted to the personal account. Occasionally the customer's bank will refuse to accept the cheque because of insufficient funds or some other reason. When this happens the cheque is returned to the business and the original entries must be cancelled. However, because of the delay between first recording the transaction and the receipt of the returned cheque, several days may elapse and this period may cover the business's year end.

When all these entries have been recorded in the cash book the balance shown will be the correct one. Even so, it will rarely agree with the balance shown in the bank statement. The reason for this is that although the bank statement is up-to-date so far as the bank is concerned it is not as up-to-date as the cash book for two reasons:

1. *Unpresented Cheques.* These represent cheques drawn by the business, but not presented for payment to the business's bank. After the entry of the cheque in the cash book it is sent to the creditor. When the creditor receives the cheque he pays it into his own bank who then pass it through the bank clearing system from whence it comes to the business's bank and is entered on the statement. The effect is that unpresented cheques will reduce the balance shown on the statements, or increase the overdraft.
2. *Unentered Deposits.* These occur when a deposit though entered in the cash book does not appear on the bank statement. Usually there is not as much delay as with cheques, but a delay of several days may be crucial when reconciling the cash book. The unentered deposits on the statement will have the effect of increasing the balance or reducing the overdraft.

The reconciliation is made in statement form starting with the original balances in the cash book, and on the bank statement as under:

Example

The cash book of J. Heath at 31st March, 19x3, showed a debit balance of £5,240, whereas the bank statement at the same date showed £8,333.
On comparing the cash book with the bank statement the following differences were obtained:

(a) A cheque paid to a creditor for £974 was entered in the cash book as £794.
(b) Dividends from investments received by the bank but not entered in the cash book amounted to £250.
(c) Bank charges not entered in the cash book of £97.
(d) A standing order for a trade subscription was not entered in the cash book for £18.
(e) Unpresented cheques amounted to £3,468.
(f) Bank deposit not credited by the bank amounted to £274.
(g) Cheques returned by the bank marked "refer to drawer" not adjusted in the cash book amounted to £56.

J HEATH
Bank Reconciliation as at 31st March, 19x3

		− £	+ £
Original cash book balance 31.3.19x3	(Debit)		5,240
Correction for cheque (£974 − £794)		180	
Dividends received from investments			250
Bank charges		97	
Standing order		18	
Returned cheque		56	
		£351	5,490
			351
Corrected cash book balance	(Debit)		£5,139
Balance per bank statement			8,333
Add Deposit not credited			274
			8,607
Less Unpresented cheques			3,468
Balance per cash book			£5,139

Explanations of the above adjustments are as follows:
The dividends when entered in the cash book, being a receipt, will increase the original balance. The bank charges, standing order, and returned cheque being credit entries will reduce the balance. The cheque being incorrectly understated will reduce the balance by the amount understated. The entries in the cash book will be as under:

CASH BOOK (Bank columns only)

		£				£
Mar. 31	Original balance	5,240	Mar. 31	Correction of cheque		180
	Dividends	250		Bank charges		97
				Standing order		18
				Returned cheque		56
				Balance		5,139
		£5,490				£5,490
Mar. 31	Balance	£5,139				

Although the bank statement shows a balance of £8,333, when the deposit is entered the balance will increase, whereas when the cheques already drawn are presented for payment the balance will reduce. Thus, when all transactions up to the 31st March, 19x3, have been entered on the bank statement the balances will coincide.

53

Should the cash book balance be a credit, the adjustments will be reversed, viz:

E. Wilson's cash book on 30th June, 19x4, gave a balance of £680 overdrawn at the bank. The bank statement at this date showed a debit of £510.

You are informed that:

(a) Unpresented cheques amounted to £350
(b) Deposits not credited on the bank statement amounted to £210
(c) Bank charges not entered in the cash book amounted to £25
(d) A bank transfer from a customer amounting to £75 had been credited to the statement but not entered in the cash book
(e) A standing order amounting to £20 had not been entered in the cash book

E. WILSON

Bank Reconciliation Statement as at 30th June, 19x4

		− £	+ £
Original cash book balance	(Overdrawn)		680
Bank charges			25
Standing order			20
Bank transfer		75	
		£75	725
			75
Corrected cash book balance	(Overdrawn)		650
Balance per bank statement	(Debit)		510
Add Unpresented cheques			350
			860
Less Deposit not credited			210
Balance per cash book			£650

It must be noted that a debit balance in the cash book represents funds in the bank, whilst a credit balance in the cash book represents an overdraft (or liability). Conversely, the balances shown on the bank statement will be the opposite entries. A debit balance in the cash book will be shown as a credit balance on the bank statement, the latter representing a liability of the bank to its customer. An overdraft being a credit balance in the cash book (a liability) will be a debit balance on the statement (an asset so far as the bank is concerned).

Occasionally questions are set where only one balance is given and it is left to the student to calculate the missing balance, e.g.:

From the following information prepare a bank reconciliation statement to show the balance in the cash book on 31st December, 19x1.

	£
1. Bank statement (credit balance)	6,300
2. Unpresented cheques	200
3. Bank charges not entered in cash book	35
4. Deposit not credited to bank statement	960
5. Dividends received by bank but not entered in cash book	15
6. Cheques returned by the bank marked "refer to drawer" not adjusted in cash book	57

Note. In this question the balance shown on the bank statement being a credit represents funds in the bank, not an overdraft.

Bank Reconciliation Statement as at 31st December, 19x1

	£	£
Balance per bank statement (credit)		6,300
Less unpresented cheques		200
		6,100
Add Deposit not credited		960
Correct cash book balance		7,060
Add Bank charges not entered in cash book	35	
Add Returned cheques not entered in cash book	57	92
		7,152
Less Dividend received not entered in cash book		15
Original cash book balance		£7,137

EXERCISES

5.1
From the following details draw up a bank reconciliation statement.

	£
Cash at bank as per bank column of the cash book	724
Unpresented cheques	280
Bank deposits entered in the cash book but not credited on the bank statement	120
Credit transfers entered as banked on the bank statement but not entered in the cash book	45
Cheque returned "refer to drawer", but not entered in cash book	15
Balance per bank statement	914

55

5.2

The cash book of E. Long showed a balance of £550 at the bank on 30th June, 19x7.

On investigation you find that:

	£
Unpresented cheques totalled	113
Deposits not credited by the bank amounted to	225
A cheque for £95 was received from a customer and discount of £5 was allowed. £100 had been entered in the bank column of the cash book	
A standing order had been paid by the bank for a trade subscription	12
A credit transfer had been received by the bank	35
Bank charges had been omitted from the cash book	18
Balance per bank statement (credit)	438

Prepare a bank reconciliation statement.

5.3

From the following details draw up a bank reconciliation statement.

	£
Cash at bank per bank column of the cash book	247
Balance per bank statement (debit)	100
Unpresented cheques	79
Deposit not entered by bank	546
Dividend received by bank not entered in the cash book	50
Cheque drawn for £672 entered in cash book as £762	
Bank charges not entered in cash book	27
Cheque returned "refer to drawer" not entered in cash book	83
Credit transfer received by bank not entered in cash book	90

5.4

From the following information prepare a bank reconciliation statement to show the balance in the cash book on 31st March, 19x5.

	£
Bank statement (credit balance)	270
Cheques amounting to £94 were drawn on 30th March but not presented for payment until 5th April	
Cheques amounting to £500 were paid into the bank on 31st March but had not been included on the bank statement	
Bank charges amounting to £8 had been omitted from the cash book	
A cheque for £22 received from B. Koss was banked on 26th March but was returned to the firm's bankers on 31st March marked "refer to drawer" and the appropriate entry was made in the bank statement. The firm's cashier was notified on the 2nd April	

5.5

From the following information prepare a bank reconciliation statement to show the balance on the bank statement on 30th June, 19x3.

	£
Balance per cash book (debit)	3,642
Unpresented cheques	3,240
Bank deposit not credited on bank statement	2,200
Bank interest debited on statement omitted from cash book	125
Bank charges omitted from cash book	45
Cheque paid, entered as £247 in cash book, should be £272	
Dividends received by the bank omitted from cash book	85

5.6

From the following information prepare a bank reconciliation statement to show the balance in the cash book on 31st August, 19x1.

Balance per bank statement £950 overdrawn.

Cheques drawn amounting to £360 had not been presented to the bank for payment

Deposits totalling £750 had not been credited by the bank

Bank charges of £140 had been omitted from the cash book

A cheque received for £60 had been returned by the bank marked "refer to drawer". No adjustment had been made in the cash book.

Dividends totalling £120 had been received by the bank but not entered in the cash book

A standing order for £14 paid by the bank had not been entered in the cash book

A cheque for £79 due to a creditor had been entered as £97 in the cash book

5.7

The following entries were from the bank columns of the cash book of T. Barber.

19x6			£	19x6				£
June	1	Balance b/fwd.	200	June	7	T. Shark		93
	6	Cash sales	80		8	F. Perch		22
	7	J. Sprat	47		9	Wages		68
	8	J. Place	52		14	S. Trout		14
	13	Cash sales	64		15	F. Perch		37
	17	P. Whelk	84		16	Wages		65
	19	Cash sales	71		17	T. Shark		29
					19	Balance	C/D	270
			£598					£598

June 19	Balance c/fwd.	£270

On 19th June he received the following statement from his bank:

19x6			Debits	Credits	Balance
			£	£	£
June	1	Balance b/fwd.			200
	8	Cash		80	280
	10	Cheque		47	327
	11	06102	93		234

57

		Debits £	Credits £	Balance £
12	06103	22		212
	06104	68		144
	Cheque		52	196
14	Cash		64	260
18	Cheque		84	344
	06107	65		279
	Dividends B.T. Ltd.		18	297
	Standing order R.A.A.C.	9		288

You are required to prepare a bank reconciliation statement as at 19th June, 19x6.

6 The Subsidiary Books

In order to prosper, a business must expand and in doing so the number of transactions will increase. Furthermore, although a small business can exist on a cash basis, i.e. paying for goods and services and receiving monies for sales at the same time as the transaction takes place, eventually it must adopt the business custom of dealing on credit.

The expansion of the business takes place in trading, thus the volume of sales transactions will increase and, of necessity to provide for the sales, also the volume of purchase transactions. Unless the business is a retail organisation such as a supermarket, where sales are conducted on a cash basis, most of the increased transactions will be dealt with on a credit basis. The latter type of transaction presents a complication in its recording as each additional item must be separately recorded in the ledger. If the number of credit sales doubles, then not only does the number of entries in the personal accounts double, but also the number of entries in the sales account. The sales account would become overloaded with items rather in the same way as the bank and cash accounts were before they were divorced from the ledger. The increase in cash sales does not affect the number of entries, only the amount of each entry is increased.

To overcome the complication of overloading the sales and purchases accounts the number of entries appearing in them must be restricted, and in order to achieve this object two subsidiary books are brought into use named the Sales and Purchases Day Books or, alternatively, Sales and Purchases Journals. They are termed day books because they are entered daily though the ledger postings may not be completed at such times.

They are not part of the ledger double-entry system, but form the basis of posting to the ledger. From this point of view they can be regarded as reference books or indeed memorandum books. The entries that are made in them originate from invoices. An invoice is a document made out by the business selling the goods and sent to the buyer giving complete details of the goods supplied, viz:

```
INVOICE          JOHN SWIFT          No. 6842
Telephone 963 84762                  84, High Street
Telegrams Hasty                      Newtun
                                     Yorks.
                                     1st June, 19x6
To: F. Yardley,
    44, Pshaw Lane,
    Tutting, Lancs.
                                        £          £
30 Sproggle sockets @ £1·50 each     45·00
20 Toggert adaptors @ £0·75 each     15·00
10 Snappet connectors @ £·50 each     5·00
                                     ─────
                                     65·00
        Less 10% Trade discount       6·50
                                               ─────
                                               58·50
Carriage                                        2·25
                                               ─────
                                              £60·75
                                               ─────
Terms: 2½% Cash discount within 7 days
```

The Sales Day Book

The entries in the Sales Day Book are based on duplicate invoices retained by the trader. They are listed in chronological order, the reference numbers of the invoices being in numerical sequence. The minimum amount of information should be noted subject to adequate references so that should a query arise in the future all details can be obtained as quickly as possible. For this reason the duplicate invoices

SALES DAY BOOK   SDB1

Date	Name	Invoice no.	Folio	£	p
19x6					
June 1	F. Yardley	6842	Y1	60	75
1	K. Jones	6843	J2	40	25
2	F. Cainen	6844	C1	50	85
3	F. Yardley	6845	Y1	75	00
3	F. Keers	6846	K4	42	30
4	D. Bamber	6847	B3	30	00
5	C. Jowett	6848	J8	35	50
6	N. Sellars	6849	S4	45	35
				£380	00

should be filed in numerical order. Only credit sales are entered in the day book.

In its simplest form the sales day book is ruled as on page 60.

At pre-determined intervals the day book is totalled and the ledger entries completed. As can be seen in the above example the invoices are numbered in numerical order. Each item is posted separately to the individual personal account, in this case a separate debtors' ledger is maintained. At the end of a week the invoices are totalled and this figure posted to the sales account in the nominal ledger. The effect of this is that instead of eight entries appearing in the sales account there is now only one. The number of postings has been cut by almost half. The double-entry system in the ledger will be as follows:

			D. BAMBER		C3
June 4	Goods	SDBL	30·00		

			F. CAINEN		C1
June 2	Goods	SDB1	50·85		

			K. JONES		J2
June 1	Goods	SDB1	40·25		

			C. JOWETT		J8
June 5	Goods	SDB1	35·50		

			F. KEERS		K4
June 3	Goods	SDB1	42·30		

			N. SELLARS		S4
June 6	Goods	SDB1	45·35		

			F. YARDLEY		Y1
June 1	Goods	SDB1	60·75		
3	Goods	SDB1	75·00		

Sales Account

	June 6	Credit sales	SDB1	380·00

The use of a sales day book improves the efficiency of the office. The book-keeping work can be split between members of the staff, postings to the personal accounts can be made daily and, provided a separate debtors' ledger is maintained, the recording of transactions does not interfere with the postings of other transactions. The totalling and posting to the nominal ledger can be selected to give the most benefit. It may be useful to know the total weekly or monthly credit sales so that a comparison can be made with previous seasonal takings or with immediate past weeks.

It is important to give adequate details in the ledger. If a query arose from F. Yardley who questioned an item on the invoice for £75·00, it is a simple matter to refer to folio 1 in the sales day book, discover the number of the invoice—6845—and from the filing system extract the duplicate invoice with all particulars contained therein and solve the query.

Where credit sales become very numerous it may be advantageous to split the debtors' ledger and day books. For example, there could be a division of the "A" to "K" debtors and the "L" to "Z" debtors. This would enable two clerks to be simultaneously engaged in entering and posting sales transactions.

The Purchase Day Book

The system applied in recording credit sales can also be used for credit purchases. A purchase day book or journal is originated and details of purchase invoices recorded. The entries are posted individually to the creditors' accounts and in total periodically to the debit of purchases account in the nominal ledger.

Two difficulties present themselves with regard to purchase invoices which are not inherent in sales invoices. Firstly, the invoice numbers will not be consecutive as each supplier will adhere to his own sequence. Secondly, the date of the invoice will seldom correspond with the date the goods are actually received. The invoice is sent by letter post when the goods are despatched and will normally be received by the buyer before the goods are delivered.

To overcome the first problem the invoices when received should be stamped with a reference number which should be in a numerical sequence. Thus it can be filed according to this system and can be easily found should reference to it be required. This reference number is entered in the purchase day book together with the original invoice number as shown at the top of the page opposite.

All details except for the reference number are taken from the original invoice. The original invoice number is recorded in case of queries from the supplier relating to a specific invoice.

The second problem is very important. The businessman only wishes to record transactions that have taken place, therefore the entries in the purchase day book must only relate to goods received. The purchase

PURCHASE DAY BOOK

Date	Name	Invoice no.	Ref. no.	Folio	£	p
June 1	P. Forrest	F.3984	364	F.10.	40	00
1	J. Oakes	A.106	365	O.2.	30	90
2	S. Spruce	P.438	366	S.7.	60	20
3	P. Forrest	F.4106	367	F.10.	40	30
4	H. Lime	L.2706	368	L.5.	52	60
5	J. Oakes	A.129	369	O.2.	26	00
				L.19.	250	00

day book therefore becomes a register of goods coming into the business. To ensure that only invoices in respect of these goods are entered it is necessary that delivery notes are matched and attached to the invoices before any entries are made.

A delivery note is a document made out by the supplier of goods giving details of the goods (except normally the price) and is sent along with the goods, viz:

```
DELIVERY NOTE    JOHN SWIFT        No. 6842
Telephone: 963 84762               84, High Street
Telegrams: Hasty                   Newtun
                                   Yorks.
                                   1st June, 19x6

To: F. Yardley,
    44, Pshaw Lane,
    Tutting, Lancs.

30  Sproggle sockets
20  Toggert adaptors
10  Snappet connectors
```

The person who accepts delivery of the goods signs the delivery note and enters the date of receipt. The delivery note is then forwarded to the book-keeper who checks it against the invoice and, if it agrees, staples the two documents together and enters the details in the purchase day book. A reference number is entered on the invoice and both documents are filed.

There is a slight problem to this system in that the entries in the purchase day book will not run in chronological order following the dates of the invoices, but in chronological order of receipt of goods. This will, however, not affect the daily posting of the day book to the personal accounts and simplifies stock-taking at the year end (see Chapter 10).

Adaptations of the Day Books

In some instances the day book becomes a complete source of information. Instead of merely recording a name and total amount due on each invoice, a complete description of the goods bought or sold is noted, viz:

SALES DAY BOOK

Date		Inv. no.	Folio	£	p	£	p
June 1	F. Yardley	6842					
	30 Sproggle sockets @ £1·50			45	00		
	20 Toggert adaptors @ £0·75			15	00		
	10 Snappet connectors @ £0·50			5	00		
				65	00		
	Less 10% Trade discount			6	50		
				58	50		
	Carriage			2	25		
			Y1			60	75

There are several disadvantages connected with this method. Firstly, it is time consuming. The time taken in entering each transaction is more than doubled. Secondly, it is repetitive as the information is already contained in the invoice, and, providing the filing system is adequate and cross-referenced, the information can be easily obtained. Thirdly, there is more chance of errors being made as more information is noted.

However, as already mentioned, all the information is contained in one location and a second advantage is that should subsequently an invoice be mislaid the information is still available.

The second amendment is in the form of analysed day books. The purpose of doing this is to provide additional information for the businessman. It is especially useful where the business deals in several distinct types of products, by showing the trading resulting from each type. Analysed final accounts can be prepared and the businessman can thus concentrate his activities on the more profitable lines or products and discard those that show a negligible profit.

ANALYSED SALES DAY BOOK

Date	Supplier	Inv. no.	Folio	Total	Furniture	Radios	Cycles
				£	£	£	£
Jan. 1	S. Row	678	R4	120	90	30	
2	A. Weaver	679	W3	50			50
3	B. Taylor	680	T1	45		45	
	D. Skegg	681	S8	160	160		
4	A. Weaver	682	W3	90	40	50	
5	W. Shore	683	S6	60			60
				525	290	125	110

The totals in the analysis columns are either posted to separate sales accounts in the ledger or to an analysed sales account. There is no limit to the number of columns that can be used in the day book. However, whatever descriptions are used in the sales day book the same should be used in the purchase day book.

In addition to purchases being bought on credit there is also the question of expenses. Not all expenses are paid for immediately on receipt of the invoice, therefore to carry out the double entry the expense must be debited and the expense creditor credited. If any of the expenses are numerous and repetitive, the same problem exists as it did for purchases. The answer is to open an expense day book which will consist of analysis columns corresponding to ledger accounts; for example, repairs, motor expenses, lighting and heating etc. The individual items are credited to their respective personal accounts, the totals under each heading debited to the nominal accounts.

In practice the purchase day book and expense day book are combined. In this case one or more analysis columns are devoted to purchases whilst the remainder cover the expenses.

Returns Books

Once a sales or purchases invoice has been entered in the books it cannot be altered, unless there has been a recording error. In a number of instances goods may have to be returned; this may be because the wrong goods were sent in the first place or the goods were faulty. Where this situation arises a credit note is issued by the supplier when the goods are returned to him. A credit note is a document made out by the original supplier giving particulars of the goods returned, reason for their return, and the value of them. This transaction negates part of the original entry.

CREDIT NOTE   JOHN SWIFT   No. CO62
Telephone: 963 84762   84, High Street
Telegrams: Hasty   Newtun
    Yorks.
    8th June, 19x6

To: F. Yardley,
    44, Pshaw Lane,
    Tutting, Lancs.

10	Snappet connectors @ £0·50 each	£5·00
	(wrong diameter)	
	Less Trade discount	0·50
		£4·50

Credit notes are usually printed in red to distinguish them from invoices.

It is usual to open separate day books for purchase returns and sales returns instead of combining them in the purchases and sales day books. The reason is because it is useful for the businessman to know why goods have been returned. If goods he has sold have been returned, it may be because slackness of his staff has resulted in wrong goods being sent, or goods have been broken in transit, or the quality is not up to specification. If there is a large number of returns, this may lead to discontented customers who might take their business elsewhere unless the businessman can rectify the situation. In the case of purchases which he has to send back it will enable him to discover which of his suppliers are more reliable than others.

An example of a sales returns day book is given opposite.

Whereas the original sales invoice was debited to the personal account and included in the total which was credited to the sales account, the returns are credited to the personal account and debited to a sales returns account in the ledger. Sales returns are also referred to as returns inward, the reason being that the goods are being sent back into the firm.

The same system is adopted for purchase returns. The original invoice is posted to the credit of the personal account and included in the total

SALES RETURNS DAY BOOK   SRB1

Date	Name	Reason	Cr. note	Folio	£	p
19x6						
June 8	F. Yardley	Wrong goods	C 062	Y1	4	50
10	K. Jones	Over supplied	C 063	J2	10	00
15	D. Bamber	Damaged	C 064	B3	7	50
20	N. Sellars	Wrong colour	C 065	S4	12	80
					£34	80

which is debited to purchases account. The credit note is entered in the purchase returns day book and debited to the personal account and credited to a purchase returns account. Purchase returns are also referred to as returns outward, as the goods are sent out of the business back to the supplier.

The filing systems and references are the same as those used for invoices. The returns books are closed off at the same time as the sales and purchases day books.

To show how the entries appear in the personal ledgers illustrations are shown below.

F. YARDLEY (Debtor)

19x6			£				£
June 1	Goods	SDB1	60·75	June 8	Returns	SDBL	4·50
June 3	”	”	75·00		Balance	C/D	131·25
			£135·75				£135·75
June 8	Balance	B/D	£131·25				

The balance due from F. Yardley £131·25 is made up of the sum of the two invoices less the value of the credit note for goods returned.

J. KILNER (Creditor)

June 6	Returns	PRB2	7·65	June 2	Goods	PDD2	75·50
	Balance	C/D	150·60	5	”	”	82·75
			£158·25				£158·25
				June 6	Balance	B/D	£150·60

At the end of the accounting year the balances in the nominal ledger are transferred to the trading account as in the example below:

Example

An extract from the trial balance of John Swift shows:

	£	£
Stock at 1st January, 19x7	6,000	
Sales		15,000
Purchases	8,000	
Returns inwards	600	
Returns outwards		400

Show how the above accounts would be recorded in the nominal ledger after transferring the balances to a trading account. Stock at 31st December, 19x7, amounted to £4,000.

Stock Account

19x6			£	19x7			£
Jan. 1	Balance	B/D	6,000	Dec. 31	Tfr. trading a/c		6,000
Dec. 31	Tfr. trading a/c		4,000				

Sales Account

Dec. 31	Tfr. trading a/c		15,000	Dec. 31	Balance	B/D	15,000

Purchases Account

Dec. 31	Balance	B/D	8,000	Dec. 31	Tfr. trading a/c		8,000

Returns Inward

Dec. 31	Balance	B/D	600	Dec. 31	Tfr. trading a/c		600

Returns Outward

Dec. 31	Tfr. trading a/c		400	Dec. 31	Balance	B/D	400

Trading Account
Year ended 31st December, 19x7

	£	£		£	£
Opening stock		6,000	Sales	15,000	
Add Purchases	8,000		*Less* Returns inward	600	14,400
Less Returns outward	400	7,600			
		13,600			
Less Closing stock		4,000			
Cost of goods sold		9,600			
Gross profit carried down		4,800			
		£14,400			£14,400
			Gross profit brought down		£4,800

It can be seen that although the returns inwards account is a debit balance, it is not transferred to the debit of trading account. Instead it is shown as a negative credit, that is, deducted from the gross value of sales. This is done to show that although £15,000 of goods were sold £600 were returned so that the net sales were £14,400. The same treatment is used in respect of purchases and returns outward.

To check that all purchase invoices have been entered correctly and that none have been omitted, use can be made of suppliers' statements. A statement is a document made out by the supplier of goods giving details of transactions involved over a particular period of time. It is sent, usually monthly, to the debtor, viz:

STATEMENT	JOHN SWIFT	84, High Street

Telephone: 963 84762 — Newtun
Telegrams: Hasty — Yorks.

30 June, 19x6

To: F. Yardley,
44, Pshaw Lane,
Tutting, Lancs.

Date	Description	Our ref.	Dr.	Cr.	Balance
May 31	Balance	—	260·00		260·00
June 1	Goods	6842	60·75		320·75
3	,,	6845	75·00		395·75
5	Cash	—		234·00	
	Discount	—		26·00	135·75
8	Credit note	C491		4·50	131·25
29	Goods	7038	80·00		211·25

Not only does a comparison between statements and day books provide a check on the accuracy of the items entered in these books, but also it verifies the balance shown in the ledger account.

6.1

You are to enter up the purchases day book from the following details, then post the items to the relevant accounts in the creditors' ledger and to show the entries in the nominal ledger at the end of the month.

19x3
June 1 Credit purchase from J. Lynch £130
3 Credit purchases from the following: D. Barnett £68, F. Hurst £117, B. Baxter £15, J. Wilson £62

6 Credit purchase from B. Baxter £43
9 Credit purchases from the following: D. Mortimer £72, F. Hurst £130, D. Barnett £15
17 Credit purchase from J. Lynch £180
24 Credit purchases from: J. Wilson £49, D. Mortimer £36
30 Credit purchases from: J. Lynch £132, D. Barnett £49

6.2
You are to enter up the sales day book from the following details, then post the items to the relevant accounts in the debtors' ledger and to show the entries in the nominal ledger at the end of the month.

19x7
Feb. 2 Credit sales to J. Edwards £310
5 Credit sales to: K. Hill £59, L. Vale £73, S. Webb £91
9 Credit sales to R. Stuart £52
14 Credit sales to: B. Charles £113, L. Vale £67, J. Edwards £141
16 Credit sales to R. Stuart £132
24 Credit sales to: J. Edwards £90, K. Hill £43, S. Webb £163
28 Credit sales to: B. Charles £68, L. Vale £48, R. Stuart £139

6.3
After entering the following in the various day books write up the personal accounts, then transfer the day book totals to the relevant nominal ledger accounts.

19x6
Oct. 1 Sold goods on credit to B. Long £80, S. Ward £125, C. Stone £62
3 Bought goods on credit from F. Riley £73, T. Short £95
4 S. Ward returned goods to us £37
8 Bought goods on credit from L. Lewis £84, B. Read £175
9 Returned goods to B. Read £52
10 Sold goods on credit to G. Tombs £84, S. Ward £45
15 Bought goods on credit from F. Riley £52, T. Short £41
17 Returned goods to F. Riley £43, T. Short £37
24 Sold goods on credit to B. Long £127, C. Stone £97
25 C. Stone returned goods to us £38
28 Bought goods on credit from L. Lewis £113, T. Short £77
29 Returned goods to L. Lewis £50
30 G. Tombs returned goods to us £23

6.4
You are to enter up the sales, purchases, and returns day books from the following details, then post the items to the relevant accounts in the personal ledgers and to show the transfers to the nominal ledger at the end of the month.

19x1
Feb. 1 Credit sales J. Swaine £250, E. Short £127, N. Sands £72
5 Credit purchases O. Reece £152, D. Poole £207, S. Pearce £57
10 Returned to D. Poole £52, S. Pearce £23

12   Credit sales N. Sands £133, E. Short £189
14   Returned from N. Sands £35, E. Short £20
15   Credit purchases E. Moore £42, D. Poole £146
20   Credit sales to J. Swain £213, L. Scott £78
     Returns from E. Short £5
23   Credit purchases O. Reece £139, S. Pearce £82
25   Credit sales E. Short £37, N. Sands £131
28   Returns from J. Swain £44, N. Sands £24
     Returns to O. Reece £38, S. Pearce £13

6.5

J. B. Williams began business on 1st July, 19x7, with capital of £800 consisting of £700 cash at the bank and £100 cash in hand.

19x7
July 1   Bought stationery paying by cheque £15
      2   Bought goods on credit from D. Rogers £97, C. Monk £116
      3   Sold goods on credit to O. Plough £36, W. Tapper £95
      4   Bought goods paying by cash £35
      5   Returned goods to D. Rogers £42
      6   Paid wages in cash £40
      8   Sold goods on credit to J. Webb £120
      9   Bought goods on credit from B. Lee £200, D. Rogers £72
     10   Returned goods to B. Lee £35
     11   Withdrew £100 from bank for cash
     12   Paid wages in cash £40
     14   Sold goods on credit to W. Tapper £92, O. Plough £72
     15   W. Tapper returned goods £30
     16   Paid D. Rogers the amount due to him by cheque
     19   Paid wages in cash £40
     24   O. Plough paid the amount due by cheque
     26   Paid wages by cash £40
     26   Cash sales for month £140
          W. Tapper returned goods £27
          Proprietor's drawings in cash £50

Enter the ledger accounts and prepare a trading and profit and loss account for the month and a balance sheet as at 26th July. The closing stock was valued at £175.

6.6

J. W. Smith commenced business on 1st December, 19x5, with capital consisting of £650 in the bank and £100 in cash.

19x5
Dec. 2   Bought goods on credit from B. Oakes £200, J. Wild £75 and
              A. Knott £166
          Paid for shop fittings by cheque £560
          Paid one month's rent by cheque £36
      4   Sold goods on credit to W. Spence £175, P. Barrow £160

71

7	Cash sales £90
10	Sold goods on credit to V. Strong £83
11	Bought goods paying by cheque £120
12	P. Barrow returned goods £38
17	W. Spence paid his account by cheque
19	Sold goods on credit to P. Barrow £140
21	Bought goods on credit from J. Wild £260
	Cash sales £120
23	Returned goods to J. Wild £37
	Paid sundry expenses by cash £15
28	Sold goods to W. Spence £84, V. Strong £162
30	V. Strong returned goods £44
	Paid B. Oakes the amount due to him by cheque
31	Paid wages in cash £125
	Drawings £60 in cash
	Paid cash into bank £100

Open all necessary books, post to ledger accounts and prepare a trading and profit and loss account for the month and a balance sheet as at 31st December, 19x5. The closing stock is valued at £200.

7 Year-end Adjustments and the Accruals Concept

The previous chapters have dealt with the recording and application of the double-entry concept. However, it would be a false assumption to presume that if final accounts are prepared from the existing entries in the books, these accounts would be correct. Some transactions that have taken place during a trading period may not wholly relate to that period, whilst others may have been omitted through lack of documentation.

The accruals concept states that the final accounts must show income and expenditure relevant to the period, not merely receipts and payments. In the case of expenditure this concept is already incorporated in transactions for credit purchases, as the account is debited immediately the goods are received. The cash element only affects the asset account of cash and the liability account of creditor.

The situation is more complicated for expenses. Normally expenses are paid as soon as an invoice is received, or very soon afterwards, but frequently there is a delay in receiving the invoice. For example, although electricity bills are rendered quarterly they refer to a period which is already in the past. If a business commences on the 1st January the first invoice will relate to the three months ended 31st March, but this invoice will not be received until towards the end of April which would be the earliest date of payment. Thus, in the first twelve months only three payments would be made, viz. 30th April, 31st July, and 31st October. This means that payments in the heating and lighting account would relate to nine months whereas the accounts are for twelve months.

The effect of this on the final accounts would be to understate the expenses for the year and, therefore, overstate the profit. The situation must be remedied and this is achieved by making a provision for the expense due, namely an accrued expense or, in short, an accrual. The amount of the accrual is normally estimated, but if the preparation of the accounts is delayed the exact amount may be ascertained.

Example

In the year ended 31st December, 19x4, the following accounts were paid in respect of electricity:

April 30th	£47	Quarter to 31st March, 19x4
July 31st	£28	30th June, 19x4
Oct. 31st	£30	30th September, 19x4

It is estimated that the amount in respect of the quarter ending on 31st December, 19x4, will be £52.

The account for heating and lighting after making provision for the accrual will be:

Heating and Lighting Account

19x4			£	19x4			£
Apr. 30 Cash	C/B		47	Dec. 31 Tfr. profit and			
July 31 ,,	,,		28	loss a/c			157
Oct. 31 ,,	,,		30				
Dec. 31 Accrual	C/D		52				
			£157				£157
				19x5			
				Jan. 1 Accrual	B/D		52

The charge to the profit and loss account is now correct as it is in respect of a full year. The account has a credit balance brought down which is a liability for, though the amount has been entered in the 19x4 accounts, it is still owing. This amount will be included in the current liabilities along with the trade creditors. The double-entry concept is applied because the item is debited above the total line and credited below in a similar manner to balances.

The same situation will arise in the following year, viz:

Example

In the year ended 31st December, 19x5, the following amounts were paid.

Jan. 31st	£52	Quarter ended 31st December, 19x4
Apr. 30th	£51	31st March, 19x5
July 31st	£33	30th June, 19x5
Oct. 31st	£34	30th September, 19x5

The amount for the quarter ended 31st December, 19x5, is estimated to be £57.

Heating and Lighting Account

19x5			£	19x5			£
Jan. 31	Cash	C/B	52	Jan. 1	Accrual	B/D	52
Apr. 30	,,	,,	51	Dec. 31	Tfr. profit and		
July 31	,,	,,	33		loss a/c		175
Oct. 31	,,	,,	34				
Dec. 31	Accrual	C/D	57				
			£227				£227
				19x6			
				Jan. 1	Accrual	B/D	57

It can be seen that the first payment of £52 is cancelled by the provision brought down so that the transfer to profit and loss account is the amount in respect of electricity used in the year 19x5. The £57 being a balance will be included in the 19x5 balance sheet as a current liability.

Provisions for accruals may have to be made in a number of expense accounts, for example, telephone, motor expenses, repairs, and wages.

On the other hand some items of expenditure have to be paid in advance, examples being rates, insurance, and road fund licences. These accounts will therefore show the expenditure paid for in the year and not the expenditure incurred during the year. Adjustments will have to be made at the year end for amounts in respect of the following period.

Example

James Long commenced business on the 1st January, 19x2. On 4th January, 19x2, he paid rates of £57 for the three months to the 31st March, 19x2. On 5th April, 19x2, he paid rates of £280 for the twelve months to 31st March, 19x3. The account, with adjustments, for the year to 31st December, 19x3, will appear as follows:

Rates Account

19x2			£	19x2			£
Jan. 4	Cash	C/B	57	Dec. 31	Prepayment	C/D	70
Apr. 5	,,	,,	280		Tfr. profit and		
					loss a/c		267
			£337				£337
19x3							
Jan. 1	Prepayment	B/D	70				

The amount of £267 transferred to the profit and loss account represents the amount of rates relating to the twelve months ended 31st December, 19x2. It is made up of £57 being three months to 31st March,

75

19x2, plus three-quarters of £280, i.e. £210, being 9 months rates to 31st December, 19x2. The £70 balance represents rates for part of the year 19x3 and will appear on the balance sheet at 31st December, 19x2, as a current asset.

In the following year the rates account would be as under if it is assumed that in 19x3 one payment of rates was made on the 6th April amounting to £320 in respect of the year to 31st March, 19x4.

Rates Account

19x3			£	19x3			£
Jan. 1	Prepayment	B/D	70	Dec. 31	Prepayment	C/D	80
Apr. 6	Cash	C/B	320		Tfr. profit and		
					loss a/c		310
			£390				£390

19x4			
Jan. 1	Prepayment	B/D	80

Similar adjustments should be made for receipts for example where property is sub-let or where a commission is received for services rendered.

Example

During the year ended 31st December, 19x2, James Long received commission of £492. At the 31st December, 19x2, he was owed £76 which he received on 9th January, 19x3.

Commission Received Account

19x2		£	19x2			£
Dec. 31	Tfr. profit and loss a/c	568	Dec. 31	Cash	C/B	492
				Amount due		76
		£568				£568

19x3			
Jan. 1	Amount due	76	

The £76 balance will appear on the balance sheet as a current asset as it is an amount due to the firm. In the account the £76 will be cancelled out when the cash is received on 9th January, 19x3.

As well as accruals and prepayments, adjustments being necessary at the year end to ensure the accounts conform to the accruals concepts, another type of provision may also be essential. This provision is in respect of stocks other than goods for resale.

Generally a certain amount of stationery and postage stamps will be kept on the premises. If a fleet of cars is kept, replacement parts may be held so that repairs can be effected without delay. If these amounts are "material", consideration of the stocks should be taken into account when the final accounts are produced.

What is material will largely depend on the size and nature of the business and the amount of stock involved. If the total value of these stocks is insignificant and would not affect the trading results, then it can be ignored. If the cost and work involved in calculating the amount outweighs the benefits achieved in including the stock, then it can also be ignored. Stocks amounting to £10 or less will have a greater effect on the profits of a small business, but will not be noticed in a large firm whose profits amount to millions of pounds. In the former business it will be material and should be included, but in the latter it is insignificant and can be ignored.

In a large firm where vast quantities of stationery are held the amount in the store room can be brought into account, but the quantities already distributed to various departments, although only partly used, are usually disregarded. The reason is that the cost and effort incurred to quantify the amount would not compensate for the benefit achieved in the accounts. Again, it is a question of the overall effect on the accounts, if it would affect the profit or total expense to any degree, it must be adjusted for in the accounts.

As stocks, in theory, are in the same nature as a prepayment the adjustment is carried out in a similar manner to the latter.

Example

James Long paid £270 for stationery in the year ended 31st December, 19x2, but at the end of the year stocks of stationery unused amounted to £56.

Stationery Account

19x2			£	19x2			£
Dec. 31	Cash	C/B	270	Dec. 31	Stock	C/D	56
					Tfr. profit and loss a/c		214
			£270				£270
19x3							
Jan. 1	Stock	B/D	56				

The £214 written off to the profit and loss account is the amount of stationery used in the year. The unused portion of £56 is carried forward to the following year. As there is a balance on the account it must be listed in the balance sheet and therefore becomes a current asset at the year end.

Many questions set in examinations do not ask for entries in the ledger accounts, but start with the trial balance and require the preparation of final accounts after dealing with accruals and prepayments. If the adjustments are concerned with expense accounts, the rule is to add the amount of the accrual to the expense account for profit and loss account purposes and include it in the balance sheet as a current liability. Prepayments are deducted from the amount shown in the trial balance for profit and loss account purposes and included as a current asset in the balance sheet, i.e.

	Profit and Loss Account	*Ledger account final balance*
Accrual	Debit	Credit
Prepayment	Credit	Debit

Example

The books of James Trafford showed the following balances at the close of business on 30th June, 19x2.

	£	£
Sales		37,910
Purchases	25,112	
Stock 1.7.19x1	7,552	
Salaries and wages	4,894	
Motor expenses	1,328	
Rent	912	
Rates	240	
Insurances	292	
Lighting and heating expenses	1,330	
Stationery	552	
Sundry expenses	230	
Motor vehicles	4,800	
Fixtures and fittings	1,200	
Debtors	9,154	
Creditors		6,090
Cash at bank	7,752	
Cash in hand	240	
Drawings	4,100	
Capital		25,688
	£69,688	£69,688

Notes at 30th June, 19x2:
1. Closing stock of goods £9,996.
2. Expenses which are owing: motor repairs £112, rent £48, electricity £52, stationery £37.

3. Expenses which have been prepaid: motor tax £50, rates £40, insurances £70.
4. Stock of stationery £25.

Prepare final accounts as at 30th June, 19x2.

JAMES TRAFFORD
Trading and Profit and Loss Account
Year ended 30th June, 19x2

	£			£
Opening stock	7,552	Sales		37,910
Add Purchases	25,112			
	32,664			
Less Closing stock	9,996			
COST OF GOODS SOLD	22,668			
Gross profit C/D	15,242			
	37,910			37,910
Salaries and wages	4,894	Gross profit B/D		15,242
Motor expenses	1,390			
Rent	960			
Rates	200			
Insurances	222			
Lighting and heating	1,382			
Stationery	564			
Sundry expenses	230			
Net profit	5,400			
	£15,242			£15,242

Balance Sheet as at 30th June, 19x2

	£	£		£	£
Capital			Fixed Assets		
Balance 1.7.19x2		25,688	Motor vehicles		4,800
Add Profit		5,400	Fixtures and fittings		1,200
		31,088			6,000
Less Drawings		4,100	Current assets		
		26,988	Stock	9,996	
Current liabilities			Stationery stk.	25	
Creditors	6,090		Debtors	9,154	
Accrued expenses	249		Prepayments	160	
		6,339	Cash at bank	7,752	
			Cash in hand	240	
					27,327
		£33,327			£33,327

79

PRINCIPLES OF ACCOUNTS

Figures in the final accounts which do not appear directly on the trial balance are calculated as under.

	Motor expenses	Rent	Rates	Insurance	Lighting	Stationery
Per trial balance	1,328	912	240	292	1,330	552
Add Accruals	112	48			52	37
	1,440	960	240	292	1,382	589
Less Prepayments	50		40	70		
Stock						25
	£1,390	£960	£200	£222	£1,382	£564

The total of accrued expenses is £249, and that of prepaid expense £160.

Unless the question specifically asks for workings there is no need to show them, although in practice it is advisable to calculate them on a separate sheet and submit them. The adjustments should never be shown in the main body of the final accounts.

EXERCISES

7.1
The final accounts of George Smith are made up to 30th June in each year. He rents two of his buildings to F. Jones and N. Murphy.

On 1st July, 19x8, there was a credit balance on the rents receivable account amounting to £150 representing one month's rent paid in advance by F. Jones, and a debit balance of £180 being one month's rent owing from N. Murphy.

During the year to 30th June, 19x9, George Smith received £1,500 from F. Jones representing the ten months to 31st May, 19x9, and from N. Murphy £2,520 representing rent for the fourteen months to 31st July, 19x9.

Show the rent receivable account in the ledger of George Smith for the year to 30th June, 19x9. Show the transfer to profit and loss account and any balances carried down.

7.2
The following account is a copy of the rent and rates account of B. Shaw for 19x3 as it appears in the ledger.

Rent and Rates Account

19x3				£	19x3				£
Jan. 8	Cash. Rates to 31.3.x3		C/B	400	Jan. 1	Balance	B/D		360
Feb. 1	Rent to 28.2.x3		C/B	480					
Apr. 7	Rent to 31.5.x3		C/B	480					
June 20	Rates to 30.9.x3		C/B	500					

80

Aug. 2	Rent to 31.8.x3	C/B	480
Nov. 1	Rent to 30.11.x3	C/B	540
8	Rates to 31.3.x4	C/B	500
Dec. 23	Rent to 28.2.x4	C/B	540

Notes

(a) The balance brought forward consisted of one month's rent at the rate of £1,920 per annum, and £200 rates.

(b) The rent was increased to £2,160 per annum from 1st September, 19x3.

You are required to close off the account as at 31st December, 19x3, showing the transfer to profit and loss account separating the rent and rates, and the balance(s) carried down.

7.3

From the following particulars write up the lighting and heating account for the year ended 30th September, 19x3. Show the transfer to profit and loss account and carry down any balances.

On 1st October, 19x2, there was a stock of fuel amounting to £76, and £43 was owing in respect of electricity.

During the year ended 30th September, 19x3, cash was paid for fuel £475, and for electricity £259.

At 30th September, 19x3, the stock of fuel amounted to £52. There were amounts unpaid for electricity for the three months ended 30th September estimated at £65 and a fuel bill of £27.

7.4

W. Snape was in business as a retail grocer and the trial balance of his books as at 30th June, 19x9, was:

	£	£
Purchases	12,800	
Sales		17,400
Rent	940	
Returns inwards	112	
Returns outwards		90
Stock at 1st July, 19x8	1,920	
Capital account		1,784
Rates	192	
Sundry debtors	1,018	
Sundry creditors		408
Shop fixtures	480	
Insurance	72	
Carriage inwards	32	
Carriage outwards	96	
Wages	1,096	
Cash in hand	68	
Cash at bank	654	
Advertising	120	
Office expenses	82	
	£19,682	£19,682

Prepare trading and profit and loss accounts for the year ended 30th June, 19x9, and a balance sheet as at that date, taking into consideration the following adjustments.

(1) The stock in hand at 30th June, 19x9, was £3,300.
(2) Prepayments were: rates £35, insurance £16.
(3) Accruals were estimated for rent £60, office expenses £18.
(4) Half the advertising expenditure related to the following year.
(5) There was a stock of stationery (included in office expenses) amounting to £15.

7.5

From the following trial balance prepare a trading and profit and loss account for the year ended 31st March, 19x6, and a balance sheet as at that date.

	£	£
Capital 1.4.19x5		17,900
Drawings	2,100	
Stock 1.4.19x5	7,450	
Purchases	46,200	
Sales		79,550
Wages and salaries	12,410	
Lighting and heating	620	
Equipment	7,200	
Carriage outwards	460	
Returns inwards	210	
Returns outwards		580
Discount allowed	570	
Discount received		630
Rent, rates, and insurance	2,230	
Motor vehicles	2,950	
Cash in hand	220	
Sundry creditors		9,850
Sundry debtors	27,840	
Bank overdraft		1,950
	£110,460	£110,460

The following information is relevant:

(1) Stock at 31st March, 19x6, amounts to £6,320.
(2) Prepayments: rates £150, insurance £76.
(3) Accruals: electricity £57, rent £250.

7.6

After his trading account for the year ended 30th June, 19x3, has been prepared, a trader's position is as follows:

	£	£
Trading account—gross profit		10,500
Plant and machinery	6,580	
Stock 30th June, 19x3	820	

	£	£
Debtors	3,250	
Creditors		2,360
Capital 1st July, 19x2		7,930
Discount allowed	450	
Discount received		370
Salaries and office expenses	2,320	
Rent, rates, and insurance	1,730	
Carriage outwards	240	
Motor expenses	1,240	
General expenses	1,000	
Drawings	1,700	
Cash at bank	1,790	
Cash in hand	40	
	£21,160	£21,160

The following information is relevant at 30th June, 19x3.

(1) Prepayments: rates £350, insurance £120, car tax £150.
(2) Accruals: rent £200, motor expenses £93, general expenses £48.
(3) Stock of stationery at 30th June, 19x3, £142 (included in general expenses).

Prepare a profit and loss account for the year ended 30th June, 19x3, and a balance sheet as at that date.

8 Year-end Adjustments— Depreciation

The preceding chapter dealt with year-end adjustments in respect of revenue expenditure and income. Further adjustments must be made in respect of certain items of capital expenditure. One of the basic concepts of accounting is to enter all transactions at cost, but in the case of fixed assets it would be incorrect to show each item continually at cost in the balance sheet. The balance sheet purports to list the assets at their true value which will, after a period of time, differ from their original price.

Generally speaking, an asset declines in value immediately after its purchase. A simple solution of showing the value of assets would be to re-value them at each year end by finding out what each would realise if sold at that time to a third party. Unfortunately, this would also be incorrect for if it was intended to sell off the assets of the business it would be forced to close down.

The assets in the balance sheet should be valued on a " going concern " basis which is a further concept of accounting. This infers that the business has an indefinite life and the values placed on assets are their worth to the business at that point in its existence. Fixed assets are held by a business for a number of years so that when a firm buys, for example, an item of machinery the price paid represents the cost of a benefit that will be recouped during the useful life of the machine. At each year end a portion of the benefit has been received so that the value of the machine represents the proportionate part of the cost in relation to the benefits still to be received. This value may bear no comparison with the amount that can be obtained by selling the machine. If an item of plant is peculiar to a specific trade, the second-hand value may be negligible whereas its value to the firm may be incalculable, especially if the machine cannot be replaced.

A plot of land, on the other hand may increase in value due to inflation, but the same plot of land may increase considerably more if used for a different purpose. Thus, freehold land in a city may be worth less if used for continuance of a business than if sold for house or flat development. The value that must be placed on it for balance sheet purposes is that relating to the continuance of the business.

The overall cost of an asset to a business is the price paid for its original value less the amount received for it when it is sold. This net amount which is spread over the life of the asset is known as depreciation and should be written off to the profit and loss accounts in proportion to the benefits derived from its use.

Two types of difficulty arise in the estimation of depreciation. Initially there is the problem of calculating the overall amount and, secondly, the allocation of the amount to specific trading periods.

With regard to the first difficulty it was stated that the total depreciation charge is calculated thus:

	£
Initial cost of asset	xxx
Less Residual value at end of useful life	xxx
Total depreciation	£xxx

Unfortunately only one factor is known with any degree of certainty, that being the initial cost. The residual value can only be estimated and this in turn will depend to some extent on how long it is intended to keep the asset. If a motor vehicle is purchased and it is intended to keep it for four years, by comparison with previous trends it may be possible to calculate the residual value reasonably accurately. However, if circumstances change and the vehicle is kept for six years, unless the decline in value is constant from year to year, the revised depreciation will not be proportionate to the original calculation.

Even if the total depreciation can be accurately determined, its allocation to individual years may almost be impossible to estimate. The annual depreciation will be charged to the profit and loss account and as the latter is based on the accruals concept, i.e. expenditure relevant to the period, the depreciation charge should be based on the benefit derived from the asset, viz.:

$$\frac{\text{Benefit received in the year}}{\text{Total estimated benefits}} \times \text{Net cost}$$

The way in which total depreciation is written off over the years depends on:

(a) *Type of Asset.* The nature of the asset itself in many instances will determine how depreciation is to be charged. Leasehold buildings

85

if properly utilised will provide constant benefits over a specified number of years so that the charge for depreciation will be constant. Machinery tends to become less efficient as it grows older, therefore the benefits decline and depreciation should be greater in the earlier years and decrease towards the end of the asset's life.

(b) *Use of Asset.* Some assets are not used continually during their lifetime because of internal or external factors. An emergency generator will only be used when the main supply fails, therefore depreciation should be charged according to use. A toll bridge is dependent on the people using it for the income gained. Due to population increase, more use may be made of the bridge the older is becomes, in which case depreciation should be low in earlier years and increase in later years.

(c) *Repairs and Maintenace.* The older an asset becomes the more likely it becomes that the repair bill will increase. So that all associated costs remain fairly constant in the profit and loss account depreciation is higher in the earlier years and lower in the later years. In earlier years high depreciation and low repairs should equate in later years with low depreciation and high repairs.

(d) *Size of Asset.* Where fixed assets comprise a number of small items of low price, e.g. tools of the trade, it is impossible to depreciate each one separately. A hammer or screwdriver may last a number of years, but the total cost is only a few pounds. The method adopted here is that of revaluation, viz.:

Loose Tools Account

19x1			£	19x1			£
Jan. 1	Balance	C/D	2,500	Dec. 31	Balance	C/D	5,800
Dec. 31	Purchases	C/B	4,000		Tfr. profits		
					and loss a/c		700
			£6,500				£6,500
19x2							
Jan. 1	Balance	B/D	700				

Stock is taken at the end of each year end and a value placed on it. The difference between this figure and the total debit is transferred to profit and loss account as depreciation (in the above example £700). This latter figure is not wholly depreciation as it includes assets that may be missing, either lost or stolen.

(e) *Type of Business.* Depreciation may be governed by the business itself. Certain trades, e.g. printing, have a recommended method of providing depreciation, in order that accounts are prepared on a standard basis and can thus be used for inter-firm comparison. If the business has a short life, depreciation must be calculated on the life of the firm and not on the life of the asset, as the latter will in many cases be greater than the former.

(f) *External Factors.* The total charge for depreciation may be influenced by outside considerations. If the business is in a rapidly changing technological trade, machines may have to be replaced within a short time by more efficient equipment. Thus, the useful life of a machine is greatly reduced and the total depreciation has to be written off in a shorter period. Where a fleet of salesmen's cars is kept, it may be necessary to replace each car within two or three years in order to present a good image to the business's customers, whereas in practice the useful life of the cars may be much longer.

To comply with the considerations detailed previously, several methods of depreciation charge-off have been devised and are described on the following pages.

The Straight Line or Fixed Instalment Method

As its name implies this method is used when the annual charge to profit and loss account is to be constant. This method is probably the easiest to apply, but is generally not the most appropriate. If efficiency of the asset declines or repairs tend to increase over its life, the charge to profit and loss account will not reflect the benefits gained.

The calculation and method of recording in the ledger are illustrated below:

A machine is bought for £6,000. It has an estimated life of three years and a scrap value of £750 at the end of its life. The machine was purchased on 1st January, 19x1.

	£
Cost of machine	6,000
Estimated residual value	750
Total depreciation	£5,250

$$\text{Annual charge} \frac{£5,250}{3} = £1,750$$

The accounts involved are the asset account and the provision for depreciation of machinery account.

MACHINERY ACCOUNT

19x1			£
Jan. 1 Purchase of machine	EDB	6,000	

Provision Depreciation of Machinery Account

19x2			£	19x1		£
Dec. 31 Balance	C/D	3,500		Dec. 31 Tfr. profit and loss a/c		1,750
				19x2		
				Dec. 31 Tfr. profit and loss a/c		1,750
			£3,500			£3,500
19x3				19x2		
Dec. 31 Balance	C/D	5,250		Jan. 1 Balance	B/D	3,500
				19x3		
				Dec. 31 Tfr. profit and loss a/c		1,750
			£5,250			£5,250
				19x4		
				Jan. 1 Balance	B/D	£5,250

The transfer to the provision for depreciation account is made at each year end, the debit appearing in the profit and loss account. The two ledger accounts are combined in the balance sheet at each year end, so that the net amount reflects the value of the asset to the firm, viz.:

Balance Sheet (Extract) at 31st December

	19x1	19x2	19x3
Fixed assets	£	£	£
Machinery at cost	6,000	6,000	6,000
Less Depreciation provision	1,750	3,500	5,250
	£4,250	£2,500	£750

It can be seen that as time passes the value to the firm decreases until 31st December, 19x3, when the value of £750 represents the amount which will be received from the sale of the machine for scrap.

The Reducing or Diminishing Balance Method

This method is designed to give a reducing charge for depreciation each year. A percentage depreciation rate is calculated which when applied

88

to the net value of the asset at each year end will reduce the item to its scrap value at the end of its life. The formula used to calculate the percentage rate is:

$$r = 1 - \sqrt[n]{\frac{s}{c}}$$

The meanings of the symbols are as follows:

r—depreciation rate required n—life of the asset
s—the residual value c—cost of the asset

Applying the formula to the example given under the straight line method, the rate will be calculated as follows:

$$r = 1 - \sqrt[3]{\frac{750}{6,000}} = 1 - \sqrt[3]{\frac{1}{8}}$$
$$r = 1 - \tfrac{1}{2} = \tfrac{1}{2} \text{ or } 50\%$$

The entries in the ledger accounts will be as under.

MACHINERY ACCOUNT

19x1			£
Jan. 1 Purchase of machine	PDB		6,000

Provision Depreciation of Machinery Account

19x2			£	19x1			£
Dec. 31 Balance	C/D	4,500		Dec. 31 Tfr. profit and loss a/c			3,000
				19x2			
				Dec. 31 – do –			1,500
		£4,500					£4,500
19x3				19x3			
Dec. 31 Balance	C/D	5,250		Jan. 1 Balance	B/D		4,500
				Dec. 31 Tfr. profit and loss a/c			750
		£5,250					£5,250
				19x4			
				Jan. 1 Balance	B/D		£5,250

Extracts from the balance sheet are:

Balance Sheet at 31st December

	19x1	19x2	19x3
	£	£	£
Fixed assets			
Machinery at cost	6,000	6,000	6,000
Less Depreciation provision	3,000	4,500	5,250
	£3,000	£1,500	£750

It will be noted that the "written down value" of the asset at 31st December, 19x3, is exactly the same as that shown in the previous example, but in 19x1 and 19x2 the values are much lower than shown in the straight line method.

The computation of the depreciation shown in the provision account is as follows:

19x1			£
Jan. 1	Cost of asset		6,000
Dec. 31	Depreciation for year at 50% of £6,000		3,000
	Written down value		3,000
19x2			
Dec. 31	Depreciation for year at 50% of £3,000		1,500
	Written down value		1,500
19x3			
Dec. 31	Depreciation for year at 50% of £1,500		750
	Written down value		£750

In the example given the amounts of depreciation are somewhat exaggerated because of the short working life of the asset. In practice asset lives tend to be much longer and the difference between the annual charges is thereby reduced.

When using the formula to calculate the rate of depreciation there must be a value given to "s". If the residual value is nil then no matter what values are given to "n" and "c" the rate would always be 100% which is obviously incorrect. Where there is in fact no residual value it is suggested that a nominal amount of £1 is inserted in the formula. This will mean that the overall depreciation will be understated by £1 but this can be adjusted in the final year, e.g.:

Plant costing £125 has a life of 3 years with no residual value. Using the formula $r = 1 - \sqrt[n]{(s/c)} = 1 - \sqrt[3]{\frac{0}{125}} = 1 - 0 = 1$ or 100% but substituting £1 for "s", $r = 1 - \sqrt[3]{\frac{1}{125}} = 1 - \frac{1}{5} = \frac{4}{5}$ or 80%

	£
Cost	125
1st year depreciation at 80%	100
Written down value	25
2nd year depreciation at 80%	20
Written down value	5
3rd year depreciation at 80%	4
Difference adjusted final year	1

In practice depreciation is charged for a complete year in the trading period when the asset is acquired irrespective of the actual date of purchase and no depreciation is charged in the year of sale or disposal. This conforms with the normal method used by the Inland Revenue for calculating allowances for expenditure on capital items. Where it is specifically requested that depreciation is to be calculated on a monthly basis, only the first and last part years are apportioned when applying the straight line method. The reducing balance method is more complicated, but the accepted method is to calculate the first year's depreciation and take the relevant proportion. The second year's charge is then based on the written down value in the normal way.

Disposals of Fixed Assets

When an asset is sold or scrapped it must be eliminated from the books of account. This is achieved by opening a disposals account in the ledger. The cost of the asset is transferred from the asset account and the depreciation in respect of the asset sold transferred from the depreciation account. If the original calculations are correct, the disposals account should balance when credited with the amount received for scrap.

Unfortunately, as was explained at the beginning of the chapter, two out of three factors involved in the calculation are only estimates. It follows that it is only when the asset is disposed of that all factors can be ascertained. Therefore, in the majority of disposals there will be slight differences which will be transferred to the profit and loss account.

Example

On 1st January, 19x1, a vehicle is purchased for £1,000. It is estimated that it will have a useful life of 5 years and then be sold for £200. The business year ended on 31st December.

On 1st January, 19x4, the vehicle was sold for £450.
Depreciation is to be calculated on the straight line method.

$$\text{Original annual depreciation} = \frac{£1,000-200}{5} = £160$$

MOTOR VEHICLES

19x1			£	19x4			£
Jan. 1	Purchase of vehicle EDB		1,000	Jan. 1	Tfr. disposals	L3	1,000

Provision Depreciation Motor Vehicles

19x4			£	19x4			£
Jan. 1	Tfr. disposals	L3	480	Jan. 1	Balance (3 years at £160 per year) B/D		480

Disposals Account

19x4			£	19x4			£
Jan. 1	Tfr. cost of vehicle	L1	1,000	Jan. 1	Tfr. deprecia-tion	L2	480
					Cash received C/B		450
				Dec. 31	Tfr. loss on sale to profit and loss a/c		70
			£1,000				£1,000

In the above example the motor vehicles and the provision for depreciation accounts are closed off. The disposals account also balances by transferring the loss of £70 to the profit and loss account. This amount represents depreciation under-provided in the previous three years. Occasionally there is a profit on sale which represents depreciation over-provided and this should be credited to the profit and loss account in the year of disposal.

Sinking Fund Method

Up to now the objects of providing depreciation have been defined as writing off the purchase price of the asset to the profit and loss account over its lifetime, and thereby reflecting the worth of the asset in the corresponding balance sheets. A further object is to provide funds for the replacement of the asset when it becomes useless.

In order not to contract the size of his business the owner should not withdraw more than the profits made. If he does so, it means that he is withdrawing his original capital thereby reducing the business liabilities and hence reducing the business assets. With reduced assets the business cannot operate on the same level as previously. By charging the profit and loss account with depreciation the profit is therefore restricted, curbing the amount that is available for drawings. Unfortunately, the savings may not increase the bank or cash balances, for the amount relative to depreciation can be used in acquiring other assets, fixed or current, with the result that when it becomes necessary to replace the asset there is no cash available.

To overcome this deficiency a sinking fund is established. This is achieved by investing an amount equivalent to the depreciation charge in securities which can be sold to realise cash for replacement of the asset. However, as the money is invested in securities interest will be received and this in turn is reinvested so that the depreciation charge can be slightly reduced. The charge for depreciation is obtained by reference to sinking fund tables.

SINKING FUND TABLES (Extract)

Amount required to be invested to provide £1

Years	4% (£)	5% (£)
4	0·2355	0·2320
5	0·1846	0·1810
6	0·1508	0·1470

Example

A machine is purchased for £4,820 on 1st January, 19x1. It has an expected life of four years. At the end of this time it will be sold for £820. A sinking fund will be opened to provide for replacement of this asset and it is estimated that an investment carrying 5% interest can be obtained.

Construct the necessary accounts to reflect the above.

The amount needed to replace the machine is £4,820, but as £820 will be received on sale the firm must contribute £4,000. By reference to the sinking fund tables £0·2320, if invested annually for 4 years at a compound interest of 5%, will amount to £1. As £4,000 is required the annual amount of investment is $4,000 \times £0·2320 = £928$.

MACHINERY ACCOUNT

19x1			£
Jan. 1 Purchase of machine			4,820

Provision Depreciation of Machinery Account

19x2			£	19x1			£
Dec. 31 Balance	C/D	1,903		Dec. 31 Tfr. profit and			
				loss a/c			928
				19x2			
				Dec. 31 Interest re-			
				ceived 5%			
				on £928	C/B	47	
				Tfr. profit and			
				loss a/c			928
			£1,903				£1,903
19x3				19x3			
Dec. 31 Balance	C/D	2,926		Jan. 1 Balance	C/D	1,903	
				Dec. 31 Interest re-			
				ceived 5%			
				on £1,903	C/B	95	
				Tfr. profit and			
				loss a/c			928
			£2,926				£2,926
19x4			£	19x4			£
Dec. 31 Balance	C/D	4,000		Jan. 1 Balance	B/D	2,926	
				Dec. 31 Interest re-			
				ceived 5%			
				on £2,926			146
				Tfr. profit and			
				loss a/c			928
			£4,000				£4,000
				19x5			
				Jan. 1 Balance			4,000

Sinking Fund Account

19x1			£	19x2			£
Dec. 31 Cash	C/B	928		Dec. 31 Balance	C/D	1,903	
19x2							
Dec. 31 Cash	C/B	975					
			£1,903				£1,903
19x3				19x3			
Jan. 1 Balance	B/D	1,903		Dec. 31 Balance	C/D	2,926	
Dec. 31 Cash	C/B	1,023					
			£2,926				£2,926

19x4				19x4			
Jan. 1	Balance	B/D	2,926	Dec. 31	Balance	C/D	4,000
Dec. 31	Cash	C/B	1,074				
			£4,000				£4,000

19x5			
Jan. 1	Balance	B/D	4,000

The amount invested in the sinking fund each year is the total of the depreciation charge for the year plus interest received in the year. At each year end the balance on the sinking fund must agree with the balance on the depreciation account.

The accounts would appear on the respective balance sheets as under:

Balance Sheet (Extract) at 31st December

	19x1	19x2	19x3	19x4
Fixed assets	£	£	£	£
Machinery at cost	4,820	4,820	4,820	4,820
Less Depreciation provision	928	1,903	2,926	4,000
	£3,892	£2,917	£1,894	£820
Investments				
Sinking fund	928	1,903	2,926	4,000

It can be seen that the total of the written down value of the machine and the sinking fund investments total £4,820 in each of the years.

If the machine is sold on 1st January, 19x5, the asset and depreciation account will be closed by transferring the balances to disposals account. The disposals account in turn will balance if the cash received for its sale is £820 as estimated.

To replace the machine the investments are sold for £4,000 which, together with the £820 received on the sale, equals the purchase price.

In practice there are several objections to this method of depreciation.

1. It is difficult, as stated, to estimate the useful life of the asset and its residual value.
2. Interest rates may vary over the years of the investment.
3. There is no guarantee that the investments can be bought or sold at a pre-determined cost price.
4. In times of inflation the replacement cost of the asset will increase and there will still be insufficient money available to buy a similar machine.
5. The interest obtained (in the above case 5%) is lower than could normally be gained by using the money invested in normal trading

95

activities. That is, cash is tied up for a number of years at a low investment return.

Plant Registers

Where only one asset of each type is held by the firm the ledger accounts will provide all the essential information. Where several assets of each type are held, e.g. a fleet of motor vehicles, a supplementary record is required. The ledger accounts will contain the cost price of all vehicles and the total depreciation written off. Particulars relating to individual vehicles are not shown, unless the ledger accounts are supported by a register. The register is not part of the double-entry system, it only analyses the two accounts.

Example

W. Smith operates a car hire business. During the four years to 30th June, 19x4, the following transactions took place.

Registration number	GY1A	GY2A	GY7B	GY8C	GY5D
Purchases year ended 30th June	19x1	19x1	19x2	19x3	19x4
Cost of vehicle	£1,000	£1,200	£1,200	£1,000	£800

During the year ended 30th June, 19x4, vehicle GY2A was sold for £575. Depreciation is calculated at 20% per annum on the reducing balance method. A whole year's depreciation is taken in the year of purchase and none in the year of sale. Amounts are taken to the nearest £1.

PLANT REGISTER

Date	Details	Total	GY1A	GY2A	GY7B	GY8C	GY5D
19x1		£	£	£	£	£	£
June 30	Purchases	2,200	1,000	1,200			
	Depreciation	440	200	240			
	Written down value	1,760	800	960			
19x2							
June 30	Purchases	1,200			1,200		
		2,960	800	960	1,200		
	Depreciation	592	160	192	240		
	Written down value	2,368	640	768	960		

19x3 June 30	£	£	£	£	£
Purchases	1,000				1,000
	3,368	640	768	960	1,000
Depreciation	674	128	154	192	200
Written down value	2,694	512	614	768	800

19x4 June 30	£	£	£	£	£	£
Purchases	800					800
	3,494	512	614	768	800	800
Sales	614		614			
	2,880	512	—	768	800	800
Depreciation	576	102		154	160	160
Written down value	2,304	410		614	640	640

Motor Vehicles Account

19x1			£	19x1			£
June 30	GY1A	EDB	1,000	June 30	Balance	C/D	2,200
	GY2A	EDB	1,200				
			£2,200				£2,000

19x1				19x2			
July 1	Balance	B/D	2,200	June 30	Balance	C/D	3,400
19x2							
June 30	GY7B	EDB	1,200				
			£3,400				£3,400

19x2				19x3			
July 1	Balance	B/D	3,400	June 30	Balance	C/D	4,400
19x3							
June 30	GY8C	EDB	1,000				
			£4,400				£4,400

19x3				19x4			
July 1	Balance	B/D	4,400	June 30	Tfr. disposals		1,200
19x4					Balance	C/D	4,000
June 30	GY5D	EDB	800				
			£5,200				£5,200

19x4			
July 1	Balance	B/D	4,000

Depreciation Motor Vehicles Account

19x2			£	19x1			£
June 30	Balance	C/D	1,032	June 30	Tfr. profit and loss a/c		440
				19x2			
				June 30	– do –		592
			£1,032				£1,032
19x3				19x2			
June 30	Balance	C/D	1,706	July 1	Balance	B/D	1,032
				19x3			
				June 30	Tfr. profit and loss a/c		674
			£1,706				£1,706
19x3				19x3			
June 30	Tfr. disposals		586	July 1	Balance	B/D	1,706
	Balance	C/D	1,696				
				19x4			
				June 30	Tfr. profit and loss a/c		576
			£2,282				£2,282
				19x4			
				July 1	Balance		1,696

Disposals Account

19x3		£	19x3		£
June 30	Tfr. cost of vehicle	1,200	June 30	Tfr. depreciation	586
				Cash proceeds	575
				Tfr. profit and loss: loss on sale	39
		£1,200			£1,200

Balance Sheet (Extract) at 30th June

	19x1 £	19x2 £	19x3 £	19x4 £
Fixed assets				
Motor vehicles at cost	2,200	3,400	4,400	4,000
Less Depreciation provision	440	1,032	1,706	1,696
	£1,760	£2,368	£2,694	£2,304

98

The total column in the plant register agrees with the total written down value in the balance sheet. It is essential that the depreciation account only contains depreciation written off vehicles which are still owned by the business. Apart from providing additional information the use of a register simplifies the entries when items are sold for the respective amounts are readily available. Also, the danger of over-depreciating individual assets is averted. When items are aggregated in the asset accounts, if the straight line method is used for depreciation, individual assets may be incorrectly depreciated beyond their cost price. In the register it will be apparent when these assets have been written down to their nil or residual value and no further depreciation is required.

Depreciation and Inflation

Because the replacement cost of fixed assets is generally higher than the original cost, depreciation by itself will not ensure that there are sufficient funds available to purchase the asset. To provide for this additional cost a further debit to the profit and loss account can be made. This is known as a plant replacement reserve and is credited to a reserve account.

The reserve account is kept entirely separate from the asset and depreciation accounts in the balance sheet and is entered as a liability of the firm immediately below the capital account.

EXERCISES

8.1
A business starts trading on 1st January, 19x1. During the four years ended 31st December, 19x4, the following transactions took place in respect of machinery.

19x1   1st January—1 machine purchased for £1,600
19x2   2nd February—2 machines costing £1,000 each
   1st November—1 machine costing £1,200
19x4   1st May—1 machine costing £400
   1st October—sold one of the machines purchased on 2nd February, £700

Write up the ledger accounts necessary to record the above taking:

(a) a depreciation rate of 10% on the straight line method, and
(b) a depreciation rate of 20% on the reducing balance method.

PRINCIPLES OF ACCOUNTS

Depreciation is taken on assets in existence at the end of each year, giving a full year's depreciation irrespective of date of purchase, and ignoring depreciation in year of disposal.

8.2

Open up all ledger accounts necessary to record the following transactions and show how they would be shown in the balance sheet at 31st December, 19x7.

19x7		£
Jan. 1	Balances brought forward	
	Machinery asset account	10,000
	Provision depreciation of machinery account	4,000
	Purchased new machinery for	12,000
Mar. 31	Machinery purchased on 1st January, 19x5, at a cost of £5,000 was sold for	2,800
Apr. 1	Purchased new machinery for	7,600
June 30	An item of machinery purchased for £4,000 on 1st April, 19x7, was sold for	4,200
Sept. 30	Balance of machinery purchased on 1st April, 19x7 was damaged beyond repair and sold as scrap for	300
Dec. 31	Purchased new machinery	5,000

Depreciation is provided at the rate of 20% per annum on the written down value and is calculated on each completed calendar month for which the machinery is held.

8.3

A business purchases a five year lease of premises for £8,000. It is decided to write off the lease and provide for its renewal by means of the sinking fund method. The necessary annual investment will obtain interest at 5% per annum and you are informed that £0·181 invested annually at 5% compound interest will amount to £1 at the end of five years.

You are required to open ledger accounts necessary to record the above for the five years.

8.4

At 30th June, 19x5, the position of a business's fixed assets were as follows:

	Cost	Total depreciation
Machinery	£96,000	£34,600
Motor vehicles	£15,800	£7,600

The following additions were made during the financial year ended 30th June, 19x6.

Machinery £8,000. Motor vehicles £4,000
Machines bought on 1st April, 19x1, for £12,000 were sold for £5,000
Vehicles bought on 1st January, 19x3, for £4,000 were sold for £1,700

Depreciation is provided at 10% on the straight line method for machinery and at 25% on the reducing balance method for motor vehicles on assets in use at the year end.

Write up the ledger accounts for the year ended 30th June, 19x6, and show the relevant entries in the profit and loss account and balance sheet.

8.5

A business engaged in motor transport had the following dealings:

19x4
Jan.   1   Purchased three vehicles for £1,600 each (nos. 1–3)
19x5
Jan.   1   Purchased two vehicles for £1,200 each (nos. 4–5)
June 30   Sold vehicle no. 2 for £1,100
19x6
Mar. 31   Purchased two vehicles for £1,500 each (nos. 6–7)

Depreciation is calculated at 25% on the reducing balance method on vehicles in use at each year end (31st December). You are required:

(a) to write up the necessary ledger accounts supported by a vehicle register, and
(b) to show what adjustment is required on the 1st January, 19x7, if the proprietor wishes to alter the method of depreciation to the straight line method, writing off the cost over five years to leave a residual value of £200 on each vehicle.

8.6

An item of plant is purchased for £1,600. It has an estimated life of four years and a residual value of £100.

Show the depreciation account and debit to profit and loss account using the following:

(1) Straight line method.
(2) Reducing balance method.
(3) Sinking fund method (assuming an investment of 5% and given that an annual investment of £0·232 will amount to £1 with compound interest of 5%).

8.7

The net profits of George Smith for 31st December, 19x1, 19x2, and 19x3 were £5,920, £6,310, and £6,374 respectively. It has now been found that the wrong method was used for depreciation of machinery and motor vehicles when calculating these profit figures.

All the assets in question were acquired on 1st January, 19x1, for £5,120 (machinery) and £25,600 (motor vehicles).

The method used was the straight line method, assuming for machinery a life of twelve years and scrap value of £320, and for the motor vehicles a life of eight years and scrap value of £1,600. The method which should have been used was the reducing balance method (machinery $12\frac{1}{2}\%$ per annum, and motor vehicles 25% per annum).

You are required to re-calculate the net profits for 19x1, 19x2, and 19x3.

8.8

The vehicles register of Harvey Jones showed the following position on 1st January, 19x8 (only extracts are shown).

	AB4A	BC8B	DE7C	FG1D	HJ3E	KL7F	Total
	£	£	£	£	£	£	£
Original value	1,000	1,200	1,500	1,200	1,600	1,400	7,900
Written down value	100	100	380	540	1,000	1,140	3,260

The vehicles are written off over five years on the straight line method of depreciation to give a residual value of £100 on each vehicle. During the year ended 31st December, 19x8, vehicles FG1D and HJ3E were sold for £500 and £800 respectively. Vehicle MN7G was acquired for £1,700.

You are required to write up the relevant ledger accounts for the year to 31st December, 19x8.

Note. Exercises relating to treatment of depreciation in the final accounts are contained at the end of the next chapter.

9 Asset Adjustment— Bad Debts and Provision for Doubtful Debts

Before the balance sheet can be said to show a true and fair view of the financial position of the business, assets other than the fixed assets will have to be investigated. Viewed from a "going concern" concept the assets in the balance sheet should represent the benefit still to be obtained by the business. The asset of debtors represents money owing to the undertaking in respect of credit sales. Unfortunately, though these debts are legally binding not all of them may be paid.

Bad Debts

Certain debtors may have become bankrupt, that is unable to pay their debts despite legal action being taken against them. The court will declare them bankrupt which means that they cannot be sued for the debt. Whatever monies they have available is shared between the people or businesses to whom they owe debts in the form of a dividend. For example, if they owe £1,000, but have only £250, then their creditors will receive 25p for every £1 that is owed. The balance of 75p in every pound is a bad debt and cannot be recovered. In other cases the debtor may just "disappear" by moving to a new locality and cannot be traced.

The amounts owing but which can never be recouped should be transferred from the debtor's account to a separate account in the nominal ledger—a "bed debts account", viz.:

B. COOKE

19x6			£	19x6		£
Feb. 2	Goods	SDB	80	June 30	Tfr. bad debts	80

Bad Debts Account

19x6		£	19x6	£
June 30	Tfr. B. Cooke	80		

The bad debts account acts as a collection centre and is transferred to the debit of profit and loss account at the end of the year. It is advisable to look through the debtors ledger at frequent intervals during the year and pursue any amounts that are overdue as this may reduce the number of possible bad debts. Where any debts prove to be bad these should be immediately written off to the bad debts account, otherwise the total of debtors would be misleading.

Provision for Doubtful Debts

The remaining debtors are those not known to be bad and the total of these is the figure which appears in the balance sheet. It is possible, though, that unforeseen circumstances will render some of these debts as bad, therefore a provision should be made to guard against this future loss. A convention has been established by accountants named the "Doctrine of Conservatism". This implies that profits should not be brought into account until they have been earned, but that provision should be made for all actual and possible losses that can be ascertained.

There is some controversy as to which period the bad debt should be related. It can be argued that the loss arises when the sale is first made or when the payment becomes due. The two dates may be in different trading periods. It is generally accepted that a provision be made in the period the sale takes place to conform with the doctrine of conservatism.

The provision is usually determined by taking a percentage of the total debtors at each year end. The percentage used is by reference to the incidence of bad debts incurred in the past or in the particular trade generally. Unlike the provision for depreciation the provision for doubtful debts is not aggregated from year to year. After the initial creation of the provision it will only require to be adjusted to result in a figure representing a percentage of the debtors. The entries are made at the end of each financial year and consist of transfers between the profit and loss account and the provision for bad debts account.

Example

M. Jones commences business on 1st January, 19x1. His debtors at
31st December, 19x1, were £8,000
31st December, 19x2, were £6,000
31st December, 19x3, were £7,000

A provision for bad debts is to be created based on 5% of debtors at the end of each year. Show the provision for doubtful debts account and extracts from the three profit and loss accounts, and the relevant balance sheets.

Provision for Doubtful Debts

19x2		£	19x1		£
Dec. 31 Tfr. profit and loss a/c (reduction of provision)		100	Dec. 31 Tfr. profit and loss a/c (5% of £8,000)		400
Balance (5% of £6,000)	C/D	300			
		£400			£400
19x3			19x3		
Dec. 31 Balance (5% of £7,000)	C/D	350	Jan. 1 Balance	B/D	300
			Dec. 31 Tfr. profit and loss a/c (increase of provision)		50
		£350			£350
			19x4		
			Jan. 1 Balance	B/D	350

Profit and Loss Account (Extract)

19x1	£	19x2	£
Dec. 31 Provision doubtful debts	400	Dec. 31 Provision doubtful debts (adjustment)	100
19x3			
Dec. 31 Provision doubtful debts (adjustment)	50		

Balance Sheet (Extract) at 31st December

	19x1		19x2		19x3	
	£		£		£	
Current assets						
Debtors	£8,000		£6,000		£7,000	
Less Provision doubtful debts	400		300		350	
		7,600		5,700		6,650

It can be seen that once the initial provision has been created the adjustment to profit and loss account can be either debit or credit depending on whether the total debtors have increased or decreased at the year end.

The entry for provision for doubtful debts that appears in the trial balance is usually that based on the debtors at the beginning of the year. Before the profit and loss can be finalised for the current year the provision must be adjusted to a percentage of the closing debtors.

Combined Bad Debts and Provision for Doubtful Debts

An alternative method of recording adjustments to debtors is to ignore a bad debts account and to enter the bad debts in the provision for doubtful debts account. The thought behind this method is that the bad debts are set off against the provision made in the preceding period.

Example

The provision for doubtful debts on 1st January, 19x6, was £500. During the year ended 31st December, 19x8, there were bad debts amounting to £300. At the end of the year the provision for doubtful debts is to be adjusted to £450.

Provision for Doubtful Debts Account

19x8			£	19x8				£
Dec. 31	Tfr. debtors (bad			Jan.	1	Balance	B/D	500
	debts)		300	Dec. 31	Tfr. to profit			
	Balance	C/D	450			and loss a/c		250
			£750					£750
				19x9				
				Jan.	1	Balance	B/D	450

The transfer to profit and loss account consists of one amount, £250, which is the balancing figure on the account. The debit in the profit and loss account is described as bad debts whereas in fact the breakdown of this figure consists of a debit of £300 for bad debts and a credit adjustment to the opening figure of £50 (i.e. £500–£450). Unless especially required it is better to open two accounts, for the two types of adjustment are completely different. Bad debts represent a loss that has actually been suffered, whereas the provision for doubtful debts is a calculation of possible future losses.

Either method will give the same result in the balance sheet.

Where a debt which has previously been written off as bad is subsequently received, wholly or in part, the entries necessary to record the transaction are to debit the cash book and credit the bad debts account. The balance on the bad debts account is then transferred to the profit and loss account in the normal way.

In addition to the general provision for doubtful debts calculated on a percentage basis, a specific provision for individual debtors may also be incorporated, e.g.

At the end of 19x9 the total debtors amount to £6,400. Included in this amount are balances due from B. Swindells, £250, and J. Loss, £150. The provision for doubtful debts should be calculated as follows:

100% for Swindells and Loss, and 4% for the remainder.

The total provision for doubtful debts would amount to:

		£
100% of £400		400
4% of £6,000		240
	Total provision	£640

Provisions for Discounts Allowed

Even after allowing for doubtful debts the amount in the balance sheet may not necessarily be the value of cash that is eventually received. As stated in Chapter 4, discounts may be offered to debtors in an attempt to induce them to pay their accounts promptly. Included in the debtors at the end of the year will be amounts that will qualify for this discount if paid within the specified time. It can be argued that provision should be made for discount allowable in respect of sales made in the current period.

Alternatively, it is suggested that the discount only becomes an expense if the cash is paid within the stipulated time and that the determining factor is the date of payment and not the date the sale was originally made. If this is the case, then no provision need be made as in this concept the accruals basis is the same as the cash basis.

If, however, a provision for discounts is required, the adjustment is made in the discount allowed account and not in a separate account. Furthermore, the discount provision should be calculated on the net debtors, i.e. the debtors less the provision for doubtful debts, as it is obvious that would be doubtful debts turn out to be bad then they will not qualify for discount. The provision for discount is deducted from the debtors in the balance sheet together with the provision for doubtful debts.

Example

C. James started trading on 1st January, 19x2. Among his transactions for the two years ended 31st December, 19x3, were discounts allowed; 19x2 £478, and 19x3 £530. His debtors at the end of 19x2 amounted to £4,000 and to £6,000 at the end of 19x3.

Provision for doubtful debts of 5%, and a provision of 2% for discounts allowed, should be created.

Show the entries in the ledger accounts for the provisions, and how debtors would be shown in the balance sheets.

Provision for Doubtful Debts Account

19x3			£	19x2		£
Dec. 31	Balance (5% of £6,000)	C/D	300	Dec. 31	Tfr. profit and loss a/c (5% of £4,000)	200
				19x3		
				Dec. 31	Tfr. profit and loss a/c	100
			£300			£300
				19x4		
				Jan. 1	Balance B/D	£300

Discount Allowed Account

19x2			£	19x2		£
Dec. 31	Discounts	C/B	478	Dec. 31	Tfr. profit and loss a/c	554
	Provision (2% of £3,800)	C/D	76			
			£554			£554
19x3				19x3		
Dec. 31	Discounts	C/B	530	Jan. 1	Provision B/D	76
	Provision (2% of £5,700)	C/D	114	Dec. 31	Tfr. profit and loss a/c	568
			£644			£644
				19x4		
				Jan. 1	Provision B/D	114

Balance Sheet (Extract) at 31st December

	19x2		19x3	
Current assets	£	£	£	£
Debtors	4,000		6,000	
Less Provision doubtful debts	200		300	
	3,800		5,700	
Less Provision discount	76		114	
		3,724		5,586

A provision can also be made for discount received based on the value of creditors shown in the balance sheet. The argument for doing this is extremely weak. The discount will only be received if the debt is paid within a specified time. Thus, at the date of the balance sheet, if a provision is made, it is a profit which has not been realised thereby breaking the convention of conservatism.

If a provision is to be made, it is dealt with as an adjustment in the discount receivable account and the debit balance remaining on this account is deducted from the total creditors in the balance sheet.

To show the effect of the provisions on questions requiring final accounts to be prepared from a trial balance, the following question and model answer is provided.

Example

The following trial balance was extracted from the books of M. Thomas at 30th June, 19x6.

	£	£
Capital		40,542
Drawings	4,296	
Debtors and creditors	15,872	10,924
Sales		163,484
Purchases	124,202	
Rent and rates	1,760	
Lighting and heating	492	
Salaries and wages	16,536	
Provision for doubtful debts, 1st July, 19x5		652
Stock in trade, 1st July, 19x5	18,548	
Insurances	344	
General expenses	1,866	
Bank balance	3,164	
Motor vehicles at cost	16,000	
Provision depreciation of motor vehicles at 1st July, 19x5		7,200
Proceeds of sale of vehicle		500

	£	£
Motor expenses	1,722	
Freehold premises at cost	20,000	
Rent received		1,500
	£224,802	£224,802

The following matters are to be taken into account:

1. Stock-in-trade, 30th June, 19x6, £19,768.
2. Lighting and heating due 30th June, 19x6, £200.
3. Rates, £80, and insurances, £94, paid in advance 30th June.
4. Of the debtors £672 are to be regarded as bad, the provision for doubtful debts is to be adjusted to 5% of the remaining debtors.
5. Rent receivable due at 30th June, 19x6, amounted to £500.
6. Depreciation has been and is to be charged on vehicles at the rate of 20% per annum on the straight line method.
7. On 1st July, 19x5, a vehicle which had been purchased for £2,000 on 1st July, 19x2, was sold for £500. The only record of the transaction is the credit of £500 to the proceeds of sale of vehicle account.

Required:
A trading and profit and loss account for the year ended 30th June, 19x6, and a balance sheet as at that date.

M. THOMAS
Trading and Profit and Loss Accounts
Year ended 30th June, 19x6

	£		£
Opening stock	18,548	Sales	163,484
Add Purchases	124,202		
	142,750		
Less Closing stock	19,768		
Cost of goods sold	122,982		
Gross profit	40,502		
	£163,484		£163,484
Salaries and wages	16,536	Gross profit	40,502
Rent and rates	1,680	Rent received	2,000
Lighting and heating	692		
Insurances	250		
General expenses	1,866		
Motor expenses	1,722		
Bad debts	672		
Increase provision doubtful debts	108		

	£			£
Depreciation motor vehicles	2,800			
Loss on sale of vehicle	300			
Net profit	15,876			
	£42,502			£42,502

Balance Sheet as at 30th June, 19x6

	£	£			£	£
Capital account			Fixed assets			
Balance 1st July, 19x5		40,542	Freehold premises			
Add Profit for year		15,876	at cost			20,000
		56,418	Motor vehicles			
Less Drawings		4,296	at cost		14,000	
			Less Deprecia-			
		52,122	tion		8,800	
						5,200
Current liabilities						25,200
Creditors	10,924		Current assets			
Accrued expenses	200		Stock		19,768	
		11,124		£		
			Debtors	15,200		
			Less			
			Provision	760		
					14,440	
			Prepaid expenses		174	
			Rent receivable		500	
			Balance at bank		3,164	
						38,046
		£63,246				£63,246

Calculations involved are:

1. Rent and rates £1,760 less £80 prepaid.
2. Lighting and heating £492 plus £200 accrued.
3. Provision for bad debts required 5% of (£15,872 less £672 bad debts) £760 less already provided at 1st July, £652.
4. Depreciation 20% of £16,000 less £2,000 in respect of vehicle sold during the year.
5. Loss on sale of vehicle.

	£
Cost of vehicle	2,000
Less Depreciation, 3 years @ £400	1,200
Written down value	800
Less Proceeds of sale	500
Loss	£300

111

6. Depreciation per trial balance £7,200 less £1,200 on vehicle sold plus £2,800 provided in current year £8,800.

EXERCISES

9.1

On 30th June, 19x2, a trader decided to raise provisions for doubtful debts based on 5% of debtors and discounts allowed based on 2% of debtors, and to maintain the provisions at that percentage at the end of each financial year. The following particulars relate to three financial years.

	19x2	19x3	19x4
	£	£	£
Debtors at 30th June	12,600	10,700	14,300
Bad debts included in above to be written off	600	700	300
Discount allowed, year ended 30th June	2,720	3,250	4,250

You are required to construct the discounts allowed account and provisions for doubtful debts account for the above periods, and to show the entries in each of the profit and loss accounts and balance sheets for each of the three years.

9.2

On the 31st March, 19x7, a trader decided to make a specific provision for the following debts.

Customer A. Sharples	£58
B. Jones	£32
C. Green	£74
D. Wilson	£140

It was also decided to make a general provision of 5% on the remaining debtors who amounted to £10,000.

During the year ended 31st March, 19x8, no further sales were made to the four debtors mentioned above. A. Sharples and B. Jones were made bankrupt and their liquidators paid a final dividend of 50p in the pound. D. Wilson paid his account in full.

On the 31st March, 19x8, it was decided to retain the provision against the debt of C. Green. Debtors at the end of the year totalled £12,119 including the amount due from C. Green. No transfers were made to bad debts account during the year. It is decided to make a general provision for doubtful debts amounting to 5% of debtors.

You are required to construct the provision for doubtful debts account for the year ended 31st March, 19x8, and to show the entries in the balance sheet at that date.

9.3

The following are the balances of the accounts of J. Bowie at 31st March, 19x5:

ASET ADJUSTMENT—BAD DEBTS AND PROVISION FOR DOUBTFUL DEBTS

	£	£
Capital		21,160
Lease of building at cost	15,000	
Motor vehicles at cost	8,000	
Provision: Depreciation of motor vehicles, 1st April, 19x4		3,500
Purchases	78,845	
Sales		103,498
Lighting and heating	1,275	
Rates	650	
Insurance	525	
Returns inwards and outwards	945	747
Bad debts	460	
Provision for doubtful debts, 1st April, 19x4		360
Debtors and creditors	9,600	7,425
Balance at bank		2,420
Stock at 1st April, 19x4	14,378	
Wages	6,432	
Drawings	3,000	
	£139,110	£129,110

Prepare trading and profit and loss accounts for the year ended 31st March, 19x5, and a balance sheet as at that date, after taking into consideration the following matters:

(1) Stock at 31st March, 19x5, amounted to £15,363.
(2) Accruals at 31st March, 19x5, to be provided, electricity £75, and a bonus to employees of £500.
(3) Insurances were paid in advance amounting to £175.
(4) The provision for doubtful debts is to be 5% of debtors.
(5) Depreciation is to be provided for the year:
    20% on motor vehicles on the reducing balance method.
    10% on the lease of building on the straight line method.

9.4
After preparing the trading and profit and loss accounts the balances remaining in a trader's books at the 31st December, 19x3, were:

	£	£
Capital		23,000
Profit year to 31st Dec., 19x3		10,300
Drawings	3,000	
Leasehold buildings at cost	15,000	
Plant and machinery at cost	12,500	
Motor vehicles at cost	12,750	
Provisions for depreciation at 1st Jan., 19x3		
Leasehold buildings		6,000
Plant and machinery		5,000
Motor vehicles		9,150

113

	£	£
Debtors	8,000	
Provision for doubtful debts, 1st Jan., 19x3		550
Stock at 31st Dec., 19x3	11,750	
Creditors		7,250
Bank overdraft		1,750
	£63,000	£63,000

Prepare a balance sheet after providing for the following:

(1) Depreciation
   Plant and machinery 10% on the straight line method.
   Motor vehicles 20% on the reducing balance method.
   The buildings were purchased on 1st January, 19x9, and are to be written off in ten equal instalments.
(2) The provision for doubtful debts is to be adjusted to 5% of debtors.

9.5
On the 31st October, 19x5, a trader decided to raise a provision for doubtful debts based on 4% of debtors and to maintain the provision at that percentage at the end of each financial year. Any bad debts were to be written off against the provision. After bad debts had been written off the debtors' balances totalled:

	£
31st October, 19x5	10,500
19x6	14,000
19x7	12,500
19x8	15,000

Bad debts written off were:

	£
Year ending 31st October, 19x5	3,200
19x6	1,750
19x7	2,200
19x8	1,875

A bad debt of £150 which had been written off in 19x5 was recovered in 19x6 and £75 which was written off in 19x7 was recovered in 19x8. Notice should be taken of these receipts in the years ended 31st October, 19x6 and 19x8.

Prepare the provision for doubtful debts account for the years 31st October, 19x5 to 19x8.

9.6
The following trial balance was extracted from the books of J. Christopher, a trader, as at 31st December, 19x4.

114

	£	£
Capital		30,000
Freehold land and buildings	14,000	
Furniture and fittings	3,000	
Motor vehicles	5,800	
Provisions for depreciation, 1st Jan., 19x4		
Furniture and fittings		2,000
Motor vehicles		4,000
Stock in trade, 1st Jan., 19x4	12,200	
Purchases and sales	117,400	138,600
Debtors and creditors	11,700	8,690
Rents received		550
Loan from J. Smith at 5% per annum		2,400
Loan interest outstanding, 1st Jan., 19x4		60
Discounts allowed and received	2,640	1,850
Provision for doubtful debts, 1st Jan., 19x4		220
Bad debts	650	
Wages and salaries	14,090	
Drawings	3,200	
General expenses	1,730	
Balance at bank	1,360	
Rates and insurances	600	
	£188,370	£188,370

The following information is relevant:

(1) Stock in trade, 31st December, 19x4, £17,000.
(2) Items outstanding at 31st December, 19x4, wages and salaries £830, general expenses £130.
(3) Rates and insurances prepaid £150.
(4) No interest was paid on the loan from J. Smith during 19x4.
(5) The provision for doubtful debts is to be adjusted to 5% of the total debtors.
(6) Depreciation should be provided as follows:
   Furniture and fittings 5% p.a. on the reducing balance method.
   Motor vehicles 25% p.a. on the reducing balance method.
(7) Part of the freehold building was let to a tenant who owed £50 at 31st December, 19x4.

You are required to prepare a trading and profit and loss account for the year 19x4 and a balance sheet as at 31st December, 19x4.

10 Stock—its Valuation and Treatment in Accounts

Having examined the fixed assets and debtors in the balance sheet and determined their values so as to represent their worth to the business as a "going concern", the next asset on which attention must be focused is stock.

To comply with the cost concept the value placed on stock should be the price paid for it. However, stock is the prime trading asset and should its value fall between the date of purchase and the business year end, the loss must be reflected in the annual accounts to comply with the convention of conservation. The stock will have depreciated in value, therefore to show a true valuation it must be included at the lower of cost or market value.

Unfortunately, this apparent unambiguous statement is capable of different interpretations.

The word "lower" can mean that each item of stock is valued under both headings and the totals compared, the lower total value being the one taken, or the lower of each individual item taken and the sum of these amounts totalled, viz:

Stock item	Cost £	Market value £
A	200	210
B	180	150
C	250	260
D	175	140
	£805	£760

If the valuation is based on aggregate figures the market value of £760 should be included in the balance sheet. If individual items are compared, then the value becomes £200+150+250+140 = £740. The lower valuation is to be preferred, but in practice the individual comparisons may take too long, and be too costly, to calculate. The question of materiality has to be considered. In the above example the difference between the two valuations is only £20 which may have an insignificant effect on the overall profits.

The market trend should give an indication of whether prices are rising or falling. If the former—stock should be valued at cost, and if the latter—stock should be valued at market value. It is accepted that either the lower valuation in aggregate or individually will satisfy the definition.

The question of what is meant by cost is the more difficult one. Stock items will be constantly purchased during the year to replace those that are sold. In a fluctuating market where supplies vary the price will both increase and decrease during the year. Where there is an inflationary economy prices will tend to rise. As the price paid for the same type of item of stock will vary during a particular trading period the difficulty at the year end is which cost price to apply. The usual practice is to sell the older item first. Therefore, if a price label is attached to each item the stock at the end of the year will bear the labels of the most recent purchases. In theory, because there is no difference between each item of identical type, it would be impossible to state from which particular purchase the item was related.

The situation of each type of stock unit can be likened to reservoirs in which the opening account is mingled with the year's purchases. The stock remaining at the end of the year can not, in theory, be allocated to a particular batch. Therefore, the cost to be placed on this stock can be any of the prices paid during the year. There are three main methods of valuing the closing stock.

1. First in, first out method—abbreviated to FIFO.
2. Last in, first out method—abbreviated to LIFO.
3. Average stock method.

The methods of calculation and the theory of each are considered in the following pages.

First In, First Out Method

This method assumes that the earliest stock purchased is the first to be sold. The closing stock therefore represents the most recent purchases and the cost price would be related to current values. This method would appear to be the most factual and is indeed used by the majority of businesses. It is the system approved by the Inland Revenue for basing taxation on the profits of the business. In reality it is obvious that where stock is composed of perishable items the older stock must be cleared before newer stock, but even in the case of non-perishable

117

stocks because goods are liable to damage, e.g. fade in colour, rust, or break, it is advantageous to sell older stock first. The mechanics of valuing stock on a FIFO basis are shown by the following illustration.

Example

The following particulars relate to purchases and sales of a particular stock unit for the three months ended 31st March.

	Purchases			Sales
	No. of units	*Price per unit*		*No. of units*
Jan. 1	800	75p.	Jan. 31	500
Feb. 1	400	62½p.	Feb. 28	600
Mar. 1	700	£1·00p.	Mar. 31	600

The stock on January 1st amounted to 200 units valued at 50p each. Compute the value of closing stock on a FIFO basis.

FIFO BASIS

			Units		Price	Value	
					p	£	£
Jan.	1	Stock		200	50		100·00
		Purchases		800 +	75		600·00
				1,000			700·00
	31	Cost of sales	200		50	100·00	
		Cost of sales	300	500 −	75	225·00	325·00 −
Feb.	1	Stock		500	75		375·00
		Purchases		400 +	62½		250·00 +
				900			625·00
	28	Cost of sales	500		75	375·00	
		Cost of sales	100	600 −	62½	62·50	437·50
Mar.	1	Stock		300	62½		187·50
		Purchases		700 +	£1·00		700·00
				1,000			887·50
	31	Cost of sales	300		62½	187·50	
		Cost of sales	300	600 +	1·00	300·00	487·50
Apr.	1	Stock		400	1·00		400·00

From an examination of the above statement it is apparent that of the 500 units sold in January, 200 units are sold from the opening stock, and 300 units are sold out of the 800 bought on 1st January. The remaining 500 units are in stock at the end of the month and are valued at 75p each.

Under this method of valuation there is no need to keep a continuous record of purchases and sales. The stock of 400 units at the end of March must be priced at the rate ruling at the date of the last purchase. If the closing stock had been 800 units, 700 of these units would relate to the purchase on 1st March. The remaining 100 units would relate to the previous purchase on 1st February.

Last In, First Out Method

This method implies that the latest units bought are the first to be sold. It assumes that the initial purchase of goods forms a "base" stock which is financed by the original capital brought into the business. This base stock should remain untouched throughout the lifetime of the business. Any sales that are made come out of purchase replacements. It is argued that sales in the trading account represent current values, therefore the cost of sales should also be at current prices. The LIFO method does, to a certain extent, provide for this ideal.

The mechanics of valuing stock on a LIFO basis are shown by using the information given in the preceding example.

LIFO METHOD

Date		Item	Units		Price	Value	
					p	£	£
Jan.	1	Stock		200	50		100·00
		Purchases		800+	75		600·00+
				1,000			700·00
	31	Cost of sales		500−	75		375·00−
Feb.	1	Stock	200		50	100·00	
		Stock	300	500	75	225·00	325·00
		Purchases		400+	62½		250·00
				900			575·00
	28	Cost of sales	400		62½	250·00	
		Cost of sales	200	600−	75	150·00	400·00
Mar.	1	Stock	200		50	100·00	
		Stock	100	300	75	75·00	175·00
		Purchases		700+	£1·00		700·00
				1,000			875·00
	31	Cost of sales		600−	1·00		600·00−
Apr.	1	Stock	200		50	100·00	
		Stock	100		75	75·00	
		Stock	100	400	1·00	100·00	275·00

In the above statement the sales of 500 units in January are made out of the 800 units purchased in that month. The closing stock comprises the original 200 units plus 300 units purchased in the month. In February, sales exceed purchases by 200 units. These will be deducted from the most recent stock purchases leaving the original 200 units plus 100 units bought in January. The final stock figure of 400 units comprises the original stock of 200 units, 100 units of stock purchased in January plus 100 surplus units purchased in March.

Average Stock Method

As its description implies, this method attempts to merge the opening stock with subsequent purchases and calculate an average price for each unit of stock. This system merges the different prices paid for stock units, whereas the two previous methods isolate the different prices. The difficulty of applying this method is that each purchase of goods will affect the price of stocks held, and calculations have to be constantly made to determine the unit price. The resulting prices may be difficult to apply and may work out at peculiar fractions of money. The closing stock price may not be an actual amount that was ever paid for goods. The justification for applying this method is that the ultimate stock valuation will lie somewhere between the two valuations under the FIFO and LIFO methods.

The mechanics are shown below, using the information contained in the two previous illustrations.

AVERAGE STOCK METHOD

			Units	Price	Value
				p	£
Jan.	1	Stock	200	50	100
		Purchases	800+	75	600+
			1,000	70	700
	31	Cost of sales	500−	70	350−
Feb.	1	Stock	500	70	350
		Purchases	400+	62½	250+
			900	66⅔	600
	28	Cost of sales	600−	66⅔	400−
Mar.	1	Stock	300	66⅔	200
		Purchases	700+	£1·00	700+
			1,000	90	900
	31	Cost of sales	600−	90	540−
Apr.	1	Stock	400	90	360

In January the opening stock was 200 units valued at £100. Before any sales are made 800 units were purchased for £600. Immediately after the purchase the stock becomes 1,000 units for which a total of £700 was paid. The average price of each unit is, therefore, £700 divided by 1,000 equalling 70p per unit. Further adjustments to the price are required after each subsequent purchase.

Effect of Stock Valuations in the Accounts

In the three illustrations the purchases for the three months were identical, viz:

	Units	£
January	800	600·00
February	400	250·00
March	700	700·00
	1,900	£1,550·00

If it is assumed that the sale of 1,700 units produced £1,500, the gross profit figures would be computed as under.

Using method	FIFO		LIFO		Average	
	Units	£	Units	£	Units	£
Opening stock	200	100	200	100	200	100
Purchases	1,900	1,550	1,900	1,550	1,900	1,550
	2,100	1,650	2,100	1,650	2,100	1,650
Closing stock	400	400	400	275	400	360
Cost of goods sold	1,700	1,250	1,700	1,375	1,700	1,290
Gross profit		250		125		210
Sales	1,700	£1,500	1,700	£1,500	1,700	£1,500

Note. The cost of sales can be obtained from totalling the amounts in the statements.

	FIFO	LIFO	Average
	£	£	£
Jan. 31st	325·00	375·00	350·00
Feb. 28th	437·50	400·00	400·00
Mar. 31st	487·50	600·00	540·00
	£1,250·00	£1,375·00	£1,290·00

121

The profits shown range from £250 to £125, and as this refers to only one line of stock, if the business deals in many varieties of goods, this difference will be greatly magnified. The reason for the difference is that the FIFO method relates historical costs to the cost of goods sold, whereas by using the LIFO method the current cost of goods sold is charged. The average stock method produces a cost somewhere between the two.

In times of rising prices and stock increases the FIFO method will give higher profits than the LIFO method. In times of falling prices the reverse will be true. As stock has to be replaced as goods are sold, and the cost of replacement is at current prices, it is argued that the LIFO method shows the correct profit.

To take what is, perhaps, an over-simplified example:

A trader commences business with capital of £100 and one unit of stock, £100. During the first month's trading he sells the unit of stock for £150. He later replaces his stock by purchasing a further unit for which, because of rapid inflation, he has to pay £150. The trading accounts will be:

	FIFO £	LIFO £
Opening stock	100	100
Purchases	150	150
	250	250
Closing stock	150	100
Cost of goods sold	100	150
Gross profit	50	—
Sales	£150	£150

The balance sheets at the end of the month would be:

	FIFO £	LIFO £
Opening capital	100	100
Profit	50	—
	150	100
Assets		
Stock	£150	£100

By using the LIFO method no profit is shown. Under the FIFO method it appears that the trader has made a profit of £50, yet at the end of the month it seems that he is in exactly the same position as he was at the start of the month. He still has only one unit of stock which is virtually the same as the one he had to start with (except that the value has changed), so how can he have made a profit?

The answer lies in the figures for stock in the respective balance sheets. The LIFO balance sheet still reflects the historical value, the FIFO balance sheet takes into account the appreciation of the stock. If the business was forced to close, it would seem improbable that the owner would sell the stock for less than its current cost price of £150.

Thus, there are advantages and disadvantages to both these systems. The FIFO method (in inflationary times) would perhaps tend to overstate profits, but would reflect the true value of stock in the balance sheet. In similar circumstances (rising prices) the LIFO method would understate profits to reflect the real gain, but the stock in the balance sheet would be under-valued. Although the average stock method attempts to reconcile the extremes of the two former methods, the values given to cost of goods sold and closing stock are not prices that have actually been paid. The overall problem is similar to depreciation as it is a matter of cost allocation. During the lifetime of the firm the total profit will be identical, no matter what method is used. It is only each year's profit that will differ. Profits will be taken earlier with the FIFO method and later with the LIFO method.

What is important is that whatever method is first chosen that method is applied during the lifetime of the firm under the convention of consistency. This means that the treatment is constant from year to year. Comparisons can be made of the annual results and provided that the basis of stock valuation is known for other firms, inter-firm results can be compared.

Should the market value of stock be lower than the cost price, then the former should be taken. Market value can have one or two meanings. The first is external to the firm and means replacement price; the second is internal and means net realisable value.

Replacement price is used when the cost price of the goods has fallen below the price actually paid. In the FIFO method it would imply that the price of goods at the balance sheet date is lower than the price paid for the last purchase. In the LIFO method it implies that the price at the date of the balance sheet is lower than the original purchase price, and in the average stock method that the price is lower than the ultimate average calculation.

Net realisable value consists of the selling price to be obtained for the goods, less the gross profit thereon, and minus any expenses which are considered necessary to sell the goods. This valuation is to be preferred to replacement price, but where it is impossible or extremely difficult to calculate, replacement price (which is generally slightly higher) can be used.

EXERCISES

10.1

Give the lowest and highest values for stock which can be shown in the accounts of a business and yet conform with accepted accounting concepts and conventions.

	Cost	Net realisable value	Replacement price
	£	£	£
Stock unit 1	700	300	400
2	1,200	1,300	1,300
3	850	840	850
4	1,100	1,200	1,300
5	550	500	450
6	900	860	900
7	1,300	1,320	1,340
8	600	580	560
	£7,200	£6,900	£7,100

10.2

A firm began the year with a stock of 1,000 identical items which cost £8 each. On 1st January the firm bought a further 3,000 items at £12 each. During the year ended 31st December the firm sold 3,200 items for £15 each.

Calculate the closing stock value and the gross profit using the following methods of stock valuation:

(a) FIFO.   (b) LIFO.   (c) Average stock.

10.3

The following particulars relate to a specific line of stock used by E. Beech.

Jan. 1 Balance 500 units costing 25p each
      2 Purchases 1,000 units costing 30p each
     10 Sales 750 units for £375
     12 Purchases 250 units costing 25p each
     31 Sales 500 units for £250

Calculate the closing stock value and the gross profit using the following methods of stock valuation:

(a) FIFO.   (b) LIFO.   (c) Average stock.

124

10.4

The following particulars relate to an identical line of stock carried by a business.

Jan.	1	Balance	1,000 units at £5 each
Feb.	28	Purchases	2,000 units at £8 each
June	30	Sales	1,000 units
Sept.	30	Purchases	1,000 units at £7 each
Dec.	31	Sales	1,500 units

The market value of the stock at 31st December was £6 per unit.

Calculate the closing stock value which would be included in the final accounts under the

(a) FIFO method.   (b) LIFO method.   (c) Average stock method.

10.5

A businessman tells you that his assets at 31st December, 19x3, comprise:

(1) Leasehold premises bought 4 years ago for £4,300 (including £300 legal fees) have 6 more years to run.
(2) A motor vehicle bought at the beginning of the current year at a wholesale price of £625. The retail price for £750 and the market value at 31st December, 19x3, is £600. The vehicle is expected to last for four years, have no residual value, and progressively lose its efficiency.
(3) Stock in trade consists of

	Cost price	Replacement price	Realisable value
	£	£	£
Item A	940	930	900
B	1,000	1,010	1,020
C	860	900	890
	£2,800	£2,840	£2,810

(4) Debtors £4,040. These include a debt of £40 from N. Brodie which is not expected to be recovered. The incidence of bad debts in this type of business is 5% and approximately half the debtors take advantage of a cash discount of 2%.

Calculate the total amount of assets which would appear in the balance sheet at 31st December, 19x3.

10.6

At the end of his first year's trading B. Smart presents you with the following balance sheet:

Balance Sheet as at 30th June, 19x2

	£		£	
Capital		Fixed assets		
Cash introduced	12,000	Leasehold property at		
Add Profit for year	6,000	cost		6,000
	18,000	Fixtures at cost		1,000
Less Drawings	4,000	Motor vehicles at cost		2,000
	14,000			9,000
Current liabilities		Current assets	£	
Trade creditors	3,200	Stock	4,050	
		Debtors	3,150	
		Balance at		
		bank	1,000	
				8,200
	£17,200			£17,200

The following matters have been ignored:

(1) Fixed assets—depreciation should be written off as follows:
   (a) Leasehold premises 10%,
   (b) Fixtures $12\frac{1}{2}\%$,
   (c) Motor vehicles 25%.
(2) Stock—it was discovered that certain items of stock costing £350 were damaged and can only be sold for £200.
(3) Debtors—a debt of £50 is regarded as bad and a provision for doubtful debts of 5% should be made on the remainder.
(4) Insurance and rates were prepaid to an amount of £100.
(5) An amount of £30 owing for electricity had been omitted.

Draw up a corrected balance sheet at 30th June, 19x2, and provide a statement showing how you have arrived at the revised profit.

11 The Journal and the Suspense Account

All entries appearing in the ledger must first be entered in a subsidiary book, that is, there must be a prime entry. In this context the cash book is regarded as being a book of prime entry though in fact it contains the cash and bank accounts which would otherwise appear in the ledger itself. As cash and bank transactions are initially entered in the cash book and then posted to a ledger account, it can be said to be a book of prime entry.

Though the majority of business transactions are automatically entered in the subsidiary books already mentioned in the text, there are some items which, because of their complexity, or because special attention to them is required, need to be entered with additional information in a special subsidiary book. This book is known as the journal. The ruling for the journal is similar to that of a day book except the two columns are headed "debit" and "credit", viz.:

JOURNAL   Dr.   Cr.

Date	Particulars	Folio	£ p	£ p
	Account to be debited		x x	
	Account to be credited			x x

As the journal is a book of prime entry both the debit and credit items have to be posted to ledger accounts or to the cash book. The journal is itself not part of the double-entry system. Its purpose is to give details of transactions which will appear in the ledger. For this reason the amount of the account to be debited is entered in the debit column, and the amount to be credited to a ledger is entered in the credit column. When listing the accounts in the particulars column, debit accounts are listed immediately against the date, whereas credit accounts are slightly inset as in the illustration above. Ledger references are noted in the folio column.

At one time a large number of entries were recorded in the journal whereas at present the journal is restricted to:

1. Opening and closing entries.
2. Entries of a complicated nature.
3. Entries which require special attention.
4. Correction of errors.

Each of these type of entries is described in the following pages.

Opening and Closing Entries

It has been assumed, up to this chapter, that all businesses have started from the moment a trader introduces his initial capital. In reality he may buy an existing business together with all its assets and possibly some of its liabilities, in which case there will be numerous accounts involved in the one transaction. At some time in the future the new owner may wish to refresh his memory regarding the individual items comprising the purchase. Unless he has a note of the transaction in the journal it will be necessary for him to inspect every ledger account to discover the initial entries.

A further factor involved is that if the business was successful before he bought it, he will probably have to pay more than the valuation of the tangible assets. The excess amount is for the purchase of "goodwill". Goodwill is known as an intangible asset and has been described in a variety of ways. Basically it is the benefit that results from acquiring an existing business rather than setting up a new business. The existing business will have acquired custom, reputation, and recognition which takes time to create in a new business. These benefits have been achieved by the previous owner and he will require recompense for his effort.

Good will should be treated in the accounts in the same way as other assets. As goodwill can only be realised when the business is sold, it is regarded as being the least realisable asset and, therefore, is placed at the top of the assets in the balance sheet.

Example

A. Jones pays £10,000 into a business bank account on 1st January, 19x7. On the same date he acquires the business of J. Amos for £6,000 paying by cheque. He acquires the following assets: fixtures £1,500, stock £3,000, debtors £750. He agrees to pay Amos's creditors totalling £550.

Show the journal entries necessary to record the above showing the amount paid for goodwill.

19x7			£	£
Jan. 1	Bank account	C/B	10,000	
	Capital account	L1		10,000
	Capital introduced by A. Jones at commencement of business			
Jan. 1	Fixtures account	L2	1,500	
	Stock account	L3	3,000	
	Debtors account	L4	750	
	Goodwill account	L5	1,300	
	Bank account	C/B		6,000
	Creditors account	L6		550
			£6,550	£6,550

Assets and liabilities acquired on
purchase of business from J. Amos

After each transaction has been recorded in the journal a brief description of it is given. The goodwill figure of £1,300 is found by deducting the total of tangible assets less liabilities taken over from the purchase consideration.

When a business ceases all the ledger accounts must be closed off. This is achieved by transferring all the assets with the exception of cash and bank into a realisation account. Any liabilities to third parties are discharged or, if they are to be taken over by the new owner, transferred into the realisation account. The money received from the sale of assets is debited to the cash book and credited to the realisation account. The difference on the realisation account is transferred to the capital account.

Example

The balance sheet of G. Wright at 31st December, 19x2, comprised:

Balance Sheet as at 31st December, 19x2 (Summarised)

	£		£
Capital account	15,000	Fixed assets (in total)	9,000
Creditors	1,000	Stock	4,000
		Debtors	2,000
		Bank	1,000
	£16,000		£16,000

On 1st January, 19x3, G. Wright sold the fixed assets, stock, and debtors to B. Other who also assumed responsibility for the creditors. B. Other paid G. Wright a cheque for £16,000 in full settlement on the same day.

Show the journal entries necessary to close the books of G. Wright.

129

		£	£
Jan. 1	Realisation account	14,000	
	Creditors account	1,000	
	Fixed assets account		9,000
	Stock account		4,000
	Debtors account		2,000
		£15,000	£15,000
	Assets and liabilities taken over by B. Other		
Jan. 1	Bank account	16,000	
	Realisation account		16,000
	Purchase consideration received from B. Other		
Jan. 1	Realisation account	2,000	
	Capital account		2,000
	Profit on sale of business transferred to capital account		
Jan. 1	Capital account	17,000	
	Bank account		17,000
	Amount due to G. Wright now paid		

Once the assets and liabilities have been transferred to the realisation account, only three accounts remain in the books, these being capital, bank, and realisation accounts. When the purchase price has been received the balance on the realisation account is transferred to the capital account. The remaining two accounts should now balance. The bank account, initially £1,000 plus £16,000 received from the purchaser, equals £17,000. The capital account initially £15,000 plus £2,000 profit on sale, equals £17,000. When repayment of capital takes place the books are finally closed.

Entries of a Complicated Nature

These entries occur when more than two accounts are involved in one transaction. The entries in the ledger would not present a clear picture of what has taken place, whereas one or two journal entries would clarify the situation. Examples under this heading are many and varied, but two illustrations are shown.

Example

S. Price acquired the lease of a shop for £4,025 from M. Jordon on 1st January, 19x3. M. Jordon had paid the rates up to 31st March, 19x3, the proportion from 1st January to 31st March being £75. He owed £50

130

for electricity up to 31st December, 19x2. The purchase price of £4,025 took these matters into account.

19x3		£	£
Jan. 1	Leasehold shop	4,000	
	Rates account	75	
	Electricity account		50
	Bank		4,025
		£4,075	£4,075

£4,025 being price paid for leasehold shop subject to adjustments for rates and electricity.

The explanation for the above entry is that although the property is worth £4,000 the rates already paid by M. Jordon should be brought into S. Price's accounts as they relate to the post acquisition period. On the other hand when the electricity account is paid by S. Price he should be compensated. The credit entry from the journal will negate the debit entry posted from the cash book.

Example

On 1st February S. Price trades in an old vehicle valued at £450 for a new one costing £1,200. He pays the difference by cheque. The old vehicle had been bought for £1,000 and depreciation amounting to £600 had been provided for it in the books.

Show the journal entries necessary to record the above.

		£	£
Feb. 1	Disposals account	1,000	
	Motor vehicles account		1,000
	Cost price of vehicle traded in transferred to disposals account		
Feb. 1	Provision. Depreciation of vehicles	600	
	Disposals account		600
	Depreciation provided on above vehicle transferred to disposals account		
Feb. 1	Motor vehicles account	1,200	
	Bank account		750
	Disposals account		450
		£1,200	£1,200

New vehicle acquired for £750 plus allowance of £450 for old one traded in.

131

The explanations given above should be self-explanatory. The original value of the car traded in should be taken out of the motor vehicles account and the total value of the new vehicle included. The balance (£50 credit) on the disposals account should be transferred to the profit and loss account at the year end. The £50 represents a profit made up as follows: value of trade-in £450 less written down value £400.

Entries which Require Special Attention

These items usually apply to transfers between ledger accounts or transactions of sufficient importance to warrant special treatment which may require authorisation by persons other than the book-keeper. The nature of these transactions will vary from business to business, but will usually include the writing off of bad debts. A bad debt represents a loss to the business and only after careful considera-tion should a debt be written off; certainly it must have the approval of someone in authority. The procedure is to journalise the transfer and have the entry initialled by the person authorising the entry, viz.:

		£	£
July 28	Bad debts account	200	
	V. Smith		200
	Bad debt written off authorised by		

Other items worthy of special attention may include purchase or disposal of fixed assets, dishonoured cheques, and year-end adjust-ments, particularly depreciation charges.

One other entry that is included under this heading is proprietor's drawings other than cash or bank. If a grocer's business is established it would seem likely that the proprietor would supply his family's needs out of the stock. If he does not pay out of his own pocket for these goods, a transfer should be made at the end of the year for the value of the goods taken. The value should be the normal selling price of the goods so that the journal entry would be

	£	£
Drawings account	500	
Sales account		500
Value of goods taken for own use		

If the value is expressed as cost price it cannot be credited to sales account. The purchases are reduced implying the total purchases were not acquired wholly for the business.

Other entries relating to drawings may be in respect of benefits received. The proprietor may use the business car for private use, or live on the business premises. If the business pays all expenses, a suitable proportion should be transferred from the expenses accounts to drawings account.

	£	£
Drawings account	450	
Motor expenses account		200
Rent and rates account		250
Transfer to ⅓ motor expenses £600 and ⅓ rent and rates £750, being proportion used for private purposes		

Correction of Errors

The last group of entries which appear in the journal concern the rectification of incorrect entries already recorded in the ledger accounts. It should be emphasised that once a transaction has been recorded it should never be altered. A second entry has to be made giving full particulars of the necessity for the correction. This group of entries can be sub-divided into two sections. The first deals with errors that are not disclosed by the trial balance, viz.: errors of omission, commission, principle, and original entry. The second deals with errors that affect the trial balance and consist of addition errors, omission of ledger balances, and posting errors. Examples of the latter are where one part of the double entry has been omitted, where both entries are recorded on the same side of the ledger, or where there has been a transposition of figures between the postings. Needless to say, all errors should be corrected before the final accounts are completed.

The first section, dealing with errors not affecting the trial balance, comprises errors within two accounts. The journal entry can, therefore, be made in the manner previously described in this chapter.

Example

At the 30th June, 19x7, the following errors were discovered in the books of J. Green. You are required to show the journal entries necessary to correct them.

1. A purchase invoice value £97 from B. Shaw was omitted from the books.

2. A sale amounting to £206 had been debited to J. King's account instead of J. King and Nephew Ltd.
3. A new typewriter costing £65 was debited to repairs account.
4. Discount allowed £98 had been entered in the cash book as £89 and this amount had been credited to B. Prince Ltd.

		£	£
30th June	Purchases account	97	
	B. Shaw		97
	Invoice from B. Shaw omitted from purchase day book		
,,	J. King & Nephew Ltd.	206	
	J. King		206
	Sales invoice debited in error to J. King		
,,	Office equipment account	65	
	Repairs account		65
	New typewriter debited in error to repairs account		
,,	Discounts allowed	9	
	B. Prince Ltd.		9
	Discount allowed £98 to B. Prince entered in cash book as £89 and posted to his account as this amount		

The second section comprises entries affecting the trial balance. This type of error affects only one ledger account so that in the normal manner a journal entry cannot be effected. To rectify this situation a suspense account is opened and an entry is made therein which will enable the totals of the trial balance to be in agreement, if the suspense account is included with the other balances. The suspense account is only temporary and will be eliminated when all the errors are corrected.

If the amount shown in the suspense account is not material to the accounts as a whole, it can be included as a current asset or current liability for interim final accounts. If it is a large amount, then the errors should be located even before interim accounts are prepared. In either case it should be eliminated before the accounts are finally drafted.

Example

At 31st March, 19x1, the trial balance of A. Morris failed to agree. The debit balances totalled £17,812 and the credit balances £17,712. The following errors were later discovered.

1. A total in the sales day book of £11,220 had been carried forward as £11,100.
2. Discount allowed amounting to £45 has been posted from the cash book to the wrong side of discounts allowed account.
3. A bad debt of £20 had been written off to bad debts account, but no entry had been made in the personal account.
4. The total in the purchase day book had been overstated by £50.

Show the journal entries necessary to correct the above and show how the entries in the suspense account would be recorded.

		£	£
Mar. 31	Suspense account	120	
	Sales account		120
	Total sales understated by £120 in sales day book		
,,	Discounts allowed account	90	
	Suspense account		90
	Correction of discounts allowed £45 posted to wrong side of a/c		
,,	Suspense account	20	
	Debtors account		20
	Debt written off as bad, but not recorded in personal account		
,,	Suspense account	50	
	Purchases account		50
	Purchases overstated in purchase day book		

Suspense Account

			£					£
Mar. 31	Sales	J	120	Mar. 31	Original difference			
	Debtors	J	20		per trial balance			100
	Purchases	J	50		Discounts allowed		J	90
			£190					£190

Some explanations for the entries may be required.

1. As debit entries are posted individually to debtors accounts only the credit entry is incorrect. The total understates the sales by £120 and thus the sales account must be increased by this amount.
2. The entry has been correctly credited to the debtors account, the discounts allowed account should be debited (not credited) with £45. To correct this credit entry made in error, the discount allowed account must be debited with twice the amount.

135

3. The bad debts account is correct, the debtors are, however, over-stated. To rectify this they must be reduced by (or credited with) the amount of £20.
4. The creditors are posted individually from the purchase day book and so are correct. The error only affects purchases which are over-stated, and must be reduced by £50.

Some questions set in examinations give a balance sheet and a list of errors which have been discovered since the preparation of that balance sheet. They require the preparation of a corrected balance sheet, entries in a suspense account, and a statement of adjusted profit. For this reason an example is shown.

Example

The balance sheet of A. Ingham as at 31st December, 19x6, is given below:

	£		£	£
Capital		Fixed assets		
Balance 1st Jan., 19x6	4,500	Fixtures and fittings		
Profit for year	4,000	at cost	1,200	
	8,500	Less depreciation	500	
				700
Less Drawings	3,000			
	5,500	Motor vehicle at cost	1,500	
		Less Depreciation	400	
				1,100
Current liabilities				1,800
Creditors	1,490			
Suspense account	10	Current assets		
		Stock	3,000	
		Debtors	1,700	
		Balance at bank	500	
				5,200
	£7,000			£7,000

Subsequently the following errors were discovered.

1. The purchase day book had been undercast by £80.
2. A new cash register costing £60 had been debited to repairs account (depreciation on fixtures is 15%).
3. A debit balance of £40 for J. Smith was omitted from total debtors.
4. An entry for £10 returns outwards was made in error in the sales book instead of the purchase returns book.

5. A cheque, £25, paid to P. Dawson (a creditor) was correctly entered in the cash book, but credited in error to his account.
6. Goods valued at £200 were taken by A. Ingham for his own use, but no entry had been made.
7. A bad debt of £25 should have been written off J. White's account.
8. £90 discount received had been correctly entered in the cash book, but had been posted to the wrong side of discounts received account.

Show the journal entries necessary to correct the above. Show a statement adjusting the original profit and a corrected balance sheet.

		£	£
31 Dec.	Purchases account	80	
	Suspense account		80
	Understatement of purchases in day book		
	Fixtures and fittings account	60	
	Repairs account		60
	Transfer cost of typewriter incorrectly debited to repairs a/c		
	Profit and loss account	9	
	Provision: depreciation fixtures		9
	Depreciation due for year on typewriter		
	Debtors—J. Smith	40	
	Suspense account		40
	Debtor omitted from final accounts		
	Sales account	10	
	Purchase returns account		10
	Returns outward incorrectly entered in sales day book		
	Creditors—P. Dawson	50	
	Suspense account		50
	Payment of £25 to P. Dawson incorrectly credited to his a/c		
	Drawings account	200	
	Sales account		200
	Value of goods taken for own use		
	Bad debts account	25	
	Debtors—J. White		25
	Amount due from J. White now written off as bad		
	Suspense account	180	
	Discount received account		180
	£90 discount received entered on debit side of discount received a/c in error		

137

Calculation of Correct Profit

	£	£
Profit per balance sheet		4,000
Purchase day book undercast	80	
Purchase of typewriter		60
Depreciation: typewriter	9	
Goods for own use		200
Bad debts	25	
Discounts received		180
	£114	4,440
		114
Adjusted profit		£4,326

Balance Sheet as at 31st December, 19x6

	£		£	£
Capital		Fixed assets		
Balance 1st Jan., 19x6	4,500	Fixtures and fittings		
Profit for year	4,326	at cost	1,260	
	8,826	*Less* Depreciation	509	
Less Drawings	3,200			751
	5,626	Motor vehicle at		
		cost	1,500	
Current liabilities		*Less* Depreciation	400	
Creditors	1,440			1,100
				1,851
		Current assets		
		Stock	3,000	
		Debtors	1,715	
		Balance at bank	500	
				5,215
	£7,066			£7,066

Workings
1. Drawings £(3,000 + 200) = £3,200.
2. Creditors £(1,490 − 50) = £1,440.
3. Fixtures and fittings £(1,200 + 60) = £1,260.
4. Depreciation on above £(500 + 9) = £509.
5. Debtors £(1,700 + 40 − 25) = £1,715.

EXERCISES

11.1
J. Carlton's balance sheet at 31st August, 19x8, was as follows:

	£		£
Capital	8,000	Office fittings	2,000
Creditors	1,000	Motor vehicles	1,500
		Stock	3,000
		Debtors	1,800
		Cash	700
	£9,000		£9,000

On 1st September, 19x8, he sold the office fittings, motor vehicles, stock, and debtors plus an amount of goodwill to B. Player for £10,000. J. Carlton paid off the creditors out of the purchase money received on 1st September.

You are required to show the journal entries necessary (a) to close off the books of J. Carlton and (b) to open the books of B. Player.

11.2

V. Blanks balance sheet at 28th February, 19x3, was as follows:

	£		£
Capital	5,200	Office fittings	1,200
Creditors	800	Motor vehicles	800
		Stock	2,000
		Debtors	1,500
		Cash	500
	£6,000		£6,000

On 1st March, 19x3, V. Blank sold the business (apart from cash) to J. Dash for £6,000 and received the purchase consideration the same date. For the purpose of his business J. Dash decided to revalue the assets as to office fittings £1,150, motor vehicles £900, stock £1,750, and to create a provision for doubtful debts of 4% of the total debtors. J. Dash introduced cash of £8,000 into the business.

You are required to show the journal entries necessary (a) to close the books of V. Blank, and (b) to open the books of J. Dash. Show also the opening balance sheet of the new business.

11.3

The trial balance of a business failed to agree and a suspense account was opened with a £50 debit balance. The following errors were later discovered.

(a) Rates paid in advance of £150 appeared as a credit balance.
(b) An item of £8 in respect of repairs had been debited to purchases account.
(c) The purchase day book had been overcast by £100.
(d) A credit note for £50 for goods returned to a supplier had been omitted from the books.
(e) A cash discount of £30 had been deducted when paying a creditor's invoice. The creditor had disallowed this discount.
(f) Rent received £75 from a sub-tenant had been incorrectly debited to rents payable account.

Show by means of journal entries how the above errors are to be corrected and write up the suspense account.

11.4

On 30th June, 19x6, the trial balance of a business failed to agree. A suspense account was opened and the final accounts prepared. The net profit was calculated at £2,500.

Further investigations showed the following errors:

(a) Returns outwards had been entered in the trial balance as £57 instead of £157.

(b) The sales day book had been overcast £400.

(c) Petty cash expenses amounting to £35 in respect of travelling expenses had not been posted to the ledger.

(d) Fixtures purchased by cheque for £70 had been entered in the cash book, but not posted to the ledger.

(e) No entry had been made in the books for goods valued at £130 taken by the proprietor for his own use.

You are required after completing the necessary journal entries (a) to calculate the true net profit, and (b) to calculate the amount by which the original trial balance failed to agree and to state which side was the larger, debit or credit.

11.5

On 31st May, 19x3, the trial balance of a business failed to agree. A suspense account was opened and interim accounts prepared which showed a net profit of £6,152. The following errors were subsequently found.

(a) A payment of £43 for advertising had been correctly entered in the cash book, but had been debited to lighting and heating account as £34.

(b) On 31st May, 19x3, goods valued at £120 (selling price) had been returned by a customer. No entry had been made in the books for the return, nor had they been included in the closing stock. The cost of these goods was £80.

(c) Discounts of £265 appearing on the debit side of the cash book and £352 on the credit side of the cash book have been posted to the wrong discount accounts.

(d) Cash sales of £120 had been correctly entered in the cash book, but had been posted to the debit of purchases account.

(e) The total of the returns outward day book (£370) had not been posted to the ledger account.

You are required after completing the necessary journal entries to (a) calculate the true net profit, and (b) to calculate the amount by which the original trial balance failed to agree, and to state which side was the larger, debit or credit.

11.6

At 30th September, 19x4, the trial balance of a business showed the following totals; debit £21,214, credit £18,762. Further investigation revealed the following errors.

(a) Goods received from a supplier amounting to £1,750 have been included in stock, but the invoice was not received until October, 19x4.
(b) The bank overdraft of £286 had been brought down as a debit balance in the cash book.
(c) £45 has been received from a debtor which had been written off as bad two years previously. The receipt was credited to a new account in the debtors ledger.
(d) An invoice for £260 had been entered in the purchase day book on 30th September, 19x4, but the goods were not received until 5th October, 19x4, and had not, therefore, been included in stock.
(e) The total of the purchase returns day book (£940) for September had been debited to sales returns account.

Show the journal entries necessary to correct the above errors and complete the suspense account.

11.7
James Long presents you with the following balance sheet as at 31st March, 19x7.

	£	£		£	£
Capital			Fixed assets		
Opening balance		4,000	Office fixtures		
Profit for year		2,500	at cost	1,242	
		6,500	Less Depreciation	563	
Less Drawings		3,500			679
		3,000	Motor vehicle at		
			cost	1,200	
			Less Depreciation	800	
Current liabilities					400
Creditors	1,814				1,079
Accrued expenses	175				
Bank overdraft	650		Current assets		
		2,639	Stock	2,500	
			Debtors	1,733	
			Prepaid expense	180	
			Suspense account	147	
					4,560
		£5,639			£5,639

On checking the books you find the following errors.

(a) An entry in the sales day book for £250 has not been posted to the debtors account.
(b) No entry has been made in the books for goods returned from a customer, nor have the goods been included in the stock. The selling price of the goods was £240, the cost price was £160.

(c) An accrual for £65 electricity was brought down as a debit balance in the ledger account.

(d) A cheque received from a debtor amounting to £175 has been posted direct to the sales account.

(e) An invoice to C. Hulme for £85 had been correctly entered in the sales day book, but was posted to his account as £58.

(f) An office desk costing £80 with a written down value of £35 had been sold for £25. The entry had been correctly entered in the cash book, but the amount had been posted to the credit of office fixtures account.

You are required to show the journal entries necessary to correct the errors, and to re-draft the balance sheet.

12 Control Accounts

During a financial year a business is engaged in hundreds, if not thousands, of transactions. Each of these transactions must be recorded within the double-entry system. It is therefore not surprising that on occasions the trial balance fails to agree. In order that errors may be located as soon as possible many businesses will draft trial balances periodically throughout the financial year. If a trial balance then fails to agree, it is assumed that the errors have been made since the last agreed trial balance, and the investigation is limited to that period of time. Even so, the number of entries, postings, and additions that will have to be verified may be considerable and a great amount of time may be taken up in order to locate the errors.

If a system is incorporated in the books that will enable the errors to be localised to a particular group of transactions, the items to be checked will be reduced and thereby the time required to find the errors will be minimised. To achieve this purpose control accounts are prepared external to, or designed within, the double-entry system. Ideally the latter method is to be preferred. As the majority of transactions concern credit sales and purchases it is usual to set up debtors and creditors control accounts.

The control accounts are constructed from total figures in order to guard against the same error being duplicated. Thus in the case of the debtors control account:

Individual Debtors	*Debtors Control Account*
1. Sales posted individually from sales day book.	Sales posted as per total in sales day book.
2. Returns posted individually from returns inwards book.	Returns posted as per total in returns book.
3. Cash posted individually from cash book.	Cash posted as per total received in cash book.
4. Discount allowed posted individually from cash book.	Discount allowed posted as per total of column in cash book.

etc.

If it is proposed to instal a complete double-entry for control accounts, two must be opened. One in the debtors ledger in which the items appear on the opposite sides to the individual debtors accounts, and one in the nominal ledger in which the entries appear on the same side as in the individual debtors accounts, viz.:

Debtors Control Account (as in the Sales Ledger)

		£				£
Jan. 31 Cash received	C/B	40,620	Jan. 1 Opening balances	B/D	10,426
Discounts allowed	C/B	2,380	31 Sales for month	SDB	90,624
Returns inwards	RIB	650			
Balance	C/D	57,400			
		£101,050			£101,050
			Feb. 1 Balance	B/D	57,400

The total balance of £57,400 should be identical to the total of the individual balances on the debtors accounts. The sales ledger balances will now be cancelled out, i.e. the sum of the individual debit balances negated by the credit balance in the control account. If the two totals do not agree, then an error has been committed and must be discovered. If they agree, it can be assumed, in the absence of any compensating errors, that all postings, additions, and balances in connection with credit sales are correct, and that if the trial balance does not agree, the mistake must lie elsewhere.

At this point the books of account contain some entries which are entered in one account, i.e. debtors control account in the debtors ledger. To complete the double entry the control account in the nominal ledger must be opened, this being a reversal of the entries already made, viz.:

Debtors Control Account (as in the Nominal Ledger)

		£				£
Jan. 1 Opening balances	B/D	10,426	Jan. 31 Cash received	C/B	40,620
31 Sales for month	SDB	90,624	Discounts allowed	C/B	2,380
			Returns inwards	RIB	650
			Balance	C/D	57,400
		£101,050			£101,050
Feb. 1 Balances	B/D	57,400			

This total is the figure entered in the trial balance because it is only necessary to show the aggregate figure for debtors in the balance sheet, and of course this figure agrees with the sum of the individual balances.

As an alternative to the system described above, the control account in the debtors ledger can be ignored, in which event the individual debtors accounts, though entered in the normal manner, are regarded as memorandum accounts only. The control account in the nominal ledger is regarded as part of the double-entry system. The balance shown in the latter account should still be agreed with the sum of the individual debtors.

A further refinement may be introduced if the number of entries in the debtors accounts increase greatly so that even if an error is localised to this area it will still entail a great amount of time to check through all the items, two debtors ledgers may be opened, e.g. A–K and L–Z. This means that all subsidiary books should be analysed to ensure that there are two totals available for each type of transaction. In the same way the debtors control account in the nominal ledger can be analysed to provide separate balances which will agree with the control accounts in each ledger. In this way the error can be localised to one or other ledger, then the work involved in discovering it will be approximately halved.

The same principles outlined in respect to debtors can also be applied to creditors. A creditors control account is opened in each creditors' ledger with the entries therein on the opposite side to those appearing in the individual account. The control account in the nominal ledger will contain aggregate entries of those appearing in the individual creditors accounts.

Control accounts are not only useful for providing a check on the postings, additions, and balances in the respective ledgers. The control accounts can be written up by a senior employee whilst the personal ledger postings can be entered by a junior clerk. The agreement of the two will provide an indication of the accuracy and efficiency of the junior employee. It will also act as a deterrent against fraud because any transfers or adjustments made in the debtors and creditors ledgers will also have to appear in the control accounts. A speedy computation of the aggregate balances will result from control accounts. If they were not kept, although individual personal accounts are available, these must be balanced and totalled before the total amount can be ascertained. If solvency (cash availability) is weak, an eye must be kept on what is owing to creditors.

PRINCIPLES OF ACCOUNTS

Other items besides the ones shown in the example in this chapter will appear in the control accounts, for example, bad debts written off, or dishonoured cheques. In addition there may be "contra" items. These occur when goods are bought from, and sold to, the same individual. For example, goods are sold to J. Watt for £120, but during the same trading period goods costing £80 are bought from him. Not only would it be reasonable to set off the debt owing to J. Watt against the amount owing from him, but in this case it would lessen the possible loss of a bad debt should J. Watt become bankrupt. The entries would be:

J. WATT (Debtors Ledger)

	£		£
Goods	120	Contra—purchases ledger	80
		Balance	40
	£120		£120
Balance	40		

J. WATT (Creditors Ledger)

	£		£
Contra—sales ledger	80	Goods	80

J. Watt will only have to pay a cheque for £40 to clear his original account. However, as the contra item is entered in both ledgers it must also be entered in the control accounts.

Care should be exercised to ensure that the control accounts reflect the individual balances in the respective ledgers. Although balances in the debtors ledger usually represent amounts owing from customers there may be credit balances. These could occur if an original invoice is paid, but then goods are returned by the customer. Where there are credit balances these must be brought down on the control account and included with the creditors balances on the balance sheet. In the same way any debit balances in the creditors ledger should be shown in the control account and included with the debtors on the balance sheet.

Example

T. Flanagan wishes to include debtors and creditors control accounts in the nominal ledger. From the particulars given below construct these accounts for the year ended 31st December, 19x3.

146

		£
Balances, 1st January, 19x3		
Sales ledger debit balances		7,300
Sales ledger credit balances		50
Purchase ledger credit balances		4,200
Purchase ledger debit balances		160
Totals for year ended 31st December, 19x3		
Credit sales		112,500
Credit purchases		88,600
Cash received from debtors		109,500
Payments to creditors including a refund of an overpayment of £30 to a customer who had made a double payment for a sale		85,800
Discounts allowed		1,250
Discounts received		500
Returns inwards		1,700
Returns outwards		1,500
Credit balances in the purchases ledger which were transferred to sales ledger accounts		250
Debit balances in the sales ledger which were transferred to purchase ledger accounts		150
Bad debts written off		100
At the 31st December, 19x3		
Sales ledger credit balances		20
Purchase ledger debit balances		70

Debtors Control Account

19x3			£	19x3				£
Jan. 1	Balances	B/D	7,300	Jan. 1	Balances	B/D		50
Dec. 31	Credit sales	SDB	112,500	Dec. 31	Cash received	C/B		109,500
	Cash paid to debtor	C/B	30		Discounts allowed	C/B		1,250
	Balances	C/D	20		Returns inwards	RIB		1,700
					Contra items Creditors control		C	250
					– do –		C	150
					Bad debts		L	100
					Balances	C/D		6,850
			£119,850					£119,850
19x4				19x4				
Jan. 1	Balances	B/D	6,850	Jan. 1	Balances	B/D		20

147

Creditors Control Account

19x3			£	19x3			£
Jan. 1	Balances	B/D	160	Jan. 1	Balances	B/D	4,200
Dec. 31	Cash pay-			Dec. 31	Purchases	PDB	88,600
	ments	C/B	85,770		Balances	C/D	70
	Discounts						
	received	C/B	500				
	Returns out-						
	wards	ROB	1,500				
	Contra items						
	Debtors						
	control	C	250				
	– do –	C	150				
	Balances	C/D	4,540				
			£92,870				£92,870
19x4				19x4			
Jan. 1	Balances	B/D	70	Jan. 1	Balances	B/D	4,540

A different type of problem arises where the balance on the control account and the total of the individual balances fail to agree. A number of errors are listed and a reconciliation is required between the two figures.

Example

The debtors control account in the general ledger shows a debit balance of £9,494, a list of balances from the sales ledger totals £8,148.

After a careful examination of the entries in the books the following errors were discovered.

1. An invoice for £120 had not been posted from the sales day book.
2. The sales day book had been overcast by £300.
3. Bad debts of £244 have been written off in the sales ledger, but no other entries have been made.
4. An account of £488 in the purchase ledger has been set off against a contra account in the sales ledger, but this is not recorded in either control account.
5. Balances totalling £178 have been left off the list of debtors.
6. Discount £10 shown in the sales ledger had been omitted from the cash book.
7. Discount allowed £12 entered in the cash book has not been posted to the customer's account.

8. An item of £86 in the sales day book has been posted as £68 in the customer's account.

Show the adjustments necessary to reconcile

(a) the balance in the debtors control account,
(b) the schedule of debtors.

Debtors Control Account

	£		£
Original balance	9,494	Sales day book	300
		Bad debts written off	244
		Creditors control contra	488
		Discount omitted from cash book	10
		Balances carried down	8,452
	£9,494		£9,494
Balances brought down	8,452		

Schedule of Debtors

	£	£
Original total		8,148
Invoice omitted		120
Balances omitted		178
Discount allowed not posted	12	
Correction of posting error (£86–£68)		18
	£12	8,464
	—	12
Total balances agreeing with control account		£8,452

EXERCISES

12.1
From the following particulars prepare the creditors control account in the nominal ledger.

		£
1st Jan.	Credit balances	6,570
	Debit balances	50
31st Jan.	Credit purchases	29,510
	Returns outwards	475
	Discounts received	1,250
	Cash paid to creditors	27,750
	Cash received from a creditor in respect of a debit balance	25
	Debtors ledger contras	520
	Debit balances	40

12.2

From the following particulars prepare the debtors control account in the nominal ledger.

		£
1st Mar.	Debit balances	8,400
	Credit balances	160
31st Mar.	Credit sales	166,900
	Cash received from debtors	151,500
	Discounts allowed	2,875
	Returns inwards	1,950
	Bad debts written off	1,875
	Cheques dishonoured by bank	120
	Cash paid to debtor re credit balance	40
	Creditors ledger contras	580
	Credit balances	90

12.3

You are required to write up the debtors and creditors control accounts in the nominal ledger from the information given below.

		£
1st Sept.	Debtors ledger—Debit balances	6,000
	Credit balances	150
	Creditors ledger—Credit balances	10,300
	Debit balances	100
30th Sept.	Credit sales	71,500
	Credit purchases	48,000
	Returns inwards	360
	Returns outwards	200
	Discount received	1,400
	Discount allowed	850
	Purchase ledger balances transferred to sales ledger	120
	Bad debts written off	100
	Cheques dishonoured by bank	60
	Cash paid to creditors	47,000
	Cash received from debtors	70,000
	Debtors ledger—Credit balances	100
	Creditors ledger—Debit balances	75

12.4

From the particulars given below write up the debtors and creditors control accounts in the nominal ledger.

		£
1st Dec.	Debtors ledger—Debit balances	6,300
	Credit balances	50
	Creditors ledger—Credit balances	4,200
	Debit balances	160

		£
31st Dec.	Credit purchases	88,580
	Credit sales	112,480
	Discounts allowed	1,240
	Discounts received	500
	Dishonoured cheques	120
	Bad debts written off	80
	Accounts settled by contra	150
	Returns inwards	1,700
	Returns outwards	1,530
	Cash paid to suppliers (including a refund of an overpayment of £30 to customer who had paid an invoice twice)	85,790
	Cash received from customers (including a bad debt previously written off as bad £60)	109,460
	Debtors ledger credit balances	20
	Creditors ledger debit balances	40

12.5
The creditors control account in the nominal ledger of B. Ware showed a balance of £8,872. The total of the balances in the creditors ledger amounted to £8,420.

The following errors were later discovered:

(1) The purchase day book had been undercast by £100.
(2) Discounts amounting to £45 had been entered in the cash book, but had not been posted to the creditors personal account.
(3) Credit balances of £60 in the purchases ledger had been listed as debit balances.
(4) Contra items, £480, made between accounts in the debtors ledger and creditors ledger had not been recorded in the control account.
(5) An old debit balance of £5 in the creditors ledger had been written off, but not recorded in the control account.
(6) An entry in the purchase day book for £57 had been posted to the creditors account as £75.
(7) A special allowance of £20 had been debited in a creditors account, but no other entry had been made.
(8) A purchase invoice for £150 had not been recorded in the books.

Show the adjustments necessary to reconcile

(a) the balance in the creditors control account,
(b) the schedule of debtors.

12.6
The following figures relating to the year 19x4 were extracted from the books of a trader.

151

		£
1st Jan.	Debit balances per debtors ledger	7,500
31st Dec.	Credit sales	96,000
	Discounts allowed	1,500
	Returns inwards	2,000
	Cash received from debtors	91,600

The total balances in the sales ledger at 31st December, 19x4, amounted to £7,990.

After the extraction of the figures and the preparation of the list shown above the following errors were discovered.

(1) A cheque received from a customer, £85, was returned by the bank. This had been entered in the cash book and personal account, but nowhere else.

(2) The sales day book had been overcast by £150.

(3) An entry in the sales day book for £90 had not been posted to the debtors account.

(4) A special allowance of £30 had been entered in a debtors account, but no other entry had been made.

(5) A debit balance of £120 had been omitted from the list of balances.

(6) Discounts allowed of £20 had been posted from the cash book to the wrong side of the debtors account.

(7) The debit side of a debtors account had been undercast by £100.

(8) A bad debt of £45 had been written off in the debtors ledger, but no entry made in the control account.

You are required to show the debtors control account for the year, and a revised list of sales ledger balances.

12.7

W. Burton operates control accounts in the nominal ledger. On 30th June, 19x7, the following amounts are extracted from his ledgers.

Debtors control account	£12,400 Dr.
Creditors control account	£7,600 Cr.
List of debtors balances	£11,510
List of creditors balances	£6,992

The following errors were later discovered.

(1) The sales day book had been overcast by £100 and the purchase day book undercast by £200.

(2) A credit balance in the purchase ledger of £300 had been omitted from the list of balances.

(3) A total figure of £350 for returns inwards for May had not been posted to the control account.

(4) A figure of £35 discount received in the cash book had been posted as £53 to the personal account.

(5) A dishonoured cheque of £80 had not been entered in the control account.

(6) An amount of £500 in the purchase ledger has been set off against a contra account in the sales ledger, but this is not recorded in either control account.

(7) Returns inwards amounting to £30 had been entered in the personal account, but not recorded anywhere else.

(8) A credit balance of £10 in the debtors ledger had been transferred to the same account in the creditors ledger, but no entry had been made in the control accounts.

You are required to show the entries in the control accounts and revised lists of balances.

13 Final Accounts—
The Modern Approach

Accountants are often accused of presenting financial results in a manner that is meaningless to anyone who has no knowledge of book-keeping. The number of people who see final accounts is increasing as the opportunities for investment in business become more popular. These people want to see trading results presented as simply as possible. Within a business it is realised that there must be integration between the different sections. Finance is concerned with all aspects of business activity whether it be manufacturing, selling, or administrative departments. To be effective any information that flows between sections must be capable of being understood without difficulty or ambiguity.

The conventional trading and profit and loss account is a continuation of the double-entry system. The cost of goods sold is calculated on the debit side whilst the sales are entered on the credit side. The difference between the two sides results in the gross profit. This figure is brought down on the credit side and expenses are listed on the debit side to produce the net profit. To a person who does not understand the basic principles of accounting this form of presentation is most confusing. He is probably used to reading a book where one reads the left-hand page from top to bottom before progressing to the right-hand page. To read a set of final accounts he is expected to absorb several lines on the left-hand side, then refer to the right-hand side before continuing again on the left-hand side of the account.

In order that the information contained in the accounts is presented as simply as possible the modern approach is to adopt a lay-out known as the narrative or vertical presentation. Instead of having debits and credits in conventional form only one main cash column is used and the entries are regarded as positive or negative, thereby conforming to basic principles.

In the trading and profit and loss account credit entries are positive $(+)$ and debit entries are negative $(-)$. To provide additional information for comparative and control purposes the profit and loss expenses are sub-divided into business functions, e.g. administrative, selling, and financial.

154

In abbreviated form the account will be presented as under:

	£	£
Sales		xxx (Cr.)
Less Cost of sales		xxx (Dr.)
GROSS PROFIT		xxx
Add Other income		xxx (Cr.)
		xxx
Less Administrative expenses	xxx	
Selling expenses	xxx	
Financial expenses	xxx	
		xxx (Dr.)
NET PROFIT		xxx (Cr.)

The balance sheet is also presented in a similar form, but differs considerably from the conventional presentation. The assets are split into two groups, fixed and current, as before, but the current liabilities are deducted from the current assets to give a figure which is known as the working capital.

When a business is first brought into existence capital will be required to purchase fixed assets which are essential to establish the business as a long-term entity. The amount of fixed assets depends on the nature of the business. A manufacturing concern will need a factory, plant, and equipment etc., but a retail business will require only fixtures and possibly a lease of premises. In addition to fixed assets a business needs further capital to furnish stock and pay day to day running expenses. This extra capital is known as the working capital and is represented in the balance sheet by the excess of current assets over current liabilities.

The description "working" refers to the use made of these assets and liabilities. Their constituent parts are changing each day. Cash is required to pay creditors who supply stock. The stock in turn is sold to debtors who pay cash, and the cycle commences again. The cash at the end of the cycle should amount to more than the opening figure as it contains the profit on goods sold. If expenses and drawings are less than the profit made, working capital will continue to increase thereby providing funds to buy additional stock and also fixed assets.

Current liabilities have to be paid out of current assets, so that the difference should always be a debit. If the liabilities exceed the assets, the business is insolvent in the short term which means that in order to pay its debts the business must sell fixed assets, thereby reducing the size of the business. To be successful the business should expand both its

155

fixed assets and working capital. The amount of working capital is obscured in the conventional balance sheet presentation.

From the total of fixed assets and working capital is deducted any long-term liabilities. The resultant figure should then agree with the balance on the capital account. An abbreviated balance sheet is shown below:

	£	£
Fixed assets		xxx
Current assets	xxx	
Less Current liabilities	xxx	
Working capital		xxx
Total net assets		xxx
Less Long-term loans		xxx
Net worth		xxx
Capital account		£xxx

Illustration. Final accounts in narrative or vertical form.

B. BANCROFT
Trading and Profit and Loss Account
Year ended 30th June, 19x3

	£	£	£
Sales			65,840
Less Opening stock		12,220	
Purchases		35,990	
		48,210	
Closing stock		4,280	
Cost of goods sold			43,930
Gross profit			21,910
Add Rent received		1,000	
Discounts received		1,140	
			2,140
			24,050
Less			
Administration expenses			
Insurances	2,000		
Lighting and heating	390		
Rent and rates	560		
General expenses	340		
		3,290	

	£	£	£
Selling expenses			
Salesmen's salaries	10,000		
Delivery expenses	2,000		
Travelling expenses	240		
Bad debts	510		
		12,750	
Financial expenses			
Discount allowed	1,200		
Bank charges and interest	70		
Loan interest	120		
		1,390	
			17,430
Net profit			£6,620

Balance Sheet as at 30th June, 19x3

	Cost £	Depreciation £	Net £
Fixed assets			
Buildings	12,000		12,000
Fixtures and fittings	2,800	800	2,000
Delivery vehicles	7,500	2,610	4,890
	£22,300	£3,410	18,890
Current assets			
Stock		4,280	
Debtors	11,000		
Less Provision doubtful debts	1,200		
		9,800	
Prepaid expenses		30	
Cash in bank		1,080	
Cash in hand		150	
		15,340	
Less Current liabilities			
Creditors	8,320		
Accrued expenses	290		
		8,610	
Working capital			6,730
			25,620
Less Loan F. Maxwell			2,000
Net worth			23,620

	Net £
Capital employed	
Opening balance	21,000
Add Profit for year	6,620
	27,620
Less Drawings	4,000
	£23,620

By presenting the accounts in this way, not only is the information presented in a logical order, but also:

1. Because there are no debit and credit sides to the statements more space is available for detailed explanations where necessary.
2. Sub-division of figures can be shown thereby providing comparisons of aggregate as well as individual items with previous years. Controls can be exercised over total expenditure of each business function.
3. Attention can be drawn to important relationships between figures which might be obscure in a conventional presentation, e.g. working capital or expenses which are fixed and those that are variable. The former tend to remain static irrespective of the sales (e.g. administration expenses) whilst the latter vary according to sales (e.g. selling expenses).
4. The lay-out lends itself admirably to systems where accounts are split over two or more distinct sets of trading results, e.g. departmental accounts (see Chapter 24).

Cash Flow Statements

Although businesses are created to make profits for their owners, a large profit does not always produce an increase in the cash or bank balances. There is no direct relationship between profits and cash balances even if drawings are restricted. If stock valued at £100 is sold on credit for £150, although a profit of £50 has been made the cash balance is unaffected because the profit has been used in providing additional credit to customers. Even if the profit had not been used in this way, if the sale had been made for cash, the money received could have been spent on fixed assets.

Because of this state of affairs accountants sometimes supplement the final accounts with a cash flow statement which explains how the opening cash and bank balances are reconciled with the closing balances.

This statement shows how funds have been raised and how they have been spent. The statement is made up by comparing the opening and closing balance sheets and by making certain adjustments to the profit.

To take a simple example—the balance sheets of J. King at 1st January and 31st December, 19x7, were as follows:

	1st January		31st December	
	£	£	£	£
Fixed assets		6,000		8,000
Current assets				
Stock	4,000		5,000	
Debtors	1,500		2,000	
Bank	750		1,000	
	6,250		8,000	
Current liabilities				
Creditors	2,000		2,700	
		4,250		5,300
		£10,250		£13,300
Capital				
Balance		10,250		10,250
Profit				6,050
				16,300
Less Drawings				3,000
		£10,250		£13,300

In the absence of information it can be assumed that expenditure has been incurred in increasing assets as under:

		£
Fixed assets	(£8,000 − £6,000) =	2,000
Stock	(£5,000 − £4,000) =	1,000
Debtors	(£2,000 − £1,500) =	500
		£3,500

On the other hand funds have been received by the profit figure of £6,050 plus increased credit facilities given by creditors (£2,700 − £2,000) = £700.

The explanation for the difference in bank balances can now be given, and a reconciliation statement is shown overleaf.

This explains why although there was a profit of £6,050 and drawings of £3,000 (i.e. a net figure of £3,050) the bank balance rose by only £250.

The above example has been simplified as all items in the balance sheet increased during the year. In practice this will not always be the case.

	£	£
Opening bank balance		750
Add Funds generated by trading profits		6,050
Funds generated by increase of creditors		700
		7,500
Less Funds expended on assets	3,500	
Drawings	3,000	
		6,500
Closing bank balance		£1,000

For example, the amount of stock held may fall which will result in funds being received, i.e. part of the asset has been sold resulting in an inflow of funds. Creditors may also fall during the year, which means that funds will have been expended in paying them off. The situation may be resolved as per the following table.

Receipt of Funds	*Expenditure of Funds*
1. Increase in capital or liability	1. Increase in asset
2. Decrease in asset	2. Decrease in liability

Unfortunately not all items entered in the accounts are concerned eventually with cash. An example of this is depreciation. The only times when cash is involved with the acquisition of a fixed asset is when it is purchased and when it is sold. Depreciation is an arbitrary amount transferred between two accounts within the books. The same type of transaction is involved when a profit or loss arises on disposal as these figures merely adjust the aggregate depreciation written off to the date of disposal. These "internal" entries have to be reversed, i.e. nullified before the cash flow statement can be completed.

The form of the cash flow statement is normally set out to show the main types of funds generated and expended. The funds generated are divided into three parts: (a) those produced by trading profits, (b) those generated by long-term borrowing, and (c) miscellaneous—usually receipts from disposals of fixed assets. Funds expended are also divided into three main types: (a) expenditure on fixed assets, (b) expenditure on working capital, and (c) expenditure lost to the business, e.g. drawings and repayment of long-term loans.

Example

The balance sheet for J. Smith at 31st December, 19x1 and 19x2, was as follows:

160

Balance Sheet as at 31st December

	19x1 £	19x2 £		19x1 £	19x2 £
Capital			Machinery at cost	10,000	11,000
Opening balance	11,500	12,500	Less Depreciation	6,000	6,000
Profit	4,000	6,000		4,000	5,000
	15,500	18,500	Freehold property		
Less Drawings	3,000	3,750	at cost	6,000	8,000
	12,500	14,750	Stock	5,000	4,500
Loan J. Jones	6,000	8,000	Debtors	3,000	4,000
Creditors	1,500	1,750	Bank	2,000	3,000
	£20,000	£24,500		£20,000	£24,500

Machinery which had cost £3,000 with a written down value of £1,000 had been sold for £1,250. The profit had been credited to profit and loss account. Mr. Smith cannot understand why although he made a profit of £6,000 in the year the bank balance only increased by £1,000. You are required to set out a statement which explains the change in the bank balance.

Before the statement can be produced it is necessary to calculate the depreciation charged in the year and whether any machinery was acquired.

	Depreciation a/c £	Machinery a/c £
Balance 31st December, 19x1	6,000	10,000
Less Amounts re machinery sold (£3,000 − 1,000)	2,000	3,000
	4,000	7,000
Amounts required to arrive at closing balances	2,000	4,000
Balances 31st December, 19x2	£6,000	£11,000

The amount debited to the profit and loss account for the year is, therefore, £2,000. Machinery costing £4,000 has been purchased during the year. A flow statement is shown overleaf.

The cash flow statement is not only a useful exercise in explaining how funds have been acquired and how they have been used. A firm must have liquid resources to meet immediate debts and if forecast cash flows are estimated there should always be sufficient funds available to meet liabilities. If forecast flow statements show that the business is likely to run into any cash difficulties in the future, then investment in

161

J. SMITH
Cash Flow Statement year ended 31st December, 19x2

	£	£	£	£
Opening bank balance				2,000
Add Profit per balance sheet			6,000	
Depreciation charged			2,000	
			8,000	
Less Profit on disposal of machinery			250	
Funds generated by trading				7,750
Outside borrowing				2,000
Cash from sale of machinery				1,250
				13,000
Less Purchase of fixed assets				
Freehold property		2,000		
Machinery		4,000		
			6,000	
Less Working capital investment				
Increase in debtors		1,000		
Decrease in stock	500			
Increase in creditors	250			
		750		
			250	
Less Drawings			3,750	
				10,000
Closing bank balance				£3,000

fixed assets should be cut back or the amount of drawings reduced. By keeping a careful watch on future cash flows a business should be able to avert any embarrassing shortages of cash or bank balances that might otherwise have arisen. This is one example where an accountant can assist management to determine future policies.

EXERCISES

13.1
From the following particulars contained in the ledger of A. Burke at 30th June, 19x4, you are required to construct a trading and profit and loss account and balance sheet in narrative form.

	£		£
Capital account	28,000	Furniture and fittings	2,520
Carriage inwards	256	General expenses	1,974
Carriage outwards	644	Insurances	246
Cash account	56	Premises at cost	16,000

	£		£
Commission received	272	Purchases	28,180
Debtors	2,956	Sales	47,076
Creditors	3,730	Returns inwards	916
Discounts allowed	448	Returns outwards	468
Discounts received	392	Stock 1st July, 19x3	7,088
Drawings	6,320	Wages and salaries	9,420
Bank deposit account	3,200	Bank overdraft	286

The stock at 30th June, 19x4, amounted to £5,240.

13.2

The following balances were extracted from the books of F. Lyon at 30th September, 19x7. You are required to prepare a trading and profit and loss account for the year ended 30th September, 19x7, and a balance sheet as at that date (both in vertical form).

	£		£
Rent and rates	400	Advertising	520
Salaries	568	General expenses	274
Heating and lighting	352	Drawings	2,020
Insurances	98	Cash in hand	32
Debtors	2,208	Land and buildings at cost	6,000
Stock 1st October, 19x6	5,236	Goodwill	1,000
Machinery at cost	7,000	Purchases	14,624
Provision for depreciation		Sales	20,196
machinery	2,000	Bank overdraft	300
Discount received	270	Creditors	786
Rent received	300		
Capital account	16,480		

The stock on 30th September, 1947, amounted to £3,716.
Rates amounting to £40 were due, but unpaid.
£100 was owing for rent by Lyon's tenant.
Depreciation is to be calculated on the machinery based on 10% of the written down value.

13.3

The following balances were extracted from the books of E. Ferguson at 31st March, 19x8. You are required to draw up the trading and profit and loss account for the year ended 31st March, 19x8, and a balance sheet as on that date, both in vertical form.

	£		£
Office salaries	8,800	Lighting and heating	250
Rent and rates	400	Bad debts	400
Insurance	140	Salesmen's salaries	6,000
General expenses	2,680	Commission paid	2,300
Bank charges	460	Carriage outwards	1,180
Discounts allowed	960	Purchases	158,690
Stock 1st April, 19x7	7,780	Sales	200,000

	£		£
Capital	51,560	Drawings	4,000
Debtors	28,460	Creditors	25,000
Plant and machinery at cost	56,000	Office fittings at cost	4,000
Provision depreciation		Provision depreciation	
machinery	15,600	fittings	2,000
Balance at bank	11,360	Cash in hand	300

(1) The stock at 31st March, 19x8, amounted to £8,000.
(2) The following amounts were owing: rent £200, lighting and heating £75.
(3) The following amounts were prepaid: rates £50, insurance £30.
(4) Depreciation is to be allowed as follows:

Plant and machinery 25% on the reducing balance method.
Office fittings   20% on the straight line method.

13.4
The balance sheets of R. Roll at 30th September, 19x7 and 19x8 are given below.

	19x7 £	19x8 £		19x7 £	19x8 £
Capital account	12,600	17,600	Office fittings		
Loan O. Dew	5,000	6,500	at cost	10,000	12,000
Creditors	5,400	6,400	Less depreciation	4,000	5,200
				6,000	6,800
			Stock	9,800	14,600
			Debtors	6,200	7,600
			Bank	1,000	1,500
	£23,000	£30,500		£23,000	£30,500

The capital amount for 19x8 is made up as follows:

	£
Balance brought forward	12,600
Profit for year	8,000
	20,600
Less Drawings	3,000
	£17,600

You are required to prepare a cash-flow statement for the year ended 30th September, 19x8.

13.5
The balance sheets of B. Powell at 31st December, 19x1 and 19x2 are given below.

	19x1 £	*19x2* £		*19x1* £	*19x2* £
Capital account	8,500	10,500	Office furniture		
Creditors	2,500	3,000	at cost	8,000	9,000
Bank overdraft	2,000	2,500	*Less* Depreciation	2,000	3,000
				6,000	6,000
			Stock	4,000	6,000
			Debtors	3,000	4,000
	£13,000	£16,000		£13,000	£16,000

Drawings for the year ended 31st December, 19x2, amounted to £3,000. During the year office furniture costing £1,000 was sold for £400. Depreciation had been provided for this item to the amount of £500. The loss on sale was debited to the profit and loss account.

You are required to prepare a cash-flow statement for the year ended 31st December, 19x2.

13.6
The balance sheets of G. Wolfe as at 31st March, 19x6 and 19x7 are given below.

	19x6 £	*19x7* £		*19x6* £	*19x7* £
Capital account	25,000	18,000	Fixtures and		
Loan B. Lamb	4,000	6,000	fittings at cost	9,000	8,000
Creditors	7,000	10,000	*Less* Depreciation	3,000	4,000
				6,000	4,000
			Freehold proper-		
			ties at cost	8,000	8,000
			Stock	12,000	15,000
			Debtors	8,000	6,000
			Bank	2,000	1,000
	£36,000	£34,000		£36,000	£34,000

No fixed assets were purchased during the year, but fixtures and fittings with a written down value of £600 were sold for £250. Drawings for the year amounted to £2,500.

You are required to prepare a cash-flow statement for the year ended 31st March, 19x7.

13.7
The balance sheets of V. Rock at 30th June, 19x4 and 19x5 are given below.

165

	19x4 £	19x5 £		19x4 £	19x5 £
Capital account	54,540	53,540	Machinery at cost	28,600	28,600
Loan from B. Owen	5,000	—	*Less* Depreciation	8,860	14,460
Creditors	11,700	10,840		19,740	14,140
Bank overdraft	9,920	—	Freehold properties	32,380	24,080
			Stock	16,600	12,240
			Debtors	12,440	9,280
			Bank	—	4,640
	£81,160	£64,380		£81,160	£64,380

The capital account for 19x5 is made up as follows:

	£
Balance brought forward	54,540
Profit for year	2,000
	56,540
Less Drawings	3,000
	£53,540

Freehold properties costing £8,300 were sold during the year for £7,500. The loss has been written off to profit and loss account

You are required to prepare a cash-flow statement to show how the bank balance has changed over the year.

14 Partnership—
Final Accounts

The previous chapters have dealt with the accounts of sole traders, but these do not comprise all businesses. When two or more persons form a relationship to carry on a business with a view to profit—a partnership is established. With the exception of accountants, solicitors, stock exchange members, or certain other professional bodies approved by the Board of Trade (where there is no restriction) a partnership is limited to twenty persons.

There are a number of advantages for establishing a partnership.

1. *There is a Division of Responsibility.* A sole trader must make all decisions by himself, whereas with a partnership the decisions are made by all the partners. When a sole trader takes a holiday, or is ill, he must leave the business in the hands of an employee, but with a partnership one of the owners can always be present.
2. *There is a Degree of Specialisation.* With each partner concentrating on the job he can do best, there is a division of labour. A sole trader has to be a "jack of all trades". This specialisation in partnerships tends to improve efficiency and thereby profitability.
3. *There is Additional Finance.* There is a limit on the amount of capital an individual can put, or is prepared to risk, in a business. As each partner contributes capital the business can expand more rapidly than a sole trader's which relies on retention of profits for increased capital. New partners can be introduced if the need arises.

Because a partnership, like a sole trader, is not a separate legal entity each partner along with the others is liable for the business debts. This means that should the business become insolvent a creditor is able to claim his debt from the partners either jointly or individually from their private resources. This gives a greater measure of security to the creditor than he possibly has when dealing with a sole trader.

Partnership Deeds or Agreements

Before a partnership is brought into being it is essential that the individuals concerned decide what conditions will apply when the partnership is formed. A written agreement is drawn up containing clauses which are designed to cover every eventuality, so that if a dispute arises in the future, reference can be made to the agreement. All partners must sign the agreement and are then bound by the conditions contained therein.

Amongst the matters dealt with would be the name of the partnership (or firm), the duration of the partnership, provisions dealing with death or retirement of any partners, and the individual rights and duties of the partners. The financial clauses are most important to the student of book-keeping and these generally deal with the contribution of capital and the division of profits, or the allocation of losses, and should contain in particular the following:

1. The amounts of capital to be contributed by the partners.
2. How much each partner can draw in anticipation of profits.
3. Whether any salaries are to be paid to the partners.
4. Whether any interest is payable on capital or current accounts.
5. Whether any interest is chargeable on drawings.
6. How the balance of profits or losses are to be divided.

The Amounts of Capital to be Contributed by the Partners

It is most important to agree on these amounts otherwise disputes may take place in the future. Not all partners are able to contribute the same proportion of capital and this is usually reflected in the division of profits. There are exceptions to this. For example, where two people enter into a partnership, one has considerable business acumen, the other has considerable wealth. Neither can successfully run a business on his own, but by combining one can supply the "brains" and the other the "money". Each contributes in his own way and, therefore, may share profits equally. Generally the capital originally contributed is fixed and is credited to each partner's capital account. Profits are usually credited to a partner's current account against which he makes his drawings.

The Restrictions in Drawings

Unlike a sole trader the capital of a partner is fixed in the partnership deed, but as profits are not known until the end of the year, and drawings are made during the year, a partner could place his current account in debit. The effect of this is that he has withdrawn part of his original capital. To attempt to overcome this situation the maximum amount of drawings allowed to each partner is stipulated in the deed. It is also advisable to list the dates on which drawings can take place, e.g. monthly or quarterly etc.

The Payment of Salaries

Strictly speaking partners cannot be paid a salary as they are owners of the firm and share in the total profits. A partner's salary is a means of sharing out the profits at the year end; it is a charge against the net profit and is credited to his current account. The question of whether any salaries should be credited to partners depends to a large extent on their work within the partnership. If some partners are more actively engaged in business affairs whilst others are non-active and regard the partnership as an investment, it may seem appropriate that the former receive a salary credit whilst the latter do not. A junior partner may only receive a small proportion of the firm's profits and is usually credited with a salary to compensate for his work within the partnership.

Interest on Capital and Current Accounts

If all partners contribute the same amount of capital, their stake in the firm is uniform and there may be no need to credit them with interest. When the capital contributions are different, the partner with the highest amount has the greater risk of losing more than the other partners. To compensate for the various amounts at risk a charge against the net profits can be made in the form of interest on capital, these amounts being credited to the partners' current accounts. In the same way, a partner who does not withdraw all he is entitled to from his current account is benefiting the firm as it can make use of the funds available. To reward the partners for balances not withdrawn interest can be credited to their current accounts.

Interest on Drawings

This adjustment has the same effect as the preceding one. The object is to reduce the amount of drawings taken from the firm. The entry is to debit the partners' current accounts with interest and add these amounts to the net profit. The longer balances are left in the firm the more benefit can be obtained so that the interest is calculated on each amount of drawings. For example, a partner withdraws £400 each quarter, i.e. 31st March, 30th June, 30th September, and 31st December. Interest is chargeable on drawings at 5% per annum. Calculate the interest to be debited to his current account.

	Amount	Rate%	Period	Fraction	Interest
31st March	£400	5	9 months	9/12ths	£15
30th June	£400	5	6 months	6/12ths	£10
30th September	£400	5	3 months	3/12ths	£5
31st December	£400	5	0 months	—	—
					£30

Balance of Profits

The remaining balance of profits after all or any of the above adjustments have been dealt with is divided between the partners in a predetermined ratio. This ratio is incorporated in the partnership deed and will depend to some extent on the amounts already agreed upon in respect of interest or salaries. In many instances this balance is divided equally as the previous adjustments should cover the different contributions made by the partners towards the business interests. If the balance is to be distributed in unequal proportions, a clause is sometimes inserted into the deed that a particular partner will receive a minimum amount. In this case the amount that may be required to make up this sum will be borne by the other partners in a proportion laid down in the deed.

The Appropriation Account

The final accounts for partnership are constructed in the same manner as those for sole traders with the addition of an account called the "Appropriation Account". Because the profit has to be divided between the partners it cannot be immediately transferred from the profit and loss account to the capital or current accounts. Instead it is brought down into the appropriation account and all the adjustments referring to partners' interests, salaries etc. are made within this account.

Example

A. Abel, B. Baker, and C. Charles are in partnership. The deed of partnership provides the following:

1. Baker shall receive a salary of £1,000, Charles shall receive a salary of £2,000.
2. Interest is allowable at 5% on their fixed capitals.
3. Interest is allowable at 5% on current account balances at the beginning of the year.
4. Interest is chargeable on drawings at the rate of 6% per annum.
5. The balance of profits is divisible, Abel 50%, Baker 30%, Charles 20%.

The net profit for the year ended 31st December, 19x3, amounted to £6,730 and you are given the following particulars.

	A. Abel £	B. Baker £	C. Charles £
Capital account 1st Jan., 19x3	6,000	5,000	4,000
Current account 1st Jan., 19x3 (credits)	1,000	500	200
Drawings.			
31st Mar., 19x3	400	400	400
30th June, 19x3	400	300	500
30th Sept., 19x3	400	400	200
31st Dec., 19x3	400	300	100

You are required to construct the appropriation account at 31st December, 19x3, and the partners' current accounts. (See page 172).

Two further points may be mentioned at this stage. If a partner makes a loan to the firm in excess of his capital, the loan interest is debited to the profit and loss account and not the appropriation account even if it is not actually paid but credited to his current account. No distinction is made between loans by partners and loans from third parties. The interest payable is therefore a charge against profits and not an appropriation or sharing of profits. If a current account in overdrawn, i.e. it has a debit balance, this should be entered as a current asset in the balance sheet and not deducted from the capital account of the partner concerned, nor from the other partners' current accounts.

171

Appropriation Account

	£	£		£	£
Salaries			Net profit brought down		6,730
B. Baker	1,000		Interest on drawings		
C. Charles	2,000		A. Abel	36	
		3,000	B. Baker	33	
			C. Charles	36	
Interest on capital					105
A. Abel	300				
B. Baker	250				
C. Charles	200				
		750			
Interest on current accounts					
A. Abel	50				
B. Baker	25				
C. Charles	10				
		85			
Balance					
A. Abel (50%)	1,500				
B. Baker (30%)	900				
C. Charles (20%)	600	3,000			
		£6,835			£6,835

Partners' Current Accounts (in columnar form)
CREDIT SIDE OF LEDGER

			Abel £	Baker £	Charles £
19x3					
Jan. 1	Balance	B/D	1,000	500	200
Dec. 31	Salaries	P & L		1,000	2,000
	Interest on capital	P & L	300	250	200
	Interest on current accounts	P & L	50	25	10
	Balance of profits	P & L	1,500	900	600
			£2,850	£2,675	£3,010
19x4					
Jan 1	Balance	B/D	1,214	1,242	1,774

DEBIT SIDE OF LEDGER

			Abel £	Baker £	Charles £
19x3					
Dec. 31	Transfer drawings account	L	1,600	1,400	1,200
	Interest on drawings	P & L	36	33	36
	Balance	C/D	1,214	1,242	1,774
			£2,850	£2,675	£3,010

The profit of £6,730 has been divided as follows:

A. Abel	£300 + 50 + 1,500 − 36	= £1,814
B. Baker	£1,000 + 250 + 25 + 900 − 33 =	2,142
C. Charles	£2,000 + 200 + 10 + 600 − 36 =	2,774
		£6,730

The Partnership Act of 1890

Although every endeavour may have been made to ensure that all eventualities have been covered in the partnership deed certain matters may be overlooked. Where omissions have occurred the provisions of the Partnership Act of 1890 will apply.

This Act covers most disputes that might arise between partners, but will only apply in the absence of any partnership agreement or clauses within the agreement.

Exceptions to the application of the Act are where the partners' conduct over a number of years implies that certain agreements have been made although not supported by written evidence. For example, if a partner had been credited with an annual salary since the inception of the partnership, it would be understood that it formed part of the original agreement.

The rules applying to the accounts are contained in Section 24 of the Act and are as follows:

1. The capital should be subscribed equally by the partners.
2. Profits and losses should be shared equally between the partners.
3. No interest is allowed on capital or current accounts.
4. No interest is to be charged on drawings.
5. No partner is entitled to receive a salary.
6. Any partner who lends the firm money in excess of the capital he has agreed to subscribe is entitled to interest at the rate of 5% per annum.
7. Every partner is entitled to inspect and copy any of the accounting records which must be kept at the place of business.

Example of Partnership Final Accounts

G. East and F. West are in partnership. The partnership deed provides:
   (a) West is to receive a salary of £2,000 per annum.
   (b) Interest at 5% p.a. is allowed on fixed capitals.

PRINCIPLES OF ACCOUNTS

(c) Interest is charged on drawings at $2\frac{1}{2}\%$ irrespective of the dates of withdrawal..
(d) Profits and losses are shared between East and West in the ratio 3:2.

The following trial balance was extracted on 30th June, 19x2.

	£	£
Capital accounts: East		20,000
West		16,000
Current accounts: East		800
West		440
Drawings: East	3,600	
West	2,800	
Shop fixtures at cost	14,000	
Office furniture at cost	600	
Provision depreciation—Fixtures 1.7.x1		2,000
—Furniture 1.7.x1		200
Debtors and creditors.	28,992	9,212
Stock 1st July, 19x1	10,520	
Purchases and sales	88,704	122,960
Carriage inwards	508	
Returns inwards and outwards	640	232
Rent and rates	5,440	
Insurances	1,268	
General expenses	2,592	
Staff salaries	14,140	
Carriage outwards	1,248	
Provision for doubtful debts 1st July, 19x1		260
Bank overdraft		3,140
Advertising	192	
	£175,244	£175,244

You are required to prepare the firm's trading and profit and loss account for the year ended 30th June, 19x2, and a balance sheet at that date taking into account the following information.

(a) Stock at 30th June, 19x2, was valued at £16,240.
(b) Rates paid in advance amounted to £352.
(c) Depreciation is to be provided—shop fixtures 10%, office furniture 20%, both on cost.
(d) The provision for doubtful debts is to be increased to £672.

174

EAST AND WEST
Trading and Profit and Loss Account
Year ended 30th June, 19x2

	£	£		£	£
Opening stock		10,520	Sales	122,960	
Purchases	88,704		*Less* Returns		
Less Returns outwards	232	88,472	inwards	640	
		98,992			122,320
Less Closing stock		16,240			
		82,752			
Carriage inwards		508			
Cost of goods sold		83,260			
Gross profit carried down		39,060			
		£122,320			£122,320
Staff salaries		14,140	Gross profit		
Rent and rates		5,088	brought down		39,060
Insurances		1,268			
General expenses		2,592			
Carriage outwards		1,248			
Increase provision doubtful					
debts		412			
Advertising		192			
Depreciation—Shop fixtures		1,400			
Depreciation—Office furniture		120			
Net profit carried down		12,600			
		£39,060			£39,060

Appropriation Account

	£	£		£	£
Salary. West		2,000	Net profit brought down		12,600
Interest on capital			Interest on drawings		
East	1,000		East	90	
West	800	1,800	West	70	160
Balance of profits					
East 3	5,376				
West 2	3,584	8,960			
		£12,760			£12,760

Balance Sheet as at 30th June, 19x2

	£	£			£	£
Capital accounts			Fixed assets			
G. East	20,000		Shop fixtures at cost	14,000		
F. West	16,000		Less Prov. depreciation	3,400		
		36,000				10,600
Current accounts			Office furniture at cost	600		
G. East	3,486		Less Prov. depreciation	320		
F. West	3,954					280
		7,440				10,880
Current liabilities			Current assets			
Creditors	9,212		Stock		16,240	
Bank overdraft	3,140		Debtors	28,992		
		12,352	Less prov.			
			d. debts	672		
					28,320	
			Prepaid exp.		352	
						44,912
		£55,792				£55,792

Details of the current account balances are given below:

Current Accounts

		East £	West £			East £	West £
19x2				19x1			
June 30	Tfr. drawings	3,600	2,800	July 1 Balance		800	440
	Interest on			June 30 Salary			2,000
	drawings	90	70	Interest on			
	Balance	3,486	3,954	capital		1,000	800
				Balance of profit		5,376	3,584
		£7,176	£6,824			£7,176	£6,824
				19x2			
				July 1 Balance		3,486	3,954

Limited Partnerships

Occasionally a person is prepared to enter into a business, but is not willing to risk losing all his assets. By registering the partnership under the Limited Partnership Act of 1907 the liability of one or more partners is restricted to the capital introduced. This means that in the event of the firm becoming insolvent the creditors would not be able to claim the amount owing to them from the private assets of the limited partners. There must be at least one general or unlimited partner in the firm. Furthermore, the limited partners cannot take part in the management of the firm.

The Business Name

As with sole traders, if a partnership trades under a name that does not consist of the true surnames of the owners, it must register the name under the Registration of Business Names Act. For example, if the name of the firm in the preceding example was George East and Frank West there would be no need to register, but if the firm traded as East, West & Company, or East West Supplies, registration would be necessary.

EXERCISES

14.1
C. Charlton, C. Clarke, and D. Hughes were in partnership. The partnership deed contains the following:

(1) The partners' fixed capitals were Charlton £24,000, Clarke £20,000, and Hughes £16,000.
(2) Clarke and Hughes were to receive salaries of £1,500 and £1,000 respectively.
(3) Interest on capital is to be calculated at 5% per annum.
(4) Charlton, Clark, and Hughes are to share profits and losses in the ratio 3:2:1.

You are given the following particulars.

	Charlton £	Clarke £	Hughes £
Current account balances (all credit) at Ist Jan., 19x7	1,000	750	500
Drawings for year 31st Dec., 19x7	4,000	3,500	2,700

The profit for the year ended 31st December, 19x7 amounted to £8,500.

You are required to prepare the appropriation account and the partners' current accounts.

14.2
Ronald, Percy, and George were in partnership. The partnership deed contains the following:

(1) The partners' fixed capitals were Ronald £10,000, Percy £6,000, and George £4,000
(2) Percy and George were to receive salaries of £2,000 and £1,000 respectively.
(3) Interest on capital is to be calculated at 5% per annum.
(4) Ronald, Percy, and George are to share profits and losses in the ratio 2:2:1.

(5) It is stipulated that George will receive a minimum (including interest and salary) of £3,000 in any year. Any sum needed to make up this amount shall be shared by Ronald and Percy in their profit sharing ratios.

The year ended 30th September, 19x8. The net trading profit amounted to £10,000.

You are required to show the appropriation account and to give a statement showing how much in total will be credited to the partners' current accounts.

14.3

Fish, Fowl, and Bird were in partnership. The partnership deed provided that:

1. Interest is credited on the partners' capital accounts at 5% per annum.
2. Interest is charged on partners' drawings at 5% per annum.
3. Bird is to receive a salary of £1,000
4. Profits are to be shared in the ratio 2:2:1.

During the year ended 30th June, 19x4, the net profit of the firm was £4,800. Drawings were: Fish £2,400, Fowl £2,000, Bird £1,600, in each case in two equal instalments on 31st December, 19x3 and 30th June, 19x4.

The partners' balances on 1st July, 19x3, were:

	Fish £	Fowl £	Bird £
Capital account	10,000	9,000	5,000
Current account (all credits)	800	600	200

On 1st January, 19x4, it was agreed that Fish should withdraw £1,000 of his capital and that Fowl should increase his capital by £1,000.

You are required to prepare the firm's profit and loss appropriation account for the year ended 30th June, 19x4, and to show the entries in the partners' capital and current accounts.

14.4

High, Wide, and Short are trading in partnership. Each is to receive interest at 5% on their capital accounts. Short is to receive a further 10% of the net profit after charging interest on the capital accounts in lieu of a salary. The balance of profits is shared in the ratio 3:2:1.

The capital accounts at 1st January, 19x7, were High £9,600, Wide £4,600, and Short £2,300. The net profit for the year ended 31st December, 19x7, was £2,165.

You are required to prepare the profit and loss appropriation account and the partners' current accounts.

14.5

Smith and Jones are partners in a retail organisation. The balances in their ledger at 30th June, 19x4, are as follows:

	£		£
Capital account Smith	16,000	Motor vehicles at cost	8,000
Jones	12,000	Provision depreciation	
Current account Smith Cr.	880	vehicles	2,080
Jones Cr.	508	Fixtures at cost	2,000
Drawings Smith	1,040	Provision depreciation	
Jones	2,400	fixtures	360
Debtors	1,720	Stock 1st July, 19x3	1,952
Returns inwards	238	Purchases	30,576
Returns outwards	630	Sales	54,300
Carriage inwards	218	Discount allowed	452
Carriage outwards	430	Discount received	626
Office expenses	1,366	Office salaries	10,872
Insurance	170	Salesmen's salaries	6,840
Goodwill	10,000	Rent and rates	916
Balance at bank	9,036	Commission received	842

The stock at 30th June, 19x4, was valued at £2,068. Motor vehicles are to be depreciated at 25% on the reducing balance method and fixtures at 10% on the straight line method. A provision for doubtful debts is to be credited at 5% of the total debtors.

The partnership agreement provides for 8% interest on capital, a salary of £1,600 to Jones, and profits to be shared Smith three-fifths and Jones two-fifths.

You are required to prepare a trading, profit and loss and appropriation account for the year ended 30th June, 19x4, and to write up the partners' current accounts.

14.6
Spence and Marks are in partnership as greengrocers. There is no partnership deed. On 31st March, 19x7, the balances in their books were

	£		£
Capital account Spence	34,000	Freehold property	52,000
Marks	26,000	Shop fittings	2,000
Current account Spence (Cr.)	6,000	Provision depreciation	
Marks (Cr.)	4,000	fittings	800
Drawings Spence	4,000	Debtors	35,120
Marks	5,600	Creditors	39,500
Purchases	143,600	Stock 1st April, 19x6	28,940
Wages	32,182	Sales	198,000
Rent and rates	2,500	Provision doubtful	
Cash at bank	10,574	debts	640
Carriage outwards	1,490	Lighting and heating	934
		Loan from Spence	8,000
		Discounts received	2,000

Stock on hand at 31st March, 19x7, was valued at £25,208. Provision for depreciation on shop fittings is to be provided at 5% on cost. The provision

179

for doubtful debts is no longer required. The loan from Spence was made on 31st December, 19x6.

You are required to prepare a trading, profit and loss and appropriation account for the year ended 30th June, 19x4, and a balance sheet as at that date.

14.7
Charles, George, and Henry have been in partnership since 1st January, 19x0. They have shared profits in the ratio of 3:2:1 respectively. At the 31st December, 19x2, it was unanimously agreed that interest at the rate of 5% per annum should have been allowed on partners' capital accounts. The following details apply to the three years.

	19x0	*19x1*	*19x2*
	£	£	£
Fixed capitals Charles	10,000	10,000	10,000
George	8,000	8,000	8,000
Henry	6,000	6,000	6,000
Drawings Charles	2,500	1,000	1,000
George	2,000	1,500	1,000
Henry	1,000	1,500	1,000
Profits	6,000	8,400	
Loss			1,200

You are required to show the partners' current accounts showing the original division of profits for 19x0 and 19x1, the adjustment necessary to effect the interest on capital, and the division of the loss for 19x2.

15 Partnership— Change in Constitution

When a partnership has been established it is inevitable that sooner or later there will be a change in its members. As the firm grows, new partners will be admitted, whilst some of the old partners will retire or die. Every change in the constitution of the firm means in effect that the old partnership ceases and a new one is formed. To ensure that the partners obtain that which is rightfully theirs, certain adjustments must be made in the accounts.

The balance sheet reflects the value of the assets on a going concern basis, but when a business ceases it is the market or realistic value that is important. Thus, when a partner leaves the firm or a new one joins there must be a re-appraisal of the asset values. A realistic value must be placed on the tangible assets and a figure calculated for goodwill. The goodwill has been built up by the old firm and all partners should benefit proportionately. In many cases goodwill is not included in the ledger because of the difficulty in evaluating it, but generally a method of calculation is included in the partnership deed for purposes of entry or exit of partners.

Retirement of a Partner

When a partner retires from a firm he will be entitled to his share of the value of the business, which is possibly not the amount due to him as shown by his capital and current accounts. For example, A, B, and C have been in partnership for many years, sharing profits equally. Their balance sheet on 31st December, 19x7, is as follows:

		£	£		£
Capital accounts	A	1,000		Fixed assets	2,000
	B	1,000			
	C	1,000		Stock	1,000
			3,000	Debtors	1,000
Current accounts	A	500		Cash	2,000
	B	300			
	C	200			
			1,000		
Creditors			2,000		
			£6,000		£6,000

181

On the 31st December, 19x7, C retires. Goodwill is valued at £3,000 and the fixed assets are to be increased to a realisable value of £2,900. A and B continue trading, sharing profits equally.

The amount due to C as per the balance sheet is £1,200 (capital £1,000 plus current account £200), but this would only be correct if the remaining figures in the balance sheet reflected their true worth. In this example they do not, therefore adjusting entries are necessary as under:

Journal entry

	£	£
Dec. 31. Goodwill account	3,000	
Fixed assets	900	
Capital account A		1,300
B		1,300
C		1,300
	£3,900	£3,900

Creation of goodwill account and increase in value of fixed assets on retirement of C.
Profits credited to capital accounts.

	£	£
Dec. 31. Capital account C	2,300	
Current account C	200	
Loan account C		2,500

Transfer of amounts due to C his retirement.

The balance sheet of A and B will now be as under:

	£	£		£
Capital account A	2,300		Fixed assets	2,900
B	2,300		Goodwill	3,000
		4,600	Stock	1,000
Current account A	500		Debtors	1,000
B	300		Cash	2,000
		800		
Loan C		2,500		
Creditors		2,000		
		£9,900		£9,900

It can be seen that the amount due to C has increased from £1,200 to £2,500, the latter being a more realistic value for his share of the net assets of the firm. The remaining partners have also increased their capital accounts by £1,300 each. However, although the new firm has the same assets as the old business their value has increased from £6,000 to £9, 900. It may be that the remaining partners wish to keep the old amounts in the books as these represented the going concern valuation. If they do, a further adjustment is necessary, viz.:

	Journal entry	£	£
Capital account A		1,950	
B		1,950	
Goodwill			3,000
Fixed assets			900
		£3,900	£3,900

Reversal of adjustments made on
    C's retirement.

The balance sheet of A and B will be revised as under:

	£	£		£
Capital account A	350		Fixed assets	2,000
B	350			
Current account A	500	700	Stock	1,000
B	300		Debtors	1,000
		800	Cash	2,000
Loan C		2,500		
Creditors		2,000		
		£6,000		£6,000

The assets are now identical with those shown on the original balance sheet, but the capital accounts of A and B are drastically reduced. At first sight this may seem to be an injustice, but on reflection, as they are now the only partners they will share in any profits that the business makes. If the business was sold in the near future and the proceeds of sale reflected the values previously calculated, there would be a profit of £3,900 which they would share equally, thereby restoring the amount reflected in the preceding balance sheet.

The situation is that A and B have purchased from C his share of the future anticipated profits from the sale of the business. At the date of C's retirement these profits are calculated at £3,900 and as the division

PRINCIPLES OF ACCOUNTS

of profits between A and B are the same proportionately they are each buying from C one-half of this amount. Instead of paying cash for this amount they are debited with the value.

Entry of a New Partner

In the same way that adjustments had to be made when a partner retired, similar adjustments must be made in the books when a new partner is admitted. The old partners must be credited with their share of profits not reflected in the books and also because their profit sharing ratios will be affected in the future they must be compensated for any reductions they will suffer.

For example, X and Y are sharing profits in the ratio 3:2. At 30th June, 19x3, their balance sheet is as under.

	£			£
Capital account X	3,000	Assets (excluding		
Y	2,000	goodwill)		5,000
	£5,000			£5,000

On Ist July they admit Z as a partner who brings in cash of £2,000. The profits in future will be shared between X, Y, and Z in the ratio of 3:2:1. Goodwill is to be valued at £3,000.

The adjustment will be to debit goodwill account with £3,000 and credit X with three-fifths, £1,800, and Y with two-fifths (£1,200) as this is the ratio that they shared profits up to the time of Z's entry. After Z has paid in his cash the balance sheet will appear as

	£		£
Capital account X	4,800	Assets	5,000
Y	3,200	Goodwill	3,000
Z	2,000	Cash (from Z)	2,000
	£10,000		£10,000

The partners may again decide that the goodwill account should not appear in the books. In which case it will be written off against the partners' capital accounts, but this time in the new profit sharing ratios, i.e. X three-sixths, £1,500, Y two-sixths, £1,000, and Z one-sixth £500. The balance sheet will now be revised to

184

	£			£
Capital account X	3,300	Assets		5,000
Y	2,200	Cash		2,000
Z	1,500			
	£7,000			£7,000

The changes from the original capital accounts are shown below.

	Original £	New £	Difference £
X	3,000	3,300	300 Cr.
Y	2,000	2,200	200 Cr.

These differences can be explained as follows.

When Z is admitted he is acquiring one-sixth of the profits which will include the profit on goodwill which is not reflected in the books. Unless an adjustment was made he would share in a profit that was earned prior to his joining the firm. He must, therefore, compensate the other partners for this amount, i.e. one-sixth of £3,000 = £500, which is the amount charged to his capital account. On the other hand the proportion of profits shared by the old partners has fallen, X from three-fifths to three-sixths, a difference of one-tenth, and Y from two-fifths to two-sixths, a difference of one-fifteenth. X must receive compensation of one-tenth of £3,000 = £300 and Y one-fifteenth of £3,000 = £200.

The rules regarding the recording of asset adjustment can be summed up as follows.

In the old partnership—adjustments are made to the asset accounts and the difference is shared between the old partners in their old profit sharing ratios.

In the new partnership—if the new values are to be retained, no further adjustments are necessary. If the old values are to be retained, the adjustments are reversed and the difference is shared between the partners in the new firm in their new profit sharing ratios.

In certain cases the new partner will not only introduce cash as capital, but will also pay in sufficient cash for his share of goodwill. This latter item may be entered in the books of the firm or be paid direct to the old partners. In these cases no goodwill account is shown in the books.

For example, D and E are in partnership sharing profits and losses 2:1. Their balance sheet as at 31st March, 19x9, is as follows:

	£		£
Capital account D	4,000	Assets (excluding	
E	2,000	goodwill)	6,000
	£6,000		£6,000

On 1st April, 19x9, they admit F as a partner. Goodwill is to be valued at £2,400 and F is to bring in capital of £2,000 and sufficient cash to purchase his share of goodwill. D, E, and F will share profits 2:1:1.

Show the entries necessary to record the above,
(a) when cash is paid direct to D and E in respect of the goodwill,
(b) when cash for goodwill is recorded in the books and paid to D and E,
(c) when cash paid for goodwill is retained within the business.

(a) In this instance no entries are necessary as the compensation to D and E is paid privately. The amounts involved are calculated as under.

F must pay one-quarter (his share of profits) of £2,400 = £600.

D will receive one-sixth (his reduction from $\frac{2}{3}$ to $\frac{1}{2}$) of £2,400 = £400.

E will receive one-twelfth (his reduction from $\frac{1}{3}$ to $\frac{1}{4}$) of £2,400 = £200.

The balance sheet of the new firm will be:

	£		£
Capital account D	4,000	Assets	6,000
E	2,000	Cash (from F)	2,000
F	2,000		
	£8,000		£8,000

(b) In this case the entries required are shown by the following journal entries:

	£	£
Cash	600	
Capital account F		600
Amount paid into firm by F in respect of purchase of goodwill		
Capital account F	600	
Cash (paid to D)		400
Cash (paid to E)		200
Amount paid to D and E in respect of purchase of goodwill by F.		

The balance sheet will be identical to the one shown in (a) previous.

(c) In this instance the £600 paid in by F will be credited to either the capital or current accounts of D and E depending on agreement. If interest is allowed on capital accounts, this will mean that D and E may receive an unfair advantage as they will receive interest on these additional amounts. The transaction is illustrated by the following journal entry:

	£	£	£
Cash account		600	
Capital account D			400
E			200
Cash introduced by F in consideration of goodwill purchased from D and E			

The balance sheet will be.

	£		£
Capital account D	4,400	Assets	6,000
E	2,200	Cash (from F)	2,600
F	2,000		
	£8,600		£8,600

Change in Profit Sharing Ratios

When a partnership has been in existence for some time, it may be necessary to change the profit sharing ratios even though there is no change in the membership. This may occur when the junior partners take a greater share of the work or responsibility, and the older partners start to take a less active part in the business. When the ratios are changed, entries must be made in the books to compensate partners who will have a reduction in their profit sharing ratio, and to charge partners who will increase their ratios. These adjustments will only be in respect of profits or losses which are undisclosed in the accounts at the date of the proposed change.

Example

R, S, and T have been in partnership sharing profits and losses 3:2:1. On 31st December, 19x3, they decide to alter the ratio to 1:2:2. Their balance sheet on 31st December, 19x3, is as follows:

187

		£		£
Capital account R		5,000	Assets	10,000
S		3,000		
T		2,000		
		£10,000		£10,000

Goodwill is estimated at £3,000. Show the revised balance sheets necessary to reflect these changes.

(a) if goodwill is to be retained within the books,

(b) if goodwill is not recorded.

(a) In this case goodwill account will be debited with £3,000 and the capital accounts credited in the old profit sharing ratios, viz.:

R 3/6ths—£1,500.   S 2/6ths—£1,000.   T 1/6th—£500.

The balance sheet will be

		£		£
Capital account R		6,500	Assets	10,000
S		4,000	Goodwill	3,000
T		2,500		
		£13,000		£13,000

(b) The adjustments can be calculated according to the gain or loss in future profit sharing ratios.

R from 3/6ths to 1/5th, a loss of 9/30ths   £3,000 = £900 Cr.
S from 2/6ths to 2/5ths, a gain of 2/30ths   £3,000 = £200 Dr.
T from 1/6th to 2/5ths, a gain of 7/30ths   £3,000 = £700 Dr.

That is S and T are acquiring goodwill from R. The balance sheet will be:

		£		£
Capital account R		5,900	Assets	10,000
S		2,800		
T		1,300		
		£10,000		£10,000

Usually when the profit sharing ratios are amended the capital accounts are adjusted to bring them into line with the divisions of profits. Partners will either pay money into the firm or withdraw amounts necessary. If, in the above case, the total accounts should remain the same the cash adjustment would be:

188

	As in balance sheet	Amount required	Adjustment
	£	£	£
R	5,900	2,000	3,900 withdrawn
S	2,800	4,000	1,200 paid in
T	1,300	4,000	2,700 paid in
	10,000	10,000	

It will be noticed that the amounts paid in balance with the amount withdrawn so that the assets previously held are unchanged.

Goodwill

The valuation of goodwill is extremely difficult to ascertain. It can only be fixed when a business is sold and the selling price agreed between buyer and seller. Goodwill is then computed as the difference in value between the net worth of the tangible assets and the selling price. Up to the moment of sale the value of goodwill is purely subjective and for this reason the method to be used in its valuation is usually detailed in the partnership deed.

Goodwill is the extra return that can be achieved by purchasing an existing business over and above the return to be made by starting a new business. It is therefore concerned with future profits. Because of this the goodwill computation is usually based on recent profits of the existing business as it is thought that these will give an indication of the profits to be earned in the future. Some of the more traditional methods are given below.

Average Profits

This method is based on a specific number of preceding years' profits. It is usually expressed as a number of years' purchase of the average profit, e.g. 2½ years' purchase of the average profits of the last 4 years. For example, if the profits have been

	£
19x1	3,000
19x2	5,000
19x3	7,000
19x4	10,000
	£25,000

The average yearly profit would be £6,250, and $2\frac{1}{2}$ years' purchase of this would be £6,250 × $2\frac{1}{2}$ = £15,625.

The $2\frac{1}{2}$ years is the estimated time it would take for a new business to build up its profits to the same amount as the established business. The £15,625 is therefore a benefit to be paid for if the old business is bought.

Weighted Average Profits

This method is a more sophisticated application of the previous one. It is contended that the more recent profits are more indicative of the future earnings of the business, and that more attention should be paid to them. To establish a more accurate average estimate of future annual profits a weighting factor is applied to each year—the highest factor in the most recent year, e.g. in the above illustration the factors might be 19x1 one, 19x2 two, 19x3 three, and 19x4 four. The average profit would be calculated

Year	Profit	Weighting	Product
19x1	£3,000	1	£3,000
19x2	£5,000	2	£10,000
19x3	£7,000	3	£21,000
19x4	£10,000	4	£40,000
		10	£74,000

The average is £74,000 divided by the sum of the weighting's 10, which equals £7,400. Two-and-a-half year's purchase would total £18,500. In this case the figure for goodwill is greater than that previously calculated. This is because annual profits were increasing. If profits had been falling the reverse would be true, i.e. the goodwill would be less.

Super Profits

This method is based on the expected return on the net value of tangible assets acquired. For example, if a person acquired the net tangible assets of a business for £24,000 and expects a return of at least $12\frac{1}{2}\%$ per annum, the profits of that business should be at least £3,000 ($12\frac{1}{2}\%$ of £24,000). If the average profits of an agreed number of years are £6,250, then an excess or super profit of £3,250 has been achieved. The figure for goodwill is then computed on a number of years' purchase of this super profit. If the number of years was agreed at five then goodwill would be valued at £16,250. The total purchase consideration would be £24,000 for the tangible assets plus £16,250 for goodwill, giving a total of £40,250.

There may be variations on the above methods. The profits of the old business may have to be adjusted, for example the elimination of certain profits which can no longer be achieved, notional salaries substituted or provisions for depreciation adjusted. The particular method should be given in the partnership agreement.

Where a number of adjustments have to be made it is convenient to open a revaluation account.

Example

S and T are in partnership sharing profits and losses equally. On 31st March they admit U as a partner, the three partners sharing profits and losses equally. For the purpose of U's entry the following adjustments were to be made.

Goodwill created of £2,000, freehold property increased from £5,000 to £6,000, provision for depreciation of machinery to be reduced by £500 and a provision for doubtful debts to be created of £200.

Revaluation Account

	£		£
Mar. 31 Tfr. provision		Mar. 31 Tfr. goodwill a/c	2,000
doubtful debts	200	Tfr. freehold	
Tfr. Capital a/c		property	1,000
S	1,650	Tfr. provision	
T	1,650	depreciation of	
		machinery	500
	£3,500		£3,500

If the above adjustments are solely for the change in constitution, the entries will be reversed in the revaluation account.

Revaluation Account

	£		£
Mar. 31 Tfr. goodwill a/c	2,000	Mar. 31 Tfr. provision	
Tfr. freehold		doubtful debts	200
property	1,000	Tfr. capital a/c	
Tfr. provision		S	1,100
depreciation of		T	1,100
machinery	500	U	1,100
	£3,500		£3,500

Where the adjustments are not to be maintained in the books, only the entries affecting capital accounts need to be posted as the other entries appear on both debit and credit sides of the realisation account.

To give an illustration of the matters dealt with in this chapter the following question and answer is set out below.

Example

Bond, Stappel, and Clip are partners sharing profits and losses 3:2:1 respectively. On 30th June, 19x6, Bond retired and Stick was admitted as a partner on 1st July, 19x6. The firm's balance sheet at 30th June, 19x6, was:

	£		£
Bond capital	20,000	Freehold premises	20,000
Stappel capital	17,000	Plant	16,000
Clip capital	7,000	Equipment	2,100
Creditors	3,200	Debtors	2,700
		Bank	6,400
	£47,200		£47,200

For the purposes of the change in constitution it was agreed that the premises should be valued at £22,000, the plant at £13,000 and the debtors at £2,500. Goodwill was to be valued at three years purchase of the average profits of the four years immediately preceding the balance sheet. These profits were

30th June, 19x3, £6,000,   19x4 £8,000,   19x5 £10,000,
19x6 £12,000

No entries were to remain in the books in respect of these transactions. The profit sharing ratios were to be equal in the new firm. Stick was to pay £20,000 into the firm, and Bond was to receive half the amount due to him, leaving the remainder on loan to the new firm.

You are required to prepare the revaluation account and the opening balance sheet of the new firm.

Revaluation Account

	£	£		£	£
June 30 Plant		3,000	June 30 Goodwill		27,000
Debtors		,200	Premises		2,000
Capital accounts					
Bond	12,900				
Stappel	8,600				
Clip	4,300	25,800			
		£29,000			£29,000

		£				£	£
July	1 Goodwill	27,000	July	1 Plant		3,000	
	Premises	2,000		Debtors		200	
				Capital			
				accounts			
				Stappel	8,600		
				Clip	8,600		
				Stick	8,600	25,800	
		£29,000				£29,000	

STAPPEL, CLIP, AND STICK
Balance Sheet as at 1st July, 19x6

	£	£		£
Capital accounts			Freehold premises	20,000
Stappel	17,000		Plant	16,000
Clip	2,700		Equipment	2,100
Stick	11,400		Debtors	2,700
		31,100	Bank	9,950
Loan from bond		16,450		
Creditors		3,200		
		£50,750		£50,750

Workings

1. Goodwill £(6,000 + 8,000 + 10,000 + 12,000) = £36,000. Therefore average profits £9,000. Three years' purchase equals £27,000.
2. Stappel capital account £(17,000 + 8,600 − 8,600) = £17,000
3. Clip capital account £(7,000 + 4,300 − 8,600) = £2,700.
4. Stick capital account £(20,000 − 8,600) = £11,400.
5. Loan from bond £(20,000 + 12,900) = £32,900 less cash repayment of £16,450 = £16,450.
6. Bank balance £(6,400 + 20,000 − 16,450) = £9,950.

EXERCISES

15.1

Brunt, Clark, and Davies are in partnership sharing profits 2:2:1. Their capitals were fixed at £6,000, £6,000 and £3,000 respectively. On 1st June, 19x5, Brunt retired and Eccles was admitted as a partner. Eccles introduced cash of £5,000 into the new firm whose profit sharing ratio was Clark 50%, Davies 25%, and

Eccles 25%. It was agreed that on the change of partnership goodwill was to be valued at £6,000.

Show the capital and loan accounts if:
(a) goodwill is to be retained in the books,
(b) goodwill is to be written off.

15.2
Foster, Greer, and Hatton are in partnership sharing profits 3:2:1. Their capital accounts were fixed at £6,000, £4,000, and £2,000 respectively. On 1st January, 19x2, Foster retired and Ince was admitted as a partner. The profit sharing ratio of the new firm was Greer 40%, Hatton 40%, and Ince 20%. For the purpose of the change goodwill was to be valued at £9,000, but was not to be retained in the books.

It is intended that the total capital should remain at £12,000 and that each partner's capital should reflect the profit sharing ratio.

You are required to state the amount that Ince is required to bring into the firm and the cash adjustment necessary for Greer and Hatton to comply with the above.

15.3
Kay, King, and Knox are equal partners sharing profits 3:1:1. Their capital accounts were fixed at £6,000, £2,000, and £2,000 respectively. On the 31st March, 19x8, King retired. Kay and Knox carried on trading sharing profits 3:2. For the purposes of the change it is agreed that goodwill is to be valued at £10,000.

It is intended that the total capital of the firm should remain at £10,000 and that each partner's capital should reflect their profit sharing ratios.

Show the cash adjustments for Kay and Knox necessary to comply with the above if:

(a) goodwill is retained in the books,
(b) goodwill is to be written off after the change.

15.4
The profits of a partnership for the last five years are as under.

19x1 £15,000, 19x2 £10,000, 19x3 £7,500, 19x4 £12,000, 19x5 £12,500.

You are required to compute the value of goodwill on the following basis:

(a) Three years purchase of the average profits of the last five years.
(b) Two and a half years purchase of the weighted average profits of the last four years. Weightings are 19x2(1), 19x3(2), 19x4(3), and 19x5(4).
(c) Three years super profits based on average profits for the last four years. The net tangible assets amount to £20,000 and a return of 15% is expected.

15.5
Blaze and Flare are in partnership sharing profits and losses equally. On 31st March, 19x5, they decide to admit Flicker as a partner and the balance sheet

194

of the firm at this date is:

	£	£		£
Capital			Goodwill	1,000
Blaze	4,000		Fittings	1,600
Flare	3,200		Stock	4,000
		7,200	Debtors	5,400
Creditors		5,600	Cash	800
		£12,800		£12,800

The following arrangements are made:

(1) Profits and losses of the new firm are to be shared Blaze 40%, Flare 40%, Flicker 20%.
(2) The goodwill of the old firm is to be increased to £4,000 and fittings revalued at £1,000.
(3) Flicker introduces as his capital £900 in cash, a motor vehicle valued at £800 and goodwill valued at £1,000.

You are required to show the balance sheet of the new firm:

(a) if all the above adjustments are retained in the books,
(b) if goodwill is to be written off.

15.6
Chadwick, Cowan, and Cross are in partnership sharing profits 4:4:2. On 31st March, 19x2, it is decided to admit Doolan. It is agreed that Doolan should pay into the business capital of £3,000 and also £2,000 for his share of the goodwill. The profit sharing ratio of the new firm was to be Chadwick 30%, Cowan 30%, Cross 30%, and Doolan 10%.
It is decided that the capital of the new firm should be £30,000 divided between the partners in their profit sharing ratios, the original partners withdrawing or paying in any sums necessary. No goodwill account was to be opened.
The balance sheet of the firm before admitting Doolan was

	£		£
Capital			
Chadwick	10,000	Assets (other than	
Cowan	6,000	cash)	22,000
Cross	8,000	Cash	5,000
Creditors	3,000		
	£27,000		£27,000

You are required to show:

(a) the entries in the partners' capital accounts,
(b) the balance sheet of the new firm.

195

16 Partnership Accounts— Dissolution and Amalgamation

The previous chapter dealt with changes in constitution of a firm which effectively meant that the old partnership closed down and a new one started. However, as at least one partner carried on in the business the book-keeping entries regarded the situation as a change rather than a closure. A full dissolution (or closing down) of a partnership takes place when all the assets have been distributed and the debts of the partnership are discharged.

A partnership comes to an end when:

1. A partner dies or retires.
2. A partner becomes bankrupt.
3. A partner becomes insane.
4. The time stipulated in the partnership deed expires.
5. The partners agree the partnership should be dissolved.

The partners should stipulate in the partnership deed how the assets are to be distributed in the event of a dissolution. If no mention is made then section 44 of the Partnership Act will apply. This states that the assets will be applied.

1. In paying the debts and liabilities of third parties.
2. In paying the partners any amounts they are due other than capital.
3. In paying the partners the amount due in respect of capital.
4. Any residue is to be divided among the partners in the proportion in which they share profits.

If the proceeds of sale of the assets are insufficient to pay off liabilities to third parties, the partners themselves must pay in sufficient amounts out of their private assets to meet the deficiency.

Dissolution means that the books of the partnership must be closed, i.e. there must be no balance left on any of the ledger accounts. This is achieved by opening a realisation account into which all assets (except for cash and bank) are transferred. Liabilities are seldom entered in this account as they are to be discharged by the firm. The only exception is when the firm is being sold as a going concern and the liabilities are to be taken over by the new owners. Costs of winding up the firm are debited to the realisation account which can be regarded as the ultimate profit and loss account—the balance being transferred into the partners' capital account. In some cases the assets may be partly distributed in specie, that is instead of being sold they are taken over by one of the partners at an agreed valuation. The book-keeping entry being to credit the realisation account and debit the partner's capital account.

A worked example is shown below.

Example

Higgs and Biggs were in partnership sharing profits 3:2. At 31st March, 19x7, their balance sheet was as under, from which date it was agreed to dissolve the partnership.

	£		£
Capital account Higgs	8,834	Leasehold premises	6,000
Biggs	9,164	Plant and machinery	5,400
		Furniture	1,240
Creditors	4,918	Motor van	560
Bank overdraft	510	Stock	3,850
		Debtors	6,376
	£23,426		£23,426

It was agreed that Biggs should take over the leasehold premises at a valuation of £7,000. The other assets were sold and realised, plant and machinery £3,600, motor van £240, furniture £580, stock £2,800, and debtors £6,042. The creditors were paid off less discounts amounting to £47, and realisation expenses amounted to £118.

Show the accounts necessary to close the partnership (ignore separate asset accounts).

Realisation Account

	£			£
31 Mar. Tfr. ledger accounts		31 Mar. Tfr cash		
Leasehold premises	6,000	proceeds		
Plant and		Plant and		
machinery	5,400	machinery		3,600
Furniture	1,240	Motor van		240
Motor van	560	Furniture		580
Stock	3,850	Stock		2,800
Debtors	6,376	Debtors		6,042
Cash realisation		Discount received		47
expenses	118	Tfr. Biggs' capital		
		a/c leasehold		
		premises		7,000
		Loss tfr. to		
		Higgs £1,941		
		Biggs 1,294		
				3,235
	£23,544			£23,544

Cash Book

	£			£
31 Mar. Realisation account		31 Mar. Balance B/D		510
Plant and machinery	3,600	Creditors		4,871
Motor van	240	Realisation ex-		
Furniture	580	penses		118
Stock	2,800	Higgs capital a/c		6,893
Debtors	6,042	Biggs capital a/c		870
	£13,262			£13,262

Creditors Account

	£		£
31 Mar. Cash	4,871	31 Mar. Balance	4,918
Realisation account			
discounts received	47		
	£4,918		£4,918

PARTNERSHIP ACCOUNTS—DISSOLUTION AND AMALGAMATION

Capital Accounts

	Higgs £	Biggs £			Higgs £	Biggs £
31 Mar. Leasehold premises		7,000	31 Mar. Balance		8,834	9,164
Loss on realisation	1,941	1,294				
Cash	6,893	870				
	£8,834	£9,164			£8,834	£9,164

Notes

(a) The discount received is debited to the creditors account and credited to the realisation account. An alternative treatment would have been to credit the partners capital accounts in their profit sharing ratios.

(b) The loss on the realisation account, £3,235, is apportioned to the partners in their profit sharing ratios.

(c) The partners have suffered a loss on their capitals invested. Higgs' capital had been reduced from £8,834 by a loss of £1,941, leaving a balance of £6,893 which he has received in cash. Biggs' capital of £9,164 has been reduced by a loss of £1,294, leaving a balance of £7,870. This amount has been settled by a cash payment of £870 and the premises valued at £7,000.

When a partner's capital account is reduced to a debit balance, he must pay into the business sufficient cash out of his private resources.

Example

Smith, Jones, and Davies are in partnership sharing profits equally. On 31st December, 19x7, they decide to dissolve the business. On that date their balance sheet was as follows

	£		£
Capital account Smith	8,000	Assets	15,000
Jones	4,000		
Davies	2,000		
Creditors	1,000		
	£15,000		£15,000

Proceeds from the sale of assets amounted to £7,500. You are required to show the accounts necessary to close the books of the partnership.

Realisation Account

	£			£
31 Dec. Tfr. Ledger accounts sundry assets	15,000	31 Dec. Cash proceeds of realisation		7,500
		Loss transferred		
		Smith	£2,500	
		Jones	2,500	
		Davies	2,500	
				7,500
	£15,000			£15,000

Cash Book

	£		£
31 Dec. Realisation account		31 Dec. Creditors	1,000
sundry assets	7,500	Capital account	
Davies capital account	500	Smith	5,500
		Jones	1,500
	8,000		£8,000

Creditors Account

	£		£
31 Dec. Cash	1,000	31 Dec. Balance	1,000

Capital Accounts

	Smith £	Jones £	Davies £		Smith £	Jones £	Davies £
31 Dec. Loss on				31 Dec. Balance	8,000	4,000	2,000
realisation	2,500	2,500	2,500	Cash			500
Cash	5,500	1,500					
	£8,000	£4,000	£2,500		£8,000	£4,000	£2,500

In the above example Davies has had to bring £500 into the firm. His total loss was, therefore, the £2,000 capital invested in the firm and the £500 out of his private assets.

A difficulty would arise if a partner was unable to bring in sufficient money to cancel out the debit balance on his capital account. This situation was omitted from the Partnership Act of 1890, but was remedied in a court case in 1904. This case was known as "Garner v. Murray" and the judge ruled that if a debit balance existed on a partner's capital account and that partner was insolvent, the amount must be borne by the other partners, not in their profit sharing ratios, but in proportion to the last agreed balances on their capital account. This is taken to mean the balances shown on the last agreed balance sheet. It must be emphasised that balances on current accounts are to be ignored when calculating this ratio. If any provisions differing from this are made in the partnership deed, then these provisions would, of course, over-rule the decision in "Garner v. Murray".

To illustrate the effect of this rule an example is shown below.

Example

Mills, Moore, and Murphy are trading in partnership sharing profits and losses in the ratio 3:2:1. The following is their balance sheet on 30th June, 19x8.

		£		£
Capital account	Mills	4,600	Sundry assets	8,620
	Moore	2,300	Cash	895
	Murphy	1,150		
Current accounts	Mills	430	Current account Murphy	975
	Moore	260		
Creditors		1,750		
		£10,490		£10,490

It was decided that the partnership should be dissolved. The assets were sold and realised £7,200, the creditors were settled for £1,700, and the costs of realisation amounted to £184. Murphy is declared insolvent, and can only pay 25p in the £1.

Show the ledger accounts necessary to close the partnership books.

Realisation Account

19x8		£	19x8			£
30 June	Tfr. sundry assets	8,620	30 June	Cash proceeds of sale		7,200
	Cash—realisation expenses	184		Discount received		50
				Loss transferred		
				Mills	£777	
				Moore	518	
				Murphy	259	
						1,554
		£8,804				£8,804

201

Cash Book

19x8		£	19x8		£
30 June	Balance	895	30 June	Creditors	1,700
	Realisation a/c			Realisation	
	sale of assets	7,200		expenses	184
	Murphy capital a/c	21		Mills capital a/c	4,211
				Moore capital a/c	2,021
		£8,116			£8,116

Creditors Accounts

19x8		£	19x8		£
30 June	Cash	1,700	30 June	Balance	1,750
	Discount received	50			
		1,750			1,750

Capital Accounts

		Mills £	Moore £	Murphy £			Mills £	Moore £	Murphy £
19x8					19x8				
30 June	Tfr. current				30 June	Balances	4,600	2,300	1,150
	a/c			975		Tfr. current			
	Loss on real-					a/c	430	260	
	isation	777	518	259		Cash			21
	Tfr. per contra	42	21			Tfr. per			
	Cash	4,211	2,021			contra			63
		£5,030	£2,560	£1,234			£5,030	£2,560	£1,234

Notes

(a) The loss on realisation is divided among the partners in their profit and loss sharing ratio.

(b) Murphy's capital account is made up as follows:

	£	£
Original balance		1,150
Less Debit balance on current a/c	975	
Share of loss on realisation	259	
		1,234
Debit balance, i.e. amount due to firm		84
Less Amount paid in, 25p in every £1		21
		63

Debit balance remaining to be borne
by other partners in their capital
ratios

Mills	£4,600 = 2		42	
Moore	2,300 = 1		21	
	£6,900	3		63

The amount of £63 is credited to Murphy's capital account and the amounts of £42 and £21 are debited respectively to Mills and Moore's capital account.

If after transferring the loss on a partner's capital account a situation arises whereby another partner's capital account is placed in debit, then that debit will be shared among the remaining partners in proportion to their last agreed capital accounts, viz.:

	A £	B £	C £	D £
Capitals as per last balance sheet	8,000	4,000	4,000	4,000
Capitals immediately after realisation of assets and payment of liabilities	9,000(Cr.)	5,000(Cr.)	200(Cr.)	2,000(Dr.)
Debit balance transferred (Garner v. Murray) 2:1:1	1,000(Dr.)	500(Dr.)	500(Dr.)	2,000(Cr.)
	8,000(Cr.)	4,500(Cr.)	300(Dr.)	Nil
Debit balance transferred (Garner v. Murray) 2:1	200(Dr.)	100(Dr.)	300(Cr.)	
Amounts finally due	£7,800(Cr.)	£4,400(Cr.)	Nil	

One other form of dissolution of partnership must be considered. This occurs when one partnership combines or amalgamates with another, to form an entirely new partnership. In this situation the assets are not realised either in the sense of being sold or distributed among the partners. The businesses continue not as separate entities but as one. The books of the old partnerships must be closed off, and a new set opened for the new firm. As no money is paid to the partners in the separate firms a notional figure must be debited to their capital accounts which represents their share of the net assets contributed to the new partnership. A realisation account is opened, but in this case all ledger balances which are taken into the new partnership are transferred therein including creditors and bank.

Example

On 31st December, A and B who are in partnership sharing profits and losses 1:1 agree to amalgamate with C and D who are in a similar trade, but share profits 2:1. Their balance sheets at that date are shown below.

		A & B £	C & D £		A & B £	C & D £
Capital accounts	A	10,000		Freehold property	4,000	
	B	10,000		Fixtures and fittings	1,000	500
	C		4,000	Stock	12,000	4,000
	D		2,000	Debtors	4,000	3,000
Creditors		3,000	3,000	Cash at bank	2,000	1,500
		£23,000	£9,000		£23,000	£9,000

It is agreed for the purposes of amalgamation that the book values of the assets are correct, no discounts will be received from the creditors, and that goodwill should be valued at £5,000 for A and B and £3,000 for C and D.

Show the realisation accounts and capital accounts in the books of the old firms, and the opening balance sheet of the new firm.

The net worths of each firm to the new partnership must first be calculated, viz.:

	A & B £	C & D £
Book value of assets	23,000	9,000
Agreed value of goodwill	5,000	3,000
	28,000	12,000
Less Creditors	3,000	3,000
Net worth	£25,000	£ 9,000

A and B's books

Realisation Account

	£		£
Tfr. sundry assets		Tfr. creditors	3,000
Freehold property	4,000	Tfr. capital accounts	
Fixtures and fittings	1,000	share of net worth	
Stock	12,000	A £12,500	
Debtors	4,000	B 12,500	
Bank	2,000		25,000
Tfr. capital accounts			
profit A £2,500			
B 2,500	5,000		
	£28,000		£28,000

204

Capital Accounts

	A £	B £		A £	B £
Share of net worth	12,500	12,500	Balance	10,000	10,000
			Profit on realisation	2,500	2,500
	£12,500	£12,500		£12,500	£12,500

In C and D's books

Realisation Account

	£		£
Tfr. sundry assets		Tfr. creditors	3,000
Fixtures and fittings	500	Tfr. capital accounts	
Stock	4,000	share of net worth	
Debtors	3,000	C £6,000	
Bank	1,500	D 3,000	9,000
Tfr. capital accounts			
profit C £2,000			
D 1,000	3,000		
	£12,000		£12,000

Capital Accounts

	C £	D £		C £	D £
Share of net worth	£6,000	£3,000	Balances	£4,000	£2,000
			Profit on realisation	2,000	1,000
	£6,000	£3,000		£6,000	£3,000

A, B, C, & D
Balance Sheet 31st December

	£		£
Capital account		Goodwill	8,000
A	12,500	Freehold property	4,000
B	12,500	Fixtures and fittings	1,500
C	6,000	Stock	16,000
D	3,000	Debtors	7,000
Creditors	6,000	Balance at bank	3,500
	£40,000		£40,000

Note

In the realisation account the figure for net worth is first credited in the total column. The split of this amount cannot be entered until the balance on the capital accounts is known. The latter is found when the profit or loss on realisation has been transferred.

In practice when the new firm has been established it may be necessary for the partners to adjust their capital accounts to a proportion more in line with their new profit sharing ratios. In some cases this will mean introducing more capital, and in others withdrawing excess amounts in cash. If goodwill is to be written off in the new firm, this is done in the new profit sharing ratios.

EXERCISES

16.1

Torr and Vose who are in partnership sharing profits and losses 3:2 decide to dissolve their partnership on 30th June, 19x5. Their balance sheet on that date is as follows.

	£		£
Capital account Torr	4,000	Fixtures	1,600
Vose	3,000	Motor vans	1,700
Sundry creditors	5,500	Debtors	5,600
		Cash	3,600
	£12,500		£12,500

The debtors realise £5,400, the fixtures £800, and one of the motor vans £1,000. The other motor van was taken over by Torr at a valuation of £800. The creditors were settled for £5,350 and expenses of dissolution amounted to £100.

Prepare the accounts necessary to close the books of the partnership.

16.2

Taylor and Turner are in partnership sharing profits and losses 2:1. On 30th September, 19x3, they decide to dissolve the partnership. The balance sheet at that date was as follows.

	£		£
Capital account Taylor	22,000	Freehold property	8,000
Turner	14,000	Furniture and fittings	790
Creditors	20,000	Stock	17,520
		Debtors	24,240
		Balance at bank	5,450
	£56,000		£56,000

206

Furniture and fittings were sold for £250, stock for £18,850. £30 of the debtors proved to be bad whilst discounts received amounted to £500. Taylor took over the property at a valuation of £10,000. The realisation expenses amounted to £110.

Prepare the accounts necessary to close the books of the firm.

16.3

Lee, Mee, and Ray were in partnership sharing profits and losses in the ratio 2:1:2. On 31st March, 19x1, they agree to dissolve the partnership, Ray deciding to carry on the business as a sole trader. The balance sheet on 31st March, 19x1 consisted of

	£		£
Capital account Lee	12,000	Land and buildings	12,000
Mee	10,000	Fixtures and fittings	1,500
Ray	7,500	Stock	10,000
Loan account Mee	6,000	Debtors	14,000
Creditors	4,500	Bank	2,500
	£40,000		£40,000

For the purposes of dissolution goodwill was valued at £5,000. The debtors realised £13,660, creditors were settled for £4,400, and dissolution expenses amounted to £410. Ray took over the land and buildings for £13,000, fixtures and fittings for £1,375, stock for £9,900, and the goodwill. He was allowed to charge a sum of £100 for his services. After payment of the sums due to Lee and Mee, Ray assumed liability for the bank overdraft.

Show the accounts necessary to close the books of the partnership.

16.4

On 31st March, 19x3, A, B, C, D, and E who trade in partnership sharing profits in the ratios of 3:3:2:2:1 respectively decide to terminate the partnership. The following details are abstracted from their balance sheet at 31st March, 19x3.

	A	B	C	D	E
	£	£	£	£	£
Capital accounts	6,000	4,000	4,000	4,000	2,000
Current accounts	1,000(Cr.)	1,000(Dr.)	3,000(Cr.)	1,200(Cr.)	1,600(Dr.)

After disposing of all the assets and paying off all partnership debts to third parties, the realisation account showed a loss of £11,000 and there was £11,600 in the firm's bank account.

B and E are declared bankrupt and can only pay 30 p and 10p respectively in the £1 towards the partnership losses.

You are required to draw up a statement showing how much is due to each partner.

16.5

Radford, Richards, and Roberts are in partnership sharing profits equally. On 30th September, 19x4, their balance sheet is as follows

	£	£		£
Capital accounts			Fixed assets	5,250
Radford	4,000			
Richards	2,000		Stock	2,750
Roberts	1,500		Debtors	2,500
	———	7,500	Cash at bank	500
Current accounts				
Radford	300		Current account	
Richards	100		Roberts	1,000
	———	400		
Loan accounts				
Radford	1,250			
Richards	850			
	———	2,100		
Creditors		2,000		
		£12,000		£12,000

Roberts was adjudicated bankrupt and the partnership was dissolved at the above date. Fixed assets, stock, and debtors realised £8,400, the creditors were repaid in full and the costs of realisation amounted to £300. Roberts was unable to contribute anything to the partnership loss.

Show the accounts necessary to close off the partnership books.

16.6

Paton and Prescot are in partnership sharing profits equally and decide to admit Price, who is a sole trader, into the partnership. The profit sharing ratios in the new firm being Paton 40%, Prescot 40%, and Price 20%. On the 31st March, 19x7, the balance sheets of the businesses were

	£	£		£
Capital account			Premises	4,000
Paton	5,000		Fixtures and fittings	1,000
Prescot	3,000		Stock	3,000
	———	8,000	Debtors	500
Creditors		700	Bank	200
		£8,700		£8,700
Capital account Price		2,600	Motor van	1,000
			Stock	1,500
Creditors		200	Debtors	300
		£,2800		£2,800

PARTNERSHIP ACCOUNTS—DISSOLUTION AND AMALGAMATION

It was agreed that
1. In the accounts of Paton and Prescot, premises be revalued at £5,000, the stock should be reduced by £600, and goodwill of £400 be created.
2. In the accounts of Price, the motor van be revalued at £800, a provision for doubtful debts of 10% of his debtors be created, and goodwill of £1,000 be created.

You are required to show the journal entries in the books of the partnership to record the above and to prepare the balance sheet of the new partnership at 1st April, 19x7.

16.7

On the 30th June, 19x6, Slight and Slater sharing profits equally decide to amalgamate with Ryan and Rowley who share profits 2:1. a new firm being created. The balance sheets of the two firms at that date being as under.

SLIGHT AND SLATER

	£		£
Capital account Slight	3,000	Property	3,000
Slater	3,000	Fixtures	500
Creditors	1,000	Stock	2,000
		Debtors	600
		Bank	900
	£7,000		£7,000

RYAN AND ROWLEY

	£		£
Capital account Ryan	3,000	Fixtures	1,500
Rowley	1,500	Stock	4,000
Creditors	1,500	Debtors	1,000
Bank overdraft	500		
	£6,500		£6,500

It was agreed that
(a) In the books of Slight and Slater the following items be revalued—property £5,000, fixtures £400, and stock £200. Goodwill attributed to the firm should be £4,000.
(b) In the books of Ryan and Rowley the following items be revalued—fixtures £1,200, stock £3,700. Goodwill attributed to the firm £3,000.
(c) The profit sharing ratio in the new firm should be—Slight 30%, Slater 30%, Ryan 20%, Rowley 20%.
(d) Goodwill was not to be shown in the books of the new firm.

You are required to show:
(a) the realisation and capital accounts in each of the old firms enabling the books to be closed,
(b) the balance sheet of the new firm.

17 Incomplete Records

It must be remembered that there is no legal compulsion for a sole trader to keep proper books of accounts. Indeed, if it was not for the taxation authorities many traders would not bother to prepare final accounts. A book-keeping system must be of benefit to the proprietor and not an end in itself. The proprietor may have little or no knowledge of double-entry book-keeping, or even if he has he may find he can obtain all the information he needs without opening a ledger. For example, he may open a cash book in which he records all receipts and payments of monies. Instead of opening a sales ledger he enters all credit sales in a note-book and when his customer pays he merely crosses out the original entry. He can obtain the names and amounts of his debtors at any time by examining the note-book and seeing which items have not been crossed out. Instead of opening a purchase ledger he may have two files, one containing paid invoices, the other unpaid invoices. When an invoice is paid he merely transfers it from one file to the other. His creditors can be ascertained by going through the unpaid file.

Obviously this system of book-keeping is not as thorough as the double-entry system and lends itself to errors. Furthermore, because all transactions are not recorded, it is difficult at some future date to look back to investigate any queries which might arise. Nevertheless, even though no or few records are maintained it is possible to construct final accounts.

The methods of construction of final accounts where there are incomplete records fall under three headings:

1. Where no records are made at all.
2. Where the records are incomplete or where some evidence of transactions is available.
3. Where a fire or some other disaster has destroyed the original books of acount.

Each of the above are dealt with under a separate section.

1. Where No Records are Kept

When a balance sheet was constructed from complete double-entries it was noticed that an increase in the capital account, in the absence of additional capital introduced, was due to retained profits which the business has made. Furthermore, the capital account was equivalent to the net worth of the business (i.e. total assets less liabilities to third parties). We can say from this that the increase in net worth represents the retained profit earned in the period between the two net worths. For example, if the net worth of a business rises from £2,000 one year to £3,500 the next year, then the retained profit is £1,500. If drawings during the year are estimated at £1,700, then the total profit for the year would have been £3,200, i.e.

Opening net worth (or capital)	£2,000
Add Profit made during year	3,200
	5,200
Less Drawings	1,700
Closing net worth (or capital)	£3,500

If an additional £1,000 had been introduced as capital during the year, then the profits for the year would have been £2,200, i.e. the increase of £3,200 would be divided between capital introduced, £1,000, and profit, £2,200.

Even if no records are kept it should be possible for a trader to produce, if given previous notice, a list of the business assets and liabilities on a specific day. The net worths at the beginning and end of a trading period are calculated by preparing a statement of affairs which is similar to a balance sheet. It is appropriate to call this list a statement rather than a balance sheet as the latter infers it is made up from balances in a ledger, and clearly this is not so if no records are maintained.

Example

From the information given below you are required to calculate the profit or loss earned by Arthur Prince in each of the two years ended 30th June, 19x3, and 30th June, 19x4.

	19x2	30th June 19x3	19x4
	£	£	£
Debtors	800	1,200	1,500
Creditors	1,000	1,500	2,750

	£	£	£
Cash	50	50	75
Bank	750(Dr.)	500(Cr.)	225(Dr.)
Loan B. Prince	—	2,000(Cr.)	1,500(Cr.)
Stock	2,500	3,000	3,500
Fixtures valued at	500	750	700
Buildings	—	4,000	4,000
Drawings (estimates)	—	2,800	2,500
Capital introduced	—	4,000	—

Statement of Affairs—30th June

	19x2		19x3		19x4	
	£		£		£	
Assets						
Buildings	—		4,000		4,000	
Fixtures	500		750		700	
Stock	2,500		3,000		3,500	
Debtors	800		1,200		1,500	
Cash	50		50		75	
Bank	750		—		225	
	4,600		9,000		10,000	
Less Liabilities						
Loan B. Prince			£2,000		£1,500	
Creditors	£1,000		1,500		2,750	
Bank overdraft		1,000	500	4,000		4,250
		£3,600		£5,000		£5,750

Calculation of net profits, year ended	30.6.x3	30.6.x4
	£	£
Closing net worth	5,000	5,750
Less Opening net worth	3,600	5,000
Increase in net worth (retained profit)	1,400	750
Add Drawings	2,800	2,500
	4,200	3,250
Less Capital introduced	4,000	
Profit for year	£ 200	£3,250

Note

The statement of affairs have been shown in vertical form for ease of effort.

Although it is impossible to present a detailed trading and profit and loss account, provided the assets and liabilities set out in the statements of affairs are correct, and the drawings are accurately calculated, the profits calculated in the above statements should be accurate.

If the statement of affairs is re-written, including the items calculated above, it is virtually impossible to distinguish it from a balance sheet drawn up from a conventional book-keeping system, viz.:

Statement of Affairs
30th June, 19x4

	£			£
Capital account			Buildings	4,000
Opening balance	£5,000		Fixtures	700
Add profits	3,250		Stock	3,500
	———		Debtors	1,500
	8,250		Bank	75
Less Drawings	2,500		Cash	225
	———	5,750		
Loan B. Prince		1,500		
Creditors		2,750		
		£10,000		£10,000

It is rare for partnerships not to keep records as it is usually a specific condition stated in the partnership deed and an implied one in the Partnership Act. If, however, no records are kept, it is necessary when computing profits by comparing net worth, those profits must be divided between the partners in their profit sharing ratios.

Example

The statement of affairs at 31st March 19x1, showed three partners as having capital accounts as follows: A £4,000, B £3,000, and C £2,000. At the 31st March, 19x2, the firm had a net worth of £10,000. During the year ended 31st March, 19x2, it was estimated that the partners' drawings were: A £2,500, B £2, 000, and C £1,500. The partners share profits—A 40%, B 30%, and C 30%.

You are required to calculate the profit for the year ended 31st March, 19x2, and the partners' capital accounts at that date.

			£
Net worth 31st March, 19x2.			10,000
31st March, 19x1 (capital accounts)			9,000
Increase in net worth			1,000
Add Drawings	A	£2,500	
	B	2,000	
	C	1,500	
			6,000
			£7,000

	A £	B £	C £
Capital accounts			
Opening Balances	4,000	3,000	2,000
Profit divided 4:3:3	2,800	2,100	2,100
	6,800	5,100	4,100
Less Drawings	2,500	2,000	1,500
Closing balances	£4,300	£3,100	£2,600

Note
The three capital accounts total £10,000 which represents the closing net worth.

2. Where Incomplete Records are Kept

This method applies when information additional to that required to prepare a statement of affairs is available. The information will generally consist of receipts and payments entered in a cash book, or an analysis of items entered on a bank statement, supported by an estimate of receipts and payments which have not gone into a bank account.

Unfortunately the information contained in the above records is inadequate to prepare a trading and profit loss account because it refers to items on a cash basis instead of an accruals basis. With available statements of affairs at the beginning and end of a trading period it is possible to adjust the figures in the cash book by building up ledger accounts where necessary and computing balancing figures. For example, if the cash paid to creditors in the cash book amounted to £17,000, provided the creditors at the beginning and end of a trading period are known, it is possible to calculate the purchases for the period, viz.:

Creditors Account

	£		£
Cash paid	17,000	Opening creditors	1,850
Closing creditors	2,200	Balance—purchases	17,350
	£19,200		£19,200

It has been assumed that the opening creditors were £1,850 and the closing figure £2,200. By opening a creditors account it is possible to enter three out of the four items. The account must balance, therefore

214

the missing figure can be determined, in this case purchases which amount to £17,350.

Alternatively, the information required can be obtained in statement form. This is done in order to save time and effort, and is illustrated in the examples given under this section. However, in the case of the purchases detailed above the computation would be:

	£
Cash paid to creditors	17,000
Less Opening creditors	1,850
	15,150
Add Closing creditors	2,200
	£17,350

The explanation of the above is that although £17,000 was paid to creditors, £1,850 referred to purchases bought in the preceding period. Only £15,150 was paid in respect of purchases made during the current period. A further £2,200 is still owing so that the total purchases amount to £17,350.

A general rule for the calculation of figures appearing in the trading and profit and loss account is to add on to the cash figure all balances referring to the current trading period and deduct all balances referring to past or future trading periods.

The calculations are shown on a "working paper" which in the case of examination questions must be shown to support the answer. In a number of cases the opening capital must be calculated by drawing up a statement of affairs.

Example

A. Short keeps a cash book as his only book-keeping record. The following is a summary of his transactions for the year ended 30th June, 19x7.

	£		£
Opening balance	1,642	Cash paid to creditors	37,248
Cash received from debtors	48,528	Salaries	4,498
Closing balance	2,060	Rent and rates	1,648
		Lighting and heating	336
		General expenses	3,562
		Drawings	4,938
	£52,230		£52,230

His assets and liabilities on the 30th June, 19x6 and 19x7 were

	30.6.19x6	30.6.19x7
	£	£
Fixed assets at cost	4,400	4,400
Stock	4,242	5,296
Debtors	6,438	6,776
Rent and rates prepaid	200	240
Creditors	3,684	3,782
Lighting and heating accrued	62	84

Fixed assets should be depreciated at 10% of cost price.

Prepare the trading and profit and loss accounts of A. Short for the year ended 30th June, 19x7, and a balance sheet as at that date.

Working Paper

Calculation of capital 30.6.19x6		£
Fixed assets		4,400
Stock		4,242
Debtors		6,438
Prepaid rent and rates		200
Cash at bank		1,642
		16,922
Less Creditors	£3,684	
Accrued lighting	62	3,746
		£13,176

Calculation of:	Purchases	Rent and rates	Lighting and heating
	£	£	£
Cash paid	37,248	1,648	336
Less Opening creditors and accruals	3,684	—	62
Add Opening prepayment	—	200	—
	33,564	1,848	274
3, *Add* Closing creditors and accruals	3,782	—	84
Less Closing prepayment	—	240	—
	£37,346	£1,608	£358

Calculation of sales		£
Cash received from debtors		48,528
Less Opening debtors		6,438
		42,090
Add Closing debtors		6,776
		£48,866

A. SHORT
Trading and Profit and Loss Account
Year ended 30th June, 19x7

	£		£
Opening stock	4,242	Sales	48,866
Add Purchases	37,346		
	41,588		
Less Closing stock	5,296		
Cost of goods sold	36,292		
Gross profit	12,574		
	£48,866		£48,866
Salaries	4,498	Gross profit	12,574
Rent and rates	1,608		
Heating and lighting	358		
General expenses	3,562		
Depreciation fixed assets	440		
Net profit	2,108		
	£12,574		£12,574

Balance Sheet as at 30th June, 19x7

		£			£
Capital account			Fixed assets at cost		4,400
Opening balance		13,176	*Less* Depreciation		440
Profit for year		2,108			3,960
		15,284	Current assets		
Less drawings		4,938	Stock	£5,296	
		10,346	Debtors	6,776	
Current assets			Prepaid expenses	240	12,312
Creditors	£3,782				
Accrued expenses	84				
Bank overdraft	2,060	5,926			
		£16,272			£16,272

Note

Care should be exercised to include bank balances or overdrafts if they are not included with the lists of assets and liabilities at the beginning and ending of a trading period.

The final accounts drawn up by this method do not differ in any way from those prepared from a complete double-entry accounting system. Full details are given as to the make up of the net profit. It is customary to call the final statement a balance sheet because the

217

working paper contains a summary of some ledger accounts and the cash book contains aggregate accounts of others not requiring adjustments.

Where details of receipts and payments of cash are picked up from bank statements, it will be necessary to find out if any business monies have not been put through the bank. Some takings may be withdrawn from the till to be used to pay expenses and drawings, the balance then being deposited in the bank. It is essential that an estimate of these cash payments is made.

Example

G. Taylor, a retailer, does not keep any books of account, but does operate a business bank account. A summary of the bank statements for the year ended 30th June, 19x9 is given below.

	£		£
Receipts from customers	8,940	Opening balance	675
Additional capital paid in	500	Payments to creditors	6,894
		Electricity	275
		Rent and rates	450
		Motor van	800
		Closing balances	346
	£9,440		£9,440

During the year he paid expenses direct from the till. His estimate of these expenses were: Wages £1,250, general expenses £350, and drawings of £25 per week.

G. Taylor is able to supply the following details of his assets and liabilities at 30th June, 19x8 and 19x9.

	30.6.19x8 £	30.6.19x9 £
Fixtures at cost	600	600
Motor van at cost		800
Stock	3,560	3,240
Debtors	750	975
Creditors	525	840
Accrued electricity	95	140
Prepaid rates	60	80
Cash in till	40	70

Depreciation is to be provided as follows: fixtures 10% on cost, motor van 20% on cost.

218

You are required to prepare a trading and profit and loss account for the year ended 30th June, 19x9, and a balance sheet as at that date.

Working Paper

Calculation. Capital at 30.6.19x8

	£	£
Fixtures		600
Stock		3,560
Debtors		750
Prepaid rates		60
Cash in till		40
		5,010
Less Creditors	£525	
Accrued electricity	95	
Bank overdraft	675	
		1,295
		£3,715

Calculation. Cash sales not banked.

	£		£
Opening balance	40	Wages	1,250
Cash sales withdrawn		General expenses	350
from till	2,930	Drawings (25x52)	1,300
		Closing balance	70
	£2,970		£2,970

Calculation of:	Purchases	Rent and Rates	Electricity
	£	£	£
Cash paid	6,894	450	275
Less Opening creditors and accrual	525		95
Add Opening prepayment		60	
	6,369	510	180
Closing creditors and accrual	840		140
Less Closing prepayment		80	
	£7,209	£430	£320

	£
Calculation of sales	
Cash banked	8,940
Cash withdrawn from till	2,930
	11,870
Less Opening debtors	750
	11,120
Add Closing debtors	975
	£12,095

G. TAYLOR
Trading and Profit and Loss Account
Year ended 30th June, 19x9

	£		£
Opening stock	3,560	Sales	12,095
Purchases	7,209		
	10,769		
Less Closing stock	3,240		
	7,529		
Gross profit	4,566		
	£12,095		£12,095
Wages	1,250	Gross profit	4,566
Electricity	320		
Rent and rates	430		
General expenses	350		
Depreciation—Fixtures	60		
Motor van	160		
Net profit	1,996		
	£4,566		£4,566

Balance Sheet as at 30th June, 19x9

	£		£	£
Capital account		Fixed assets		
Opening balance	3,715	Fixtures at cost	600	
Add Capital introduced	500	*Less* Depreciation	60	
Profit for year	1,996	Motor van at cost	800	540
	6,211	*Less* Depreciation	160	
Less Drawings	1,300			640
	4,911	Current assets		1,180
Current liabilities		Stock	3,240	
Creditors	£840	Debtors	975	
Accrued expenses	140	Prepaid expenses	80	
	980	Balance at bank	346	
		Cash in hand	70	
				4,711
	£5,891			£5,891

Notes
1. In this example a cash summary must be constructed in order to determine the amount of cash sales withdrawn from the till. It is necessary to take into account the opening and closing cash balances for this purpose.
2. The profit and loss account must be debited with expenses paid by cash out of the till in addition to bank payments.

3. Destruction of Books of Original Entry

When a fire or flood destroys the books of accounts it is probable that the disaster also destroys certain assets. When this occurs it makes it impossible for the proprietor to make up a statement of affairs. For example, the stock may be totally destroyed in which case it will be impossible to physically make a stock-taking. Unless stock control records are kept, and these too may have been destroyed, some other means of calculating the missing value must be found.

Fortunately there is an acceptable method which is based on the gross profit percentage or margin. This consists of the relationship between the gross profit and the sales or turnover, the former being expressed as a percentage of the latter, viz.:

	£	£
Sales		40,000
Opening stock	7,946	
Purchases	28,432	
	36,378	
Closing stock	4,378	
Cost of goods sold		32,000
Gross profit		£ 8,000

$$\text{The gross profit percentage} = \frac{8,000}{40,000} \times 100 = 20\%$$

The gross profit margin tends to remain stable between one period and another in the same business, especially if that business is a retail organisation. The effect of this is that if certain figures can be obtained it is possible to calculate one that is missing.

Example

On 28th February a fire occurred at the premises of A. Baker totally destroying his stock. From an examination of his bank statements it has been possible to estimate his sales from 1st January as £25,000 and his purchases as £19,684. His accounts for the year ended the previous 31st December, showed closing stock as £6,742, and the gross profit percentage as 20%

You are required to calculate the value of stock destroyed by fire.

		£
(1) Opening stock		6,742
Purchases for two months		19,684
		26,426
(2) Sales for two months	£25,000	
Less Gross profit 20%		
of £25,000	5,000	
Cost of goods sold		20,000
(3) Value of stock destroyed		£ 6,426

The explanation for the above calculation is as follows:

1. The cost of goods sold cannot be determined in the normal manner because the value of closing stock is missing. Nevertheless, the calculation is started by adding purchases to the opening stock giving a value of £26,426.

222

2. The cost of goods sold can be obtained by deducting the amount of profit made from the value of sales and as the gross profit percentage is known this can be easily achieved.
3. The figure of £26,426 obtained in (1) above must be reduced by the closing stock to give the cost of goods sold which has been estimated in (2) above, £20,000. The closing stock can, therefore, be obtained by deducting the £20,000 from £26,426.

As an alternative to using the gross margin it is possible to use the "mark-up". Mark-up is the profit expressed as a percentage of the cost of the goods as opposed to gross margin which is the profit as a percentage of sales, viz.:

	£
Cost of goods	100
Profit	25
Selling price	£125

The margin or gross profit is
$$\frac{25}{125} \times 100 = 20\%$$

The mark up is
$$\frac{25}{100} \times 100 = 25\%$$

A relationship exists between the two percentages, for if one is known it is simple to find the other. In the example given the mark-up is 25% and the margin is 20%. If these percentages are changed to fractions they become one quarter and one fifth; that is the denominator has increased by one. If the fraction mark-up is two ninths the gross profit would be:

	£
Cost of goods	90
Mark-up 2/9ths	20
Selling price	£110

The gross profit fraction would be $\frac{20}{110} = \frac{2}{11}$, in this case the denominator has increased by two.

Therefore, to convert the mark-up fraction to the gross profit fraction all that is necessary is to take the mark-up numerator as being constant and to add this number to the denominator for the gross profit fraction, e.g.

Mark-up fraction		Gross profit fraction

$$\frac{3}{8} \qquad \frac{3}{8 + 3} = \frac{3}{11}$$

$$\frac{2}{5} \qquad \frac{2}{5 + 2} = \frac{2}{7}$$

To illustrate the use of this technique allied to incomplete records the following problem is typical of questions asked in examinations.

Example

C. Barr, who is in business as a stationer, has his shop totally destroyed by fire on 25th March, 19x2. He has an adequate fire insurance and wishes you to calculate the claim for loss of stock from the insurance company and to prepare his accounts for the period 1st January, 19x2, to 25th March, 19x2.

All his books and records have been destroyed in the fire, but you are able to obtain the following information.

Balance Sheet as at 31st December, 19x1

	£			£
Capital account	4,500	Fixtures at cost	£400	
		Less Depreciation	140	260
Creditors	1,750	Stock		3,980
Accrued electricity	30	Debtors		840
rent	100	Bank		1,275
		Cash in till		25
	£6,380			£6,380

An analysis of his bank statements from 1st January to the 25th March shows the following:

	£		£
Opening balance	1,275	Amounts paid to suppliers	5,984
Cash deposited from customers	7,385	Rent and rates	350
		Lighting and heating	230
		Insurances	80
		New fixtures	50
		Closing balance	1,966
	£8,660		£8,660

C. Barr takes money out of the till to pay sundry expenses which he estimates to have been—wages £360, cash purchases £160, sundry expenses £120, and drawings £600.

On 25th March, 19x2, his creditors amounted to £1,926, his debtors amounted to £750, electricity owing was £20, and insurances prepaid £60.

As well as the destruction of the stock the fixtures were entirely burned as was £20 in bank notes contained in the till. The insurance company agreed to settle these further claims for £280.

The normal mark up in C. Barr's business was 25%

Working Paper

Calculation of cash summary

	£		£
Opening balance	25	Wages	360
		Purchases	160
Balance representing money		Sundry Expenses	120
withdrawn from till	1,235	Drawings	600
		Closing balance destroyed	20
	£1,260		£1,260

Calculation of:	Purchases	Rent and Rates	Lighting	Insurances
	£	£	£	£
Per Bank statement	5,984	350	230	80
Cash summary	160			
	6,144	350	230	80
Less Opening creditors and accruals	1,750	100	30	
	4,394	250	200	80
Add Closing creditors and accruals	1,926		20	
Less Closing prepayment				60
	£6,320	£250	£220	£20

Calculation of sales:

	£
Per Bank statement	7,385
Cash summary	1,235
	8,620
Less Opening debtors	840
	7,780
Add Closing debtors	750
	£8,530

225

Calculation. Loss on fixtures destroyed

	£
Written down value 1.1.19x2	260
Additional purchases	50
	310

	£	
Amount of claim	£280	
Less In respect of cash destroyed	20	
		260
		£ 50

Claim for loss of stock

		£
Stock 1.1.19x2		3,980
Add Purchases to 25.3.19x2		6,320
		10,300
Sales to 25.3.19x2	£8,530	
Less profit therein		
Mark-up 25% = 1/4th		
Margin 20% = 1/5th	1,706	6,824
Value of stock destroyed		£3,476

C. BARR

Trading and Profit and Loss Account

Period 1st Jan, 19x2, to 25th March, 19x2

	£		£
Opening stock	3,980	Sales	8,530
Purchases	6,320	Insurance claim for	
	10,300	loss of stock	3,476
Gross profit	1,706		
	£12,006		£12,006
Wages	360	Gross profit	1,706
Rent and rates	250		
Lighting and heating	220		
Insurances	20		
Sundry expenses	120		
Loss on fixtures	50		
Net profit	686		
	£ 1,706		£ 1,706

Balance Sheet as at 25th March, 19x2

	£		£
Capital account		Current assets	
Opening balance	4,500	Debtors	750
Add Profit for year	686	Prepaid Insurance	60
	5,186	Claim: Insurance Co.	3,756
Less Drawings	600	Balance at bank	1,966
	4,586		
Current liabilities			
Creditors £1,926			
Accrued lighting 20			
	1,946		
	£6,532		£6,532

Note

The insurance claim shown in the balance sheet is made up of £280 claim for fixtures and cash lost plus £3,476 for loss of stock.

Changes in Gross Profit Percentage

Although it has been stated that the gross profit percentage tends to be constant there can be exceptions to this rule.

1. If the cost of the goods sold increases but the selling price is not put up in the same proportion, the margin percentage will either increase or decrease depending on whether the selling price is proportionately higher or lower than the original cost price.
2. If a greater or smaller proportion of special allowances or trade discounts is made in one trading period as compared with the average allowed.
3. If there is a change in the method of stock valuation or some of the stock has become damaged or obsolete and has to be written off.
4. If the business deals in several lines of goods, each one having a different mark-up. If the relative proportions of goods sold alters, this will have an effect on the aggregate gross profit percentage.
5. If some external factor alters the difference between cost price and selling price, for example the change from purchase tax to value added tax.

If any of the above changes have occurred, allowance must be made

227

if the margin percentage is used to calculate any items. Even with adjustments being made the resultant figure may not be as accurate as when the margin is constant.

EXERCISES

17.1
On the 31st December, 19x5, J. Nuttall presents you with the following figures. He started trading on 1st January, 19x3, with capital of £4,000. He asks you to prepare statements showing his annual profits for the three years.

	31st Dec., 19x3 £	31st Dec., 19x4 £	31st Dec., 19x5 £
Cash at bank	1,950		650
Bank overdraft		1,450	
Debtors	750	850	1,275
Creditors	2,300	1,800	2,000
Fittings at cost	200	400	400
Motor vehicle at cost	1,200	1,200	1,200
Prepaid rates	60	80	85
Accrued electricity	45	60	50
Stock	3,400	3,300	4,200
Loan S. Nuttall	1,000	1,500	1,000
Drawings	2,500	3,000	2,000

Note
Mr. Nuttall requires that fittings be depreciated at 5% on cost each year and motor vehicles 20% on cost each year. The figures shown above are the aggregate purchases. No fixed assets have been sold.

17.2
A, B, C, and D who share profits in the ratios 3:3:2:2 present you with the following information,

	30th June, 19x7 £	30th June, 19x8 £	30th June, 19x9 £
Cash at bank	1,750	850	1,875
Debtors	3,200	3,500	4,125
Creditors	2,300	3,200	3,400
Stock	6,450	5,450	6,250
Fixed assets	12,000	11,500	11,000
Prepaid rent	100	120	140
Loan F	1,200	2,400	1,000
Accrued rates	50	70	90
Drawings A	2,000	1,500	2,500
B	2,400	1,500	2,000
C	1,700	1,400	1,800
D	1,500	1,200	1,700

The capital accounts at 1st July, 19x6, were as follows:
A £8,000, B £6,000, C £4,000, and D £2,000.
You are required to show the entries in the partners' capital accounts for the period 1st July, 19x6, to 30th June, 19x9.

17.3
S. Rudd furnishes you with the following details of his financial position as at 31st December, 19x7 and 19x8.

	31st Dec., 19x7 £	31st Dec., 19x8 £
Cash at bank	520	
Bank overdraft		252
Shop fixtures at cost	500	500
Debtors	730	592
Creditors	482	328
Stock	1,064	1,358

Notes
(a) During 19x7 and 19x8 Rudd has withdrawn £100 in cash each month for his own expenses.
(b) Rudd estimates that the shop fixtures have fallen in value at the rate of 10% per annum on written down value.
(c) An examination of the individual debtors' accounts at 31st December, 19x8 reveals that £28 should be written off as bad debts.

You are required to prepare a statement showing what profit has been made up for the year ended 31st December, 19x8, and to state the balance on Rudd's capital account as at that date.

17.4
B. Sunley has not kept proper books of account, but is able to present you with the following information:

Summary of Bank Statement
Year ended 31st March, 19x3

	£		£
Trading receipts banked	35,685	Balance 1.4.19x2	1,050
		Payments to creditors	30,150
		Rent and rates	480
		Lighting and heating	300
		General expenses	945
		Drawings	1,350
		Balance 31.3.19x3	1,410
	£35,685		£35,685

Balances at	31st March, 19x2	31st March, 19x3
	£	£
Motor vehicles	4,350	3,600
Stock	4,500	6,300
Debtors	2,250	2,550
Creditors	1,800	2,025
Prepaid rates	60	80
Accrued general expenses	180	135

You are required to prepare a trading and profit and loss account for the year ended 31st March, 19x3, and a balance sheet at that date.

17.5

The following information has been taken from the incomplete records of Parke and Scott.

Balances as at	30th June, 19x2	30th June, 19x3
	£	£
Debtors	8,540	10,360
Creditors	16,720	14,420
Bank	240 (Dr.)	
Stock	11,680	14,780
Fixtures and fittings	4,140	
Motor vehicle	800	
Capital—Parke	4,000	
Scott	4,000	
Current account—Parke	480 (Cr.)	
Scott	200 (Cr.)	

	£
Receipts during year	
Cash sales	6,560
Debtors for credit sales	63,280
Payments during year	
Creditors for credit purchases	51,500
Salaries and wages	6,500
Rent	600
Rates	240
Motor expenses	1,240
Sundry expenses	5,126
Drawings—Parke	4,200
Scott	3,900
Heating and lighting	2,580

Notes
(1) Rates amounting to £160 for the half-year ending 30th September, 19x3, were due but, unpaid.
(2) Rent had to be prepaid to the amount of £200.

(3) Depreciation should be provided by the reducing balance method at 10% on fixtures and fittings, and 20% on the motor vehicle.

You are required to prepare trading, profit and loss, and appropriation accounts for the year ended 30th June, 19x2, and balance sheet at that date.

17.6

The following is a summary of the bank account of Robson for the year ended 30th September, 19x6:

	£		£
Balance 1.10.19x5	1,028	Payments to suppliers	37,572
Sales deposits	48,744	Rent and rates	1,542
Balance 30.9.19x6	236	General expenses	3,394
		Drawings	7,500
	£50,008		£50,008

An amount of £4,236 was taken from the shop till and used to pay wages of £2,560; the balance was proprietor's drawings.

The following information was obtained:

	30.9.19x5	30.9.19x6
	£	£
Debtors	4,480	5,380
Creditors	3,890	3,418
Stock	4,860	6,300
Furniture	2,000	2,000
Prepaid rates	84	90
Accrued general expenses	162	238

During the year ended 30th September, 19x6, discounts received from creditors amounted to £300. The creditors at 30th September, 19x5, included an amount of £120 owing to a customer who had overpaid his account. This amount was set off against sales to him in the current year.

You are required to prepare a trading and profit and loss account for the year ended 30th September, 19x6, and a balance sheet as at that date.

17.7

The balance sheet of B. Stafford at 31st December, 19x2, was:

	£		£
Capital	6,440	Premises	3,000
		Fixtures and fittings	500
Creditors	600	Stock	1,600
		Debtors	500
		Cash at bank	1,440
	£7,040		£7,040

On the 15th June, 19x3, cash and certain records were stolen from the office safe.

From the remaining records it was established that the following transactions had taken place between 1st January and 15th June, 19x3:

	£
Expenses paid	4,300
Cash and credit purchases	21,300
Cash and credit sales	28,640

On the 16th June, the following balances were extracted from the books: Debtors £720, creditors £860, bank balance £2,280, stock was valued at £1,300. Stafford had withdrawn £1,000 for his own use during this period.

You are required:
(a) To prepare a statement showing the amount of the insurance claim to be made for the cash stolen.
(b) To prepare a trading and profit and loss account for the period, and a balance sheet as at 15th June, 19x3.

17.8

On the evening of 19th September, 19x7, part of the stock of J. Pearson was destroyed by fire. Goods valued at £750 were untouched by the fire and some of the remainder could be sold for £65. From the information given below you are required to prepare a statement showing the amount of the claim from the insurance company.

	£
Stock. 31st Mar., 19x6	4,826
31st Mar., 19x7	5,720
Sales year ended 31st Mar., 19x7	41,734
Sales 1st Ap., 19x7, to 19th Sept., 19x7	22,680
Purchases year ended 31st Mar., 19x7	36,666
Purchases 1st Ap., 19x7, to 19th Sept., 19x7	19,957

17.9

On 28th April, 19x3, a fire destroyed the stock and fittings belonging to C. Lewis.

His balance sheet on 31st December, 19x2, contained the following:

	£		£
Capital	9,000	Shop fittings	750
		Motor vehicle	1,200
Creditors	2,800	Stock	4,985
Accrued electricity	40	Debtors	3,750
Accrued general expenses	160	Prepaid rates	60
		Balance at bank	1,255
	£12,000		£12,000

An analysis of his bank statements from 1st January to 28th April, 19x3, revealed:

	£
Cash deposits from cash and credit sales	29,974
Capital introduced	1,000
Payments to creditors	25,715
Rent and rates	650
Lighting and heating	310
Motor expenses	430
General expenses	1,120
Drawings	850
Shop fittings	60

Cash had been taken from the till to pay wages £1,460, purchases £300, and general expenses £90.

At 28th April, 19x3, debtors owed £4,200, there was £3,100 owing to creditors, expenses due but not yet paid were electricity £75, general expenses £120.

The insurance company agreed that the claim for fittings destroyed should amount to £725.

You are required to prepare:

(a) A statement showing the amount that should be claimed from the insurance company.

(b) A trading and profit and loss account for the period up to the fire and a balance sheet as at 28th April, 19x3.

Note

The normal mark-up for this type of business is 20%.

17.10

After the close of business on 30th June, 19x6, the day's takings were stolen from the safe of B. Tomkins. The cash book and nominal ledger were also found to be missing.

You are able to ascertain the following details.

(1) Balances at 30th June, 19x6, bank £2,100 (Dr.), debtors £4,580, creditors £6,486, general expenses accrued £250.

(2) Transactions during the period 1st April, 19x6, to 30th June, 19x6, were purchases £16,760, cash and credit sales £21,680, wages and salaries £2,300, general expenses £1,470, fixtures purchased £200, and drawings £800.

(3) The whole of the takings had been paid into the bank with the exception of those stolen.

(4) The value of stock on hand taken immediately after the burglary amounted to £3,800, but it was thought that some other items of stock had been stolen.

(5) The normal mark-up for this business is 33⅓% on cost.

233

(6) The balance sheet as at 31st March, 19x6, was:

	£		£
Capital	4,460	Shop fixtures	600
		Stock	3,750
Creditors	5,272	Debtors	4,162
Accrued expenses	180	Bank	1,400
	£9,912		£9,912

You are required to prepare:
(a) Statements showing the claims to be made against the insurance company.
(b) A trading and profit and loss account for the three months ended 30th June, 19x6, and a balance sheet as at that date.

18   Non-trading Organisations

The prime purpose in establishing a business is to make a profit. On the other hand a number of institutions are formed to provide a service to the public or restricted to the members of the particular institution. These institutions comprise charities, sports, and social clubs. The income of these institutions may not be limited to membership subscriptions, but may also include receipts from sale of drinks or, in the case of a golf club, receipts from the sale of equipment. Nevertheless, the main object of the society or club is not to make a profit but to cover the costs of running the activities which may include providing fixed assets, e.g. a pavilion or club house.

Because the institution is not formed to trade or make a profit the final accounts do not include a profit and loss account. In fact, except for the larger societies, it is unlikely that a complete double-entry system of book-keeping is maintained. Usually a cash book is written up supported by a register of members. For the smaller institutions a summary of the cash book is prepared each year and distributed to the members. This summary is known as a Receipts and Payments Account.

The disadvantage of the receipts and payments account is that it shows only monies received and paid during the year, and not the true income and expenditure for the year. Any invoices which have not been paid will not be reflected in the account submitted to members, nor will mention be made of any assets acquired in previous years which are still in existence. To overcome these disadvantages an income and expenditure account is drawn up and at the same time a balance sheet is shown.

The income and expenditure account takes the place of a profit and loss account. Income is shown on the credit side and expenditure on the debit side. The compilation of the income and expenditure account is based on the same principles used in the preparation of business accounts from incomplete records. That is, by basing the figures on the cash summary (receipts and payments account) suitably adjusted for items accrued or prepaid. The balance on this account is not described as net profit or loss, but as a surplus or deficiency for the year.

One problem that exists is with regard to subscriptions. If any subscriptions are in arrear at the end of the year, it may be argued that these should be ignored, for unless the member willingly pays them it is very rare for the institution to sue for them. Normally, the person concerned is suspended from membership. Furthermore, to show the subscriptions in arrear as a debt due to the institution in the balance sheet might be considered as contravening the convention of conservatism. However, unless specially told to ignore subscriptions in arrear the student should make all adjustments indicatèd.

Example

The receipts and payments account shows total subscriptions received in the year ended 31st December, 19x8, as £2,300.

At 31st December, 19x7, subscriptions paid in advance totalled £80 whilst those in arrear amounted to £120. At 31st December, 19x8, subscriptions in arrear were £150 and subscriptions paid in advance totalled £60.

Calculate the net amount of subscriptions in respect of the year ended 31st December, 19x8.

	£	£
Cash received during 19x8		2,300
Subscriptions in advance 31.12.19x7		80
arrear 31.12.19x7	120	
arrear 31.12.19x8		150
advance 31.12.19x8	60	
	£180	2,530
	—	180
Subscriptions for 19x8		£2,350

The explanation for the above computation is as follows:

1. Additions to £2,300. The subscriptions in advance at December, 19x7, are in respect of 19x8 so must be added to the cash received in 19x8. The subscriptions in arrear at December, 19x8, are also in respect of 19x8 and must be included in that year.
2. Subtractions from £2,300. The amount of £2,300 includes £120 subscriptions which relate to 19x7 and £60 subscriptions which relate to 19x9. As the amount required relates to 19x8 both these items must be deducted.

Wherever income and expenditure can directly be related, as, for example, the costs and receipts from a special event, it is normal to link these in the income and expenditure account and extend the difference, viz.:

	£	£
Christmas dance expenses	350	
Less Dance receipts	317	
Loss on Dance		33

In the balance sheet the members share of the net assets may be described as capital as in a normal business balance sheet or as "Reserve" or "Accumulated Fund".

As in incomplete records a working paper is necessary to calculate figures that appear in the income and expenditure account.

Example

The treasurer of a social club has prepared the following receipts and payments account for the year ended 30th June, 19x3.

Receipts and Payments Account
Year ended 30th June, 19x3

Receipts	£	Payments	£
Balance at bank 1.7.19x2	84	Rent of rooms	180
Subscriptions	1,124	Wages of caretaker	650
Entrance fees	50	Purchase sports equipment	280
Sale of refreshments	760	Dance expenses	205
Sale of dance tickets	298	Refreshment supplies	664
		Secretary's expenses	120
		Balance at bank 30.6.19x3	217
	£2,316		£2,316

The members require an income and expenditure account for the year ended 30th June, 19x3, and a balance sheet as at that date.

You ascertain the following information:

1. At 30th June, 19x2, assets comprised: furniture £960, sports equipment £380, subscriptions in arrear £28, liabilities were accrued rent £60 and subscriptions in advance £44.
2. At 30th June, 19x3, assets comprised: furniture £864, sports equipment £520, subscriptions in arrear £35, liabilities were accrued rent £120, accrued wages £25, and subscriptions in advance £18.

Working Paper

	£	£
Calculation: Opening capital		
Furniture		960
Sports equipment		380
Subscriptions in arrear		28
Balance at bank		84
Accrued rent	60	
Subscriptions in advance	44	
	104	1,452
	—	104
		£1,348

	£	£
Calculation: Subscriptions		
Cash received		1,124
Subscriptions in arrear June, 19x2	28	
advance June, 19x2		44
arrear June, 19x3		35
advance June, 19x3	18	
	£46	1,203
	—	46
		£1,157

Calculation of:	Rent £	Wages £
Cash paid	180	650
Less Accrual 30.6.19x2	60	
	120	
Add Accrual 30.6.19x3	120	25
	£240	£675

Calculation of depreciation on	Furniture £	Equipment £
Opening balance	960	380
Additions		280
	960	660
Less Closing value	864	520
	£96	£140

Income and Expenditure Account
Year ended 30th June, 19x3

	£		£	£
Caretaker's wages	675	Subscriptions		1,157
Rent of rooms	240	Entrance fees		50
Secretary's expenses	120	Sale of refreshments	760	
Depreciation—Furniture	96	Cost of refreshments	664	
Equipment	140	Profit	—	96
Surplus for year	125	Sale of dance tickets	298	
		Cost of dance	205	
		Profit		93
	£1,396			£1,396

Balance Sheet as at 30th June, 19x3

	£	£		£	£
Capital account			Fixed assets		
Balance 1.7.19x2	1,348		Furniture	960	
Surplus for year	125		*Less* Depreciation	96	
		1,473			864
Current liabilities			Sports equipment	660	
Accrued rent	120		*Less* Depreciation	140	
Accrued wages	25				520
Subscriptions in					1,384
advance	18				
		163	Current assets		
			Subscriptions in		
			arrear	35	
			Balance at bank	217	
					252
	£1,636				£1,636

When a club runs a trading activity amongst its members so as to make a profit, e.g. a bar for the sale of drinks, it is usual to separate this activity from the income and expenditure account and prepare a trading account. The profit on this account is transferred to the credit of the income and expenditure account.

It is common practice when a person is paid to run a bar or other trading activity to pay him, in addition to a wage, a commission based on the profit made. This is a an inducement for him to encourage custom, for the greater the profit the greater will be the benefit both to him and the club. The exact wording of the basis on which the commission is to be calculated is extremely important. It can be a certain percentage of the profits either before or after the calculation of such commission.

Example

The profits made in a bar trading account were calculated at £4,400. The barman is entitled to a commission of 10%. Calculate the commission if it is based on

(a) 10% of the profits before charging such commission.
(b) 10% of the profits after charging such commission.

For the purpose of (a) the calculation is straight-forward, i.e.

$$\frac{10}{100} \times 4{,}400 = £440$$

To calculate (b) the computation is more complicated. The fractions to be set against the profit consist of the numerator being constant, but the denominator will consist of 100 plus the numerator, i.e.

$$\frac{10}{110} \times 4{,}400 = £400$$

The bar profit is now reduced from £4,400 less the commission of £400 to £4,000. The commission is now 10% of this latter amount.

Example

The following is the receipts and payments account of the Drincup Rugby Club for the year ended 31st March, 19x4.

Receipts	£	Payments	£
Cash in hand 1.4.19x3	15	Groundsman's wages	850
Cash in bank 1.4.19x3	257	Barman's wages	520
Subscriptions	905	Rent of ground	540
Bar takings	6,003	Repairs to pavilion	267
Sale of dance tickets	490	Rugby equipment	140
Donations	20	New mower (less £40 received for old one)	340
		Bar purchases	3,569
		Expenses of dance	630
		Insurances	150
		Secretarial expenses	95
		Cash in hand 31.3.19x4	25
		Cash at bank 31.3.19x4	564
	£7,690		£7,690

You are given the following information.

1. As at 31st March, 19x3, the book values of the fixed assets were—
   Club house £2,200 (cost £3,000), motor mower £70 (cost £250),
   equipment £300.
2. The other current assets and liabilities were:

	31st March, 19x3	31st March, 19x4
	£	£
Bar stock at cost	1,683	1,427
Creditors for bar purchases	237	320
Creditors for secretarial expenses	27	36
Creditors for rent	60	120
Subscriptions in arrear	14	28
Subscriptions in advance	35	21

3. Depreciation is to be written off the fixed assets as: Club house
   £200, mower £38, equipment £90.
4. The barman is entitled to a commission of 5% of the profits made on
   the bar after charging such commission.

Prepare an income and expenditure account (showing a separate bar
trading account) for the year ended 31st March, 19x4, and a balance
sheet as at that date.

Working Paper

		£	£
Calculation: Opening capital			
	Club house		2,200
	Mower		70
	Equipment		300
	Cash in hand		15
	Cash at bank		257
	Bar stock		1,683
	Subscriptions in arrear		14
	Creditors—Bar purchases	237	
	Secretarial expenses	27	
	Rent	60	
	Subscriptions in advance	35	
		£359	4,539
		—	359
			£4,180

241

Calculation of:	Bar purchases	Secretarial expenses	Rent
	£	£	£
Cash payments	3,569	95	540
Less Opening accrual	237	27	60
	3,332	68	480
Add Closing accrual	320	36	120
	£3,652	£104	£600

	£	£
Calculation: Subscriptions		
Cash received		905
Subscriptions in arrear 31.3.19x3	14	
advance 31.3.19x3		35
advance 31.3.19x4	21	
arrear 31.3.19x4		28
	£35	968
	—	35
		£933

	£
Calculation: Loss on sale of mower	
Written down value	70
Less Value received	40
	£30

	£
Calculation: Equipment	
Balance brought forward	300
Additions during year	140
	440
Less Depreciation	90
	£350

DRINCUP RUGBY CLUB
Bar Trading Account year ended 31st March, 19x4

	£		£
Opening stock	1,683	Bar takings	6,003
Add Purchases	3,652		
	5,335		
Less Closing stock	1,427		
	3,908		
Barman's wages	520		
Barman's commission	75		
Profit carried down	1,500		
	£6,003		£6,003

Income and Expenditure Account
Year ended 31st March, 19x4

	£	£		£
Groundsman's wages		850	Subscriptions	933
Rent of ground		600	Donations	20
Repairs to pavilion		267	Profit bar trading	1,500
Insurances		150	Deficit for year	16
Secretarial expenses		104		
Expenses of dance	630			
Less sale of tickets	490			
Loss		140		
Loss sale of mower		30		
Depreciation club house		200		
Mower		38		
Equipment		90		
		£2,469		£2,469

243

Balance Sheet as at 31st March 19x4

	£	£		£	£
Capital account			Fixed assets		
Balance at 31.3.19x3		4,180	Club house at cost	3,000	
Less Deficit for year		16	Less Depreciation	1,000	
		4,164			2,000
Current liabilities			Mower at cost	380	
Creditors			Less Depreciation	38	
Bar supplies	320				342
Secretarial expenses	36		Equipment at		
Rent	120		valuation		350
Barman's com-					2,692
mission	75				
Subscriptions in ad-			Current assets		
vance	21		Bar stock	1,427	
		572	Subscriptions in		
			arrear	28	
			Cash at bank	564	
			Cash in hand	25	
					2,044
		£4,736			£4,736

Note. The barman's commission is calculated as follows:

The profit before charging commission is £6,003 − (3,908 + 520) = £1,575.
The commission is therefore

$$\frac{5}{105} \times 1,575 = £75$$

As it has not been paid before the year end it must also appear as a current liability.

EXERCISES

18.1
From the following particulars and the notes attached relating to the Inner Archery Club, prepare the final accounts of the club for the year ending 31st December, 19x7.

Receipts and Payments Account

	£		£
Balance in hand 1.1.19x7	250	Repairs to equipment	120
Subscriptions	785	Purchase new equipment	200
Locker rents	42	Expenses dances and socials	320

	£		£
Receipts from dances and socials	438	Repair and decoration of club house	150
Sale of old lawn mower	20	Rent of ground	400
Sale of equipment	50	Secretarial expenses	80
		Balance in hand 31.12.19x7	315
	£1,585		£1,585

At 1st January, 19x7, the club owned a club house costing £1,000, equipment valued at £250, a mower valued £30. The club owed a catering bill of £39 and secretarial expenses of £25. Subscriptions in arrear were £35 and paid in advance £20. At 31st December, 19x7, in addition to the club house, equipment was valued at £350. The club owed dance expenses £22 and secretarial expenses £45. Subscriptions in arrear were £25 and in advance £50.

18.2
The following is the receipts and payments account of the Overzealous Social Club for the year ending 31st December, 19x8:

	£		£
Balance in hand 1.1.19x8	922	Payments. Bar supplies	32,284
Subscriptions for 19x7	96	Furniture	4,300
19x8	8,072	Rent and rates	2,520
19x9	388	Wages	15,140
Bar sales	49,246	Printing, stationery etc.	690
Hire of rooms	230	General expenses	2,814
		Balance in hand 31.12.19x8	1,206
	£58,954		£58,954

The following information is available:

(a)

	31.12.19x7 £	31.12.19x8 £
Bar stocks	2,864	3,220
Creditors bar stocks	3,550	3,970
Due to club for hire of rooms	24	60
Rent outstanding	500	
Wages outstanding		180
Furniture	10,500	
Subscriptions in advance	206	
Subscriptions in arrear		148

(b) Provision is to be made for depreciation of furniture £1,250.

You are required to prepare a bar trading account and income and expenditure account for the year ended 31st December, 19x8, and a balance sheet as at that date.

245

18.3

The receipts and payments account of the Downtown Social Club for the year ended 30th June, 19x1, is given below:

	£		£
Balance	692	Staff salaries	3,254
Subscriptions	3,188	Bar supplies	3,686
Bar receipts	5,564	Rent, rates, insurance	254
Games room receipts	820	Furniture (bought 1st	
Receipts from socials	704	January, 19x1)	600
Entrance fees	288	Printing	126
		General expenses	658
		Cost of socials	760
		Repairs and cleaning	238
		Lighting and heating	178
		Games room expenses	466
		Balances	1,036
	£11,256		£11,256

You are required to prepare a bar trading account and income and expenditure account for the year ended 30th June, 19x1, and a balance sheet at that date, taking into account the following information:

(a) Subscriptions include £66 in arrear and £80 in advance.
(b) Creditors for bar supplies were—31.6.19x0 £286, 30.6.19x1 £364.
(c) Bar stock on 30.6.19x0 was £327, and on 30.6.19x1 £397.
(d) Staff salaries owing 30.6.19x1 were £74.
(e) Provide for depreciation on furniture @ 10% p.a. The value of this asset on 30.6.19x0 was £700.
(f) The bar steward is entitled to a commission of 10% on the bar profits after charging the commission.

18.4

The following particulars apply to the Overair Social Club:

	30.9.19x6	30.9.19x7
	£	£
Bar stock	100	145
Creditors—Bar purchases	150	130
Rent		70
Subscriptions in arrear	25	30
Subscriptions in advance	10	60
Equipment (estimated value)	550	560

Receipts and Payments Account
Year ended 30th Sept., 19x7

	£		£
Opening cash balances	500	Rent and rates	360
Donations	300	Repairs to property	290

	£		£
Subscriptions	460	Caretaker's wages	1,000
Bar sales	3,790	Purchase equipment	150
Hall lettings	30	Bar purchases	2,720
Sale of raffle tickets	320	Heating and lighting	200
		Bar steward's wages	400
		Secretarial expenses	50
		Closing cash balances	230
	£5,400		£5,400

The bar steward is entitled to a commission of 5% on the bar profits after charging his wages and commission.

You are required to prepare a bar trading account and an income and expenditure account for the year ended 30th September, 19x7, and a balance sheet at that date.

18.5
The receipts and payments account of the Town Supporters Club is given below.

Receipts and Payments Account
Year ended 30th June, 19x6

	£		£
Opening bank and cash		Wages	3,407
balance	1,068	Bar steward's salary	1,200
Subscriptions	2,900	Purchase bar supplies	7,945
Sale of programmes	1,672	Rent and rates	330
Bar receipts	11,596	Purchase souvenirs	1,783
Donations	1,240	Printing of programmes	1,480
Sale of souvenirs	2,516	Donation Town Football	
		Club	4,000
		Closing bank and cash	
		balance	847
	£20,992		£20,992

You are given the following information.
(a) Assets and liabilities

	30.6.19x5	30.6.19x6
	£	£
Clubhouse	9,000	9,000
Equipment (cost £3,000)	1,900	1,800
Bar stock	684	1,057
Creditors—Bar purchases	768	842
Souvenir purchases	148	215
Printing	195	84
Subscriptions in advance	84	74
arrear	140	210

247

(b) The bar steward is entitled to a commission of 10% of the bar profits after charging his salary and commission.

You are required to prepare a bar trading account and an income and expenditure account for the year ended 30th June, 19x6, and a balance sheet as at that date.

18.6
The following is a summary of the amounts received and spent by the Classical Debating Society from its date of commencement on 1st April, 19x3, to 31st March, 19x4.

	£
Purchase of Buildings	5,000
Equipment	1,600
Refreshments	7,384
Wages paid	1,040
Rates and insurance paid	160
Printing, postage, and telephone paid	96
Bank interest and charges paid	58
Electricity paid	216
Loan repaid to H. Short	1,000
Subscriptions received	1,050
Receipts from sale of refreshments	8,566
Loan from bank	2,000
Loan from H. Short	6,000
General expenses paid	234

Notes
(a) All the receipts and payments went through the bank.
(b) Refreshments on hand at 31st March, 19x4, amounted to £280.
(c) The following amounts were owing on 31st March, 19x4: loan interest H. Short £300, refreshments £475, electricity £84.
(d) At the year end insurance was prepaid amounting to £35.
(e) At the year end subscriptions in advance amounted to £35.

You are required to prepare:

(1) a receipts and payments account for the year ended 31st March, 19x4,
(2) an income and expenditure account for the same year, and
(3) a balance sheet as at 31st March, 19x4.

19 The Interpretation of Final Accounts

The compilation of the trading and profit and loss accounts and the balance sheet represents the end product of a series of transactions which have taken place over a particular period of time. However, the recording or mechanical aspect is only one facet in accounting. The proprietor of the business can make use of the final accounts as a form of control and also to diagnose the strengths and weaknesses of the undertaking. It is of no benefit to the owner if the firm is making handsome trading profits, if by doing so the liquidity (or cash resources) is placed in jeopardy. By correctly interpreting the accounts dangerous trends can be averted in the future by installing more conservative policies.

The preparation of final accounts is concerned with historical accounting, in that the transactions have already taken place. The interpretation of final accounts is concerned with the current or future position of the firm and the implementation of controls and policies.

The businessman is concerned with two main problems. The first is the profitability of the business—is it sufficient for the amount of effort and capital he has put in? The second is the financial stability of the business—is it strong enough to ensure its continued existence both in the short and long terms?

To compare two or more sets of accounts a series of ratios have been developed. The reason for this is that if one is comparing a relationship between two figures because of the magnitude of the amounts, it is sometimes difficult to see at a glance which set of accounts produces the better situation, whereas if both sets of figures are reduced to the same base, the difference between them can be seen at once.

The ratios involved are:

1. Return on capital invested.
2. Gross profit percentage.
3. Stock turnover rate.
4. Net profit percentage.
5. Expenses ratios.

6. Return on assets employed.
7. Proprietorship ratio.
8. Working capital ratio.
9. Acid test or solvency ratio.

Before applying the ratios several points have to be borne in mind. Ratios are not an end in themselves; they only provide pointers, and any conclusions must be supported by other evidence. Balance sheet ratios are made up from figures which relate to a precise moment in time. The position may radically alter within a very short time, therefore any conclusion reached may be affected by future events. When comparing accounts of two widely differing businesses it is usual for ratios to be quite different yet give the same conclusion. For example, a large engineering concern will have a smaller turnover of stock than a retail greengrocer, yet each may be justified in the amount of stock carried.

To illustrate the mechanics and interpretation of ratios the following example is given representing the accounts of a business for two consecutive years.

Trading and Profit and Loss Accounts

	£	Year 1 £	£	Year 2 £
Sales		200,000		250,000
Opening stock	28,000		22,000	
Purchases	144,000		193,500	
	172,000		215,500	
Less Closing stock	22,000		25,500	
Cost of goods sold		150,000		190,000
Gross profit		50,000		60,000
Administrative expenses	15,000		17,500	
Selling expenses	20,000		25,000	
Financial expenses	5,000		2,500	
		40,000		45,000
Net profit		£10,000		£15,000

Balance Sheet

	£	Year 1 £	£	Year 2 £
Fixed assets		135,000		144,000
Current assets				
Stock	22,000		25,500	
Debtors	20,000		25,000	
Cash	8,000		500	
	50,000		51,000	
Current liabilities—creditors	25,000		30,000	
Working capital		25,000		21,000
		160,000		165,000
Less Long-term loan		60,000		60,000
		£100,000		£105,000
Capital employed				
Opening balance		96,000		100,000
Add Profit		10,000		15,000
		106,000		115,000
Less Drawings		6,000		10,000
		£100,000		£105,000

Return on Capital Employed

This ratio is designed to show whether the businessman is justified in continuing the business or in closing it down. It is calculated by expressing the profit earned in a given period as a percentage of the owner's capital. To be strictly accurate the denominator should be the average capital employed during the period, but as a matter of convenience the balance at the year end is usually taken.

The results of the two years in the illustration are:

Year 1 $\dfrac{10,000 \times 100}{100,000} = 10\%$

Year 2 $\dfrac{15,000 \times 100}{105,000} = 14\cdot3\%$

From the above results it can be seen that there has been a marked improvement over the two years. The next consideration is to compare the return achieved by the business with the possibility of what could be obtained if the business was sold and the proceeds invested in securities. The dividend which would be thus obtained is then added to the salary which the businessman could command if he worked elsewhere together with an additional percentage for the risk involved in carrying on his own business.

If the latter amount is greater than the sum realised by the business, then a possibility arises that the business should be terminated. Other considerations affect the decision such as if the return on capital continues to increase, the situation may be totally reversed. An individual may prefer to work for himself rather than for someone else, and to allow for this he may be prepared to suffer some pecuniary loss.

Gross Profit Percentage

This ratio has already been mentioned in Chapter 17 and consists of the gross profit expressed as a percentage of net sales or turnover. The ratio is not only concerned with profitability, but also acts as a control on trading account entries.

In the example given the results are:

Year 1 $$\frac{50,000 \times 100}{200,000} = 25\%$$

Year 2 $$\frac{60,000 \times 100}{250,000} = 24\%$$

There has been a drop of 1% in the second year which represents a loss of £1 for every £100 of sales. This loss could have arisen from:

(a) Cash stolen from the till in respect of cash sales. In this case a stricter control must be installed. This could be achieved by installing a recording cash register which lists all takings which must be balanced with the cash at the end of each day; or by insuring that sales are made by one assistant, but money is received by a cashier, thus creating a division of responsibility.

(b) Stock stolen either by employees or customers. To overcome this difficulty a more rigid form of stock control should be put into operation or the stock itself should be more strategically placed so that pilferage can be cut to the minimum.

(c) Accounting entries may be incorrectly recorded. The closing stock figure may have been incorrectly calculated, or purchase invoices may have been entered but the goods themselves not received until after the year end, in which case they will not have been included in the closing stock. In any event, the accounting system would need tightening up.

(d) A change in selling policy. The selling price of the goods may have been reduced in order to create an increased volume. In this example sales have increased from £200,000 in Year 1 to £250,000 in Year 2. The effect of this is that although the gross profit percentage has fallen the absolute profit is increased. The same effect is felt if the cost of goods increases, but the selling price is not increased in the same proportion.

A reason must be found for the decrease in the ratio, for if it is not due to (c) and (d) above, a loss of 1% on £250,000 or £2,500 has been incurred.

A rise in the gross profit percentage could be attributed to:

(a) incorrectly overstating the closing stock,
(b) omitting purchase invoices from the records,
(c) increasing the selling price of the goods.

Stock Turnover Rate

This ratio is applied to judge the effective use of stock and is obtained by dividing the cost of goods sold by the average stock held. In practice the average stock should be based on weekly or monthly stocks held, but in exercises it is usual to take the average of the opening and closing annual stocks, viz.:

Year 1 $\quad \dfrac{150,000}{\frac{1}{2}(28,000+22,000)} = \dfrac{150,000}{25,000} = 6\times$

Year 2 $\quad \dfrac{190,000}{\frac{1}{2}(22,000+25,500)} = \dfrac{190,000}{23,750} = 8\times$

To interpret the results in the first year the annual cost of goods sold was £150,000, the average stock was £25,000 which means that the stock was sold 6 times in the year or, alternatively, there was sufficient stock on hand to satisfy (12/6) two months sales. In the second year the stock turnover had risen to 8 times or, alternatively, there was (12/8) 1½ months sales on hand.

Provided that the level of stocks is sufficient to provide for all sales, it is more efficient to keep stock to a minimum. Less cash is used to pay for the goods, leaving more money available to meet other expenses.

253

The larger the stock the greater the chance of pilferage, breakage, and obsolescence, not to mention the costs involved in storing and insurance of it. Therefore, the higher the stock turnover the greater is the efficiency.

Net Profit Percentage

The net profit is the ultimate profit made by trading and is the difference between the gross profit and the expenses incurred in running the business. To judge whether the trading profitability has increased or decreased a ratio is prepared which expresses the net profit as a percentage of the net sales. This ratio is often linked with return on assets employed which is described later.

In the example given:

$$\text{Year 1} \qquad \frac{10,000 \times 100}{200,000} = 5\%$$

$$\text{Year 2} \qquad \frac{15,000 \times 100}{250,000} = 6\%$$

There has been an increase of 1% in the second year. This is despite a drop of 1% in the gross profit ratio. If the latter was caused by a drop in selling price, the policy has been justified in the overall increase in net profit from £10,000 to £15,000. In addition there has been a saving in the expense incurred in running the business, and to find out where the saving of 2% has occurred it is necessary to express the expenses as a percentage of sales.

Expense Ratios

Expenses are divided into three main types; fixed, variable, and semi-variable. Fixed expenses are those incurred for the general running of the business. They are not affected by the volume of sales. Administration expenses are usually given as an example of these. It takes a clerk the same amount of time to enter an invoice for £2,000 as it does for an invoice amounting to £200. On the other hand certain expenses vary according to sales, for example salesmen's commission. Some expenses fall between the previous two types and these are termed semi-variable. An example of these would be lighting and heating if overtime is worked.

In the illustration it is possible to see the absolute changes between expenses, but not the relative changes. For this reason expense ratios are prepared.

	Year 1		Year 2	
	£	%	£	%
Administrative expenses	15,000	7·5	17,500	7·0
Selling expenses	20,000	10·0	25,000	10·0
Financial expenses	5,000	2·5	2,500	1·0
Net profit	10,000	5·0	15,000	6·0
Gross profit	50,000	25·0	60,000	24·0
Sales	£200,000	100·0	£250,000	100·0

From the above it can be seen that although selling expenses have risen from £20,000 to £25,000 the relative increase has been nil, as in both years it is 10% of sales. This could be expected as selling expenses are generally variable. Although administration expenses have fallen from 7·5% to 7·0% the absolute amount has risen by £2,500. In view of the fact that these expenses tend to be fixed, this increase may be excessive and investigations should be made to see where it has occurred so that economies may be made in the future. Not only has the percentage fallen for financial expenses but also the absolute amounts. Thus there have been savings of 0·5% for administrative expenses and 1·5% for financial expenses which accounts for the difference of 2% mentioned in the preceding ratio.

Return on Assets Employed

This ratio is used to test the effective use of the assets of the business. It is calculated by expressing the net profit as a percentage of the total assets. To provide an accurate comparison the average value of assets employed during the year should be taken, but as this may be impossible to achieve the assets at the year end are usually taken. There is some discussion as to whether it is better to take the total assets less current liabilities as the denominator, the reason being that the balance sheet presents a situation at a fixed time, and is liable to great changes within a very short time, particularly with current assets and current liabilities. By subtracting current liabilities from the total assets a figure is obtained which corresponds to capital employed and long-term liabilities which tends to be constant in the short term. As this ratio attempts to show the efficiency of asset usage, goodwill, and other intangible assets are sometimes excluded from the calculation. Whichever method is adopted, provided it is used consistently, a comparison can be made.

255

In the illustration the ratios would be:

Year 1 $$\frac{10,000 \times 100}{135,000 + 50,000} = \frac{1,000,000}{185,000} = 5\cdot4\%$$

Year 2 $$\frac{15,000 \times 100}{144,000 + 51,000} = \frac{1,500,000}{195,000} = 7\cdot7\%$$

The results indicate that not only has the absolute profit increased but also the relative profit has improved. That is, the assets are being used to produce a greater proportionate profit. The business is more efficient in the second year.

Another ratio used to illustrate the use of assets is the sales/assets ratio, viz.:

Year 1 $$\frac{\text{Sales}}{\text{Assets}} = \frac{200,000}{185,000} = 1\cdot1$$

Year 2 $$\frac{\text{Sales}}{\text{Assets}} = \frac{250,000}{195,000} = 1\cdot3$$

For every £1 of assets, sales in Year 1 amounted to £1·1, whereas in Year 2 sales had increased to £1·3.

Proprietorship Ratio

The previous ratios have been concerned with profitability and efficiency. The next consideration is that of solvency. In Chapter 13 it was found that there was no correlation between profits and cash. A businessman may become a little too greedy, and in order to increase profits has to borrow money either in the form of loans or by acquiring increased credit facilities which he is unable to repay. He may over-invest in fixed assets or in stock, thereby leaving himself short of liquid resources to pay short-term debts or expenses. This is known as over-trading and is the cause of most business failures.

The businessman must keep a careful watch on his business assets and liabilities, and should the situation start to deteriorate steps should be taken to rectify the state of affairs before it becomes critical. The financial stability has to be approached from two aspects, the long term and the short. A guide to long-term stability is the proprietorship ratio which is calculated by expressing the capital employed as a percentage of the total assets. In the example given the ratios are:

Year 1 $$\frac{100,000 \times 100}{185,000} = 54 \cdot 2\%$$

Year 2 $$\frac{105,000 \times 100}{195,000} = 53 \cdot 8\%$$

The position has slightly worsened in the second year. The owner has a claim on 53·8% of the total assets compared with 54·2% in the previous year. This means that third parties have a claim on nearly half the value of the assets. It may become increasingly difficult for the business to obtain credit in the future, and should the long-term debts be due within the next few years the business would find it very difficult to repay them. The proprietorship ratio should never fall below 60% in ordinary circumstances.

Working Capital Ratio

To judge the business short-term stability the working capital ratio is used. This is calculated by dividing the current assets by the current liabilities. Current liabilities have to be paid out of money produced by current assets. If the latter are insufficient to do this, fixed assets must be sold to realise cash. Unfortunately, if this has to be done, then the scope of business activity will be diminished and the future profits will 'fall.

The ratios provided by the example are:

Year 1 $$\frac{50,000}{25,000} = 2$$

Year 2 $$\frac{51,000}{30,000} = 1 \cdot 7$$

The interpretation of these figures is that for every £1's worth of liabilities in Year 1 there were £2's worth of assets; in Year 2 this had fallen to £1·7's worth of assets. The security for creditors has fallen. It is difficult to say at this stage if this represents a critical situation. At one time it was regarded that a ratio of 2:1 was essential, but the amount would vary from business to business. What is important is the trend of the ratio and certainly in the illustration it is worsening.

Acid Test or Solvency Ratio

This ratio is a refinement of the previous one in that it gives the cash cover for current liabilities. Only current assets which are expressed in cash or which are guaranteed of producing cash are taken into account. This means that stock and work in progress will be omitted. The reason for this is that stock must be sold to a debtor or customer before receipts are guaranteed, whereas current liabilities are committed debts. In the example the ratio would be:

$$\text{Year 1} \qquad \frac{20,000 + 8,000}{25,000} = 1\cdot1$$

$$\text{Year 2} \qquad \frac{25,000 + 500}{30,000} = 0\cdot9$$

The ratio has fallen in Year 2. There was £1·1's worth of liquid assets for each £1 of liabilities which is quite adequate. In Year 2 the cover had fallen to £0·9. In addition to paying current liabilities the business has to find cash to pay the day-to-day running expenses so that the position in Year 2 would appear to be critical.

There is no overall ideal ratio although 1:1 may be taken as a rule of thumb measure. If the business in the example is that of a supermarket where stock is sold quickly and debts realised within a short time, money would soon flow into the firm. However, because of the incidence of debtors it would appear that the business operates on a credit basis and, therefore, it would be some time before money is received from the sale of current stock.

From the few ratios described in this chapter it should be possible to see that a great deal of information can be obtained from the final accounts. In this example, though profitability and efficiency have increased, these have been achieved at the cost of financial stability. It would seem that the business is overtrading and unless steps are taken to curtail sales, or bring in extra capital, the position could become very precarious in the future. The accountant can, therefore, provide the basis for deciding future management policies which will provide for healthy expansion.

EXERCISES

19.1
For the year ended 30th June, 19x3, the items in a businessman's trading account were as follows:

Stock 1.7.19x2 £6,550, stock 30.6.19x3 £7,850, sales £49,760, purchases £39,000, returns inwards £1,760, returns outwards £1,700.

(a) You are required:
  (1) To state the cost price of goods sold.
  (2) To state the amount of business turnover.
  (3) To calculate the stock turnover.
  (4) To state the gross profit percentage.
(b) On the assumption that during the following year turnover will increase by 25%, that the gross profit percentage and the rate of stock turnover will be unchanged, you are required to draw up an estimated trading account for the year ended 30th June, 19x4.

19.2
P. Norman carries on business as a retailer. His average stock is £8,000 and is turned over five times in each trading year. The average mark up is 25%, the fixed expenses amount to £4,000, and the variable expenses to 10% of turnover.

(a) Calculate the trading and profit and loss accounts for the year.
(b) If the stock turnover increases to 6 times in a year, all other items being as above, what additional profit would be made?

19.3
N. Peters carries on business as a retailer, During the year ended 31st March, 19x8, the business made a gross profit of $33\frac{1}{3}\%$ on a turnover of £75,000 and a net profit of 10%. His rate of stock turnover was 8.

By reducing his selling prices by 4% N. Peters estimates that whilst carrying the same average stock his stock turnover will increase to 12 in the following year, while his expenses will increase by £4,500.

You are required:

(a) To calculate the trading and profit and loss account for the year ended 31.3.19x8. There has been no change in the value of opening and closing stocks.
(b) To estimate the trading and profit and loss account for the following year.

19.4
The following items appeared in the trading account of a business for the year ended 31st December, 19x3.

Stock 1.1.19x3 £5,936, stock 31.12.19x3 £4,544, purchases £61,488, sales £83,840.

If the ratio of gross profit to turnover was reduced by 5%, by how much would the rate of stock turnover have to increase to maintain the same gross profit? Assume the average stock is the same as for 19x3.

19.5
The following is the balance sheet of B. Low as at 31st December, 19x4.

	£		£
Capital		Motor vehicles	1,800
Opening balance	8,000	Plant and machinery	2,000
Profit for year	3,000	Premises	4,000
	11,000	Stock	3,000
Less Drawings	2,000	Debtors	2,200
		Bank	1,940
	9,000	Cash	60
Long-term loan	3,000		
Creditors	3,000		
	£15,000		£15,000

You are required to calculate:

(1) Return on capital invested.
(2) Return on assets employed.
(3) Proprietorship ratio.
(4) Working capital ratio.
(5) Acid test ratio.

19.6
The final accounts of two firms are shown below. Compute three ratios which suggest that firm A is stronger than firm B, and three which suggest firm B is stronger than firm A.

Trading and Profit and Loss Accounts

	Firm A £	Firm B £
Sales—Cash		34,000
Credit	48,000	6,000
	48,000	40,000
Less Cost of goods sold	24,000	30,000
Gross profit	24,000	10,000
Less Expenses	22,000	8,000
Net profit	£2,000	£2,000

Balance Sheets

	Firm A £	Firm B £
Capital accounts	21,000	9,000
Long-term loans	6,000	5,000
Creditors	9,000	6,000
Bank overdraft	4,000	
	£40,000	£20,000
Freehold property	6,000	9,000
Equipment	8,000	3,000
Stock	14,000	5,000
Debtors	12,000	1,000
Bank	—	2,000
	£40,000	£20,000

19.7
C. Long purchased a business for £50,000 and commenced trading on 1st April, 19x6. From the following information you are required to prepare, in as much detail as possible, a trading and profit and loss account for the year ended 31st March, 19x7, and a balance sheet as at that date.

Drawings during the year	£5,000
Fixed assets as at 31st March, 19x7	£50,000
Working capital at 31st March, 19x7	£30,000
Long-term loan at 31st March, 19x7	£20,000
Working capital ratio at 31st March, 19x7	2:1
Acid test ratio at 31st March, 19x7	1·5:1
Ratio of sales to total assets	1·5:1
Stock turnover rate during the year	8

(*Note.* The opening and closing stocks were identical.)
Debtors at the year end amount to 20% of turnover.

20 Manufacturing Accounts

Where a business manufactures the goods it trades in, a further section is necessary to complete the final accounts. A retailer or wholesaler buys goods in a completed form and these are debited to the trading account. A manufacturer will not have an account for purchases of goods for resale, but instead will have a number of accounts in his ledger concerned with the costs involved in making those goods. These accounts must be summarised in a manufacturing account and the total, which represents the cost of goods produced, is then transferred into the trading account in place of purchases.

The manufacturing account is built up in a particular manner so as to emphasize certain elements of cost. These consist of:

    (a) Prime cost.
    (b) Factory cost.
    (c) Factory or production cost of goods completed.

Prime costs consist of the items directly attributed to the product itself and consist of direct materials, direct labour, and direct expenses. The word "direct" implies that they are an integral part of the product as opposed to indirect or factory expenses which relate to the running of the factory. Direct materials consist of all materials which are used in the product itself together with the cost of carriage inwards on those materials. Direct labour consists of the wages, salaries, and bonuses paid to operatives engaged in manufacturing the product. Amounts paid to supervisory or maintenance employees are not direct labour. Direct expenses are other items which do not fall under the two preceding headings, but can be identified with the product, for example royalties paid on a production basis.

The items comprised in the calculation of prime costs are all variable expenses, that is they increase or decrease according to the level of production.

Factory cost is the total cost of running the factory for a specific period of time. It is composed of prime cost plus factory overhead or indirect expenses. Factory overheads are all those expenses which are necessary to operate the factory, but which cannot be directly attributed to the product itself. They include wages and salaries paid to supervisory (including foremen) and service employees, rent, rates, heating and lighting of the factory, and depreciation of machinery used in production. In general, indirect expenses tend to be fixed in nature because they have to be paid irrespective of the amount of goods produced by the factory.

Factory cost of goods completed is the final calculation in the manufacturing account and represents the cost of goods which have been completely finished and have reached the condition in which they are sold. Unless the manufacturing process is extremely quick there will always be a number of goods in the factory which are partly finished. These goods will contain some or all of the direct material necessary for their completion, plus a proportion of the total direct labour expense costs. An adjustment must be made in the manufacturing account for these items, which are known as work in progress, to determine the cost of goods actually completed. The calculation consists of taking the factory cost and adding on the opening work in progress and subtracting the closing work in progress.

To illustrate the preparation of a manufacturing account and the transfer to the trading account the following example is given.

Example

The following figures were extracted from the books of a manufacturer at 31st December, 19x3.

	£
Stocks at 1.1.19x3	
Raw materials	16,000
Work in progress	10,000
Finished goods	24,000
Purchases of raw material	55,000
Carriage inwards	1,200
Manufacturing wages	28,000
Supervisory wages	7,600
Rent and rates	4,600
Heating, lighting, and cleaning	7,000
Office salaries	6,400
Plant and machinery at cost	68,000
Sales	140,600

The following information is relevant.

(a) Stocks at 31.12.19x3.

	£
Raw materials	20,000
Work in progress	19,000
Finished goods	14,400

(b) Rent and rates are to be apportioned 75% to the factory, 25% to administration.

(c) Heating, lighting, and cleaning expenses are to be apportioned 80% to the factory, 20% to administration.

(d) Plant and machinery is to be depreciated 5% on the straight line method.

You are required to prepare manufacturing, trading, and profit and loss accounts for the year ended 31st December, 19x3.

Manufacturing, Trading and Profit and Loss Accounts
Year ended 31st December, 19x3

	£	£				£
Raw materials			Factory cost of goods			
Opening stock		16,000	completed	C/D		91,250
Purchases		55,000				
Carriage inwards		1,200				
		72,200				
Less Closing stock		20,000				
Cost of materials						
consumed		52,200				
Direct wages—						
manufacturing		28,000				
PRIME COST		80,200				
Add factory over-heads						
Indirect wages—						
supervisory	7,600					
Rent and rates (75%)	3,450					
Heating, lighting and cleaning (80%)	5,600					
Depreciation— machinery	3,400					
		20,050				
		100,250				91,250

	£		£
FACTORY COST OF			
PRODUCTION	100,250		91,250
Add Opening work in progress	10,000		
	110,250		
Less Closing work in progress	19,000		
	£91,250		£91,250
Finished goods		Sales	140,600
Opening stock	24,000		
Cost of goods completed	91,250		
	115,250		
Less Closing stock	14,400		
COST OF GOODS SOLD	100,850		
Gross profit C/D	39,750		
	£140,600		£140,600
Office salaries	6,400	Gross profit B/D	39,750
Rent and rates (25%)	1,150		
Heating, lighting, and cleaning (20%)	1,400		
Net profit	30,800		
	£39,750		£39,750

Notes

1. In the balance sheet at 31st December, 19x3, there will be included under current assets the following:

	£	£
Stock of raw material	20,000	
Work in progress	19,000	
Stock of finished goods	14,400	
		53,400

2. Occasionally, if production of finished goods is below demand, finished goods may be purchased from an external supplier. In this case the total of these purchases is entered directly in the trading account with the cost of goods completed.

In the preceding example no profit was shown in the manufacturing account. The gross profit brought down in the profit and loss account represents the profits made by manufacturing and in selling the finished product. It is of great importance to the owner to know how much additional profit he is making by manufacturing the goods himself instead of buying them in their finished state from an outside supplier. Obviously, if it is costing him more to make them in his factory than to buy them from an external supplier, it would be more profitable to close the factory down and buy the finished goods direct.

To show how much profit the factory has made the finished goods are transferred from the manufacturing account to the trading account at the market value or at a value decided upon by the owners. The resultant profit is then transferred to the profit and loss account together with the now reduced profit from the trading account. The net profit will be unaffected as all that has happened is that the total gross profit has been apportioned between the manufacturing and selling functions of the business.

Example

The following balances have been extracted from the books of a manufacturer at 31st December, 19x7.

	£
Stocks at 1st January, 19x7	
Raw materials	5,600
Work in progress	7,200
Finished goods	26,000
Purchases raw material	44,000
Manufacturing wages	108,000
Supervisory wages	12,000
Factory power	2,800
Factory rates	4,400
Repairs to machinery	3,600
Depreciation on machinery	7,200
Office—Salaries	17,000
Rates	1,600
Expenses	12,000
Sales	296,000

The following information is relevant.

Stocks at 31st December, 19x7	
Raw materials	4,600
Work in progress	6,200
Finished goods	24,000

The value of goods completed during the year on the open market at trade price was £257,000.

Manufacturing, Trading, and Profit and Loss Accounts
Year ended 31st December, 19x7

	£	£			£
Raw materials			Market value of		
Opening stock		5,600	goods completed C/D		257,000
Purchases		44,000			
		49,600			
Less Closing stock		4,600			
Cost of materials					
consumed		45,000			
Direct wages—					
manufacturing		108,000			
PRIME COST		153,000			
Add Factory overheads					
Indirect wages					
supervisory	12,000				
Factory power	2,800				
Factory rates	4,400				
Repairs to					
machinery	3,600				
Depreciation of					
machinery	7,200				
		30,000			
FACTORY COST OF					
PRODUCTION		183,000			
Add Opening work					
in progress		7,200			
		190,200			
Less Closing work					
in progress		6,200			
FACTORY COST OF					
GOODS COMPLETED		184,000			
Manufacturing profit C/D		73,000			
		£257,000			£257,000

267

	£			£
Finished goods		Sales		296,000
Opening stock	26,000			
Market value of goods				
completed	257,000			
	283,000			
Less Closing stock	24,000			
COST OF GOODS SOLD	259,000			
Gross profit C/D	37,000			
	£296,000			£296,000
Office—Salaries	17,000	Manufacturing		
Rates	1,600	profit	B/D	73,000
Expenses	12,000	Gross profit on		
Net profit	79,400	trading	B/D	37,000
	£110,000			£110,000

Where there are warehouse expenses given in the list of balances it is usual to include these in the trading account. These expenses are concerned with the storage and packing of the finished product and for this reason they are regarded as not being a selling expense but as part of the cost of goods sold.

Valuation of Work in Progress and Finished Goods

Work in progress and finished goods are usually valued at factory cost, that is, the amount of direct material used in the partly finished goods, labour costs and direct expenses incurred in bringing the goods up to their present state, plus a proportion of the factory overheads.

There are objections to this method, however, and it has been suggested that work in progress and finished goods should be valued at prime cost. The argument being that factory overheads are fixed expenses and generally can be regarded as calendar costs; that is, related to a particular period rather than to production. For that reason the whole of factory overheads should be written off in the year they are incurred instead of being reduced by some element being carried forward in the closing value of work in progress and finished goods.

It is further argued that valuing work in progress and finished goods at factory cost contravenes the convention of conservatism in that it anticipates profits, viz.:

The following particulars relate to the production and sales of a certain line of goods.

	Year 1 £	Year 2 £	Year 3 £
Prime costs	2,400	3,200	1,600
Factory overheads	2,000	2,000	2,000
	units	units	units
Sales at £10 per unit	450	750	600
Production	600	800	400

There is no work in progress at the end of each of the years.
In summary form the manufacturing and trading accounts would be:

(a) Valuing stocks of finished goods at factory cost and using the FIFO method.

	Year 1		Year 2		Year 3	
	units	£	units	£	units	£
Sales	450	4,500	750	7,500	600	6,000
Opening stock	Nil	—	150	1,100	200	1,300
Prime cost	600	2,400	800	3,200	400	1,600
Factory overheads		2,000		2,000		2,000
	600	4,400	950	6,300	600	4,900
Less Closing stock	150	1,100	200	1,300	—	—
Cost of goods sold	450	3,300	750	5,000	600	4,900
Gross profit		£1,200		£2,500		£1,100

The closing stocks are calculated as follows:

Year 1   The closing stock is 150 units (production 600 less sales 450). The factory cost attributed to this amount is

$$\frac{150 \times 4,400}{600} = \text{£}1,100$$

Year 2   The closing stock is 150 units brought forward plus 800 units produced less 750 units sold. As goods sold are based on the principle of first in first out, the 200 units of stock in hand relate to the current year's production so the value attributed to these is

$$\frac{200}{800} \times 5,200 \text{ (the factory cost)} = \text{£}1,300$$

269

Year 3 There is no closing stock, the opening stock of 200 units plus the 400 units produced in the period equal the number of units sold.

(b) Valuing stocks of finished goods at prime cost and using the FIFO method.

	Year 1		Year 2		Year 3	
	Units	£	Units	£	Units	£
Sales	450	4,500	750	7,500	600	6,000
Opening stock	—	—	150	600	200	800
Prime cost	600	2,400	800	3,200	400	1,600
Factory overheads		2,000		2,000		2,000
	600	4,400	950	5,800	600	4,400
Less Closing stock	150	600	200	800	—	—
	450	3,800	750	5,000	600	4,400
Gross profit		£700		£2,500		£1,600

The number of units of closing stock are identical to the former example, but the values are calculated as under:

Year 1
$$\frac{150 \times 2,400}{600} \text{ (prime cost)} = £600$$

Year 2
$$\frac{200 \times 3,200}{800} \text{ (prime cost)} = £800$$

Because the production and sales of units during the three years are identical and there is no opening or closing stock at the beginning and end of the three-year period, the aggregate profits in each method will agree, but a comparison of the annual profits shows the following result:

	Factory cost £	Prime cost £
Year 1	1,200	700
Year 2	2,500	2,500
Year 3	1,100	1,600
	£4,800	£4,800

It will be noticed that valuing closing stock of finished goods at factory cost produces higher profits in the first year and lower in the third year. The argument for valuing stock on this basis is that the amount shown in the balance sheet presents a more accurate picture of the market

270

value of the goods, whereas valuing them at prime costs understates their value. Furthermore, a number of factory overheads are not completely fixed in nature. For example, depreciation may be written off on a machine hour rate, additional heating and lighting is required for overtime working, the number of supervisory staff depends on the number of operatives. These examples show that some of the factory overheads are at least semi-variable and should be included in the valuation of closing stock of finished goods and work in progress.

The problem of valuation is somewhat similar to the problems involved in the valuation of closing stocks of goods purchased for resale outlined in Chapter 10. Whichever method is decided upon that method should be applied consistently so that the accounts are comparable from year to year.

EXERCISES

20.1
From the following information prepare a manufacturing, trading, and profit and loss account for the year ended 30th June, 19x5.

		£
Stocks 1st July, 19x4		
	Raw materials	6,000
	Work in progress	2,000
	Finished goods	9,000
Sales		160,000
Purchases of raw materials		44,000
Carriage inwards		5,500
Carriage outwards		1,400
Direct wages—factory		60,000
Indirect wages—factory		10,000
Factory rent and rates		600
Office rent and rates		500
Factory heat, light, and power		3,000
Office heat, light, and power		1,900
Office salaries		7,000
Salesmen's salaries		11,000
Repairs to plant and machinery		400
Depreciation plant and machinery		5,600
Sundry factory expenses		200
Stocks 30th June, 19x5		
	Raw materials	3,000
	Work in progress	5,000
	Finished goods	7,000

20.2

From the following information prepare manufacturing, trading, and profit and loss accounts for the year ended 30th September, 19x4.

	£
Stocks 1st October, 19x3	
Raw materials	18,000
Work in progress	3,000
Finished goods	3,500
Sales	810,000
Purchases raw materials	290,000
Carriage inwards	2,000
Factory—Direct wages	280,000
Indirect wages	34,000
Overhead expenses	20,000
Depreciation—Plant and machinery	30,000
Factory buildings	1,500
Office buildings	400
Office salaries	42,000
Office expenses	38,000
Carriage outwards	5,000
Discount allowed	6,000
Discount received	4,000
Stocks 30th September, 19x4	
Raw materials	14,000
Work in progress	6,000
Finished goods	26,000

20.3

From the following particulars relating to J. Blower, a manufacturer of machine components, prepare a manufacturing, trading, and profit and loss account for the year ended 31st December, 19x2.

	£
Stocks 1st January, 19x2	
Raw materials	50,000
Work in progress	14,500
Finished goods	50,000
Purchases raw material	95,000
Sales	193,000
Factory—Direct wages	20,000
Indirect wages	5,500
Office salaries	10,400
Carriage inwards	2,500
Carriage outwards	7,500
Factory overhead expenses	21,500
Repairs to plant and machinery	5,400
Office expenses	8,500
Salesmen's salaries	13,500

	£
Stocks 31st December, 19x2	
Raw materials	57,000
Work in progress	9,000
Finished goods	73,000

Note. Profit on factory production is taken in the manufacturing account and for this purpose the market value at trade price of the goods completed in the year was estimated at £180,000.

20.4

From the following particulars prepare a manufacturing, trading, and profit and loss account for the year ended 31st March, 19x7.

	£
Stocks 1st April, 19x6	
Raw materials	23,200
Work in progress	7,700
Finished goods	10,500
Purchases raw materials	65,000
Factory—Direct wages	25,600
Indirect wages	5,100
Office salaries	12,200
Warehouse wages	4,600
Carriage inwards	450
Rent and rates—Factory	2,600
Office	800
Warehouse	500
Factory power	6,000
Factory indirect expenses	4,500
Office expenses	3,000
Warehouse expenses	2,800
Sales	165,300
Stocks 31st March, 19x7	
Raw materials	17,600
Work in progress	8,500
Finished goods	9,200

Note. Profit is taken in the manufacturing account for goods produced. The trade price of these was estimated at £130,000.

20.5

From the following information you are required to prepare manufacturing, trading, and profit and loss accounts for the year ended 30th June, 19x8, and a balance sheet as at that date.

	£
Capital account	68,850
Buildings at cost	36,000
Plant and machinery at cost	34,500

273

	£
Stocks 1st July, 19x7	
Raw materials	4,500
Work in progress	6,900
Finished goods	5,400
Debtors	19,500
Creditors	9,750
Prepaid expenses 30th June, 19x8	2,850
Accrued expenses 30th June, 19x8	3,450
Provisions for depreciation 1st July, 19x7	
Buildings	6,000
Plant and machinery	15,000
Drawings	12,000
Cash at bank	4,500
Sales	138,000
Carriage inwards	900
Salesmen's salaries and expenses	7,500
Bad debts	75
Heat and light—Factory	500
Offices	250
Wages—Factory direct	22,650
Factory indirect	6,075
Rates—Factory	600
Office	300
Printing and stationery	3,150
Purchases raw materials	31,800
finished goods	34,350
Office expenses	1,800
Factory overhead expenses	3,000
Motor vehicle expenses	1,950

The following information is relevant:

(a) Stocks 30th June, 19x8

	£
Raw materials	3,000
Work in progress	6,750
Finished goods	1,150

(b) Depreciation is to be provided for

	£
Plant and machinery	3,000
Factory buildings	1,500
Office buildings	500

20.6

The following balances were extracted from the books of J. Pillar as at 31st March, 19x9.

	£
Capital account	59,360
Drawings	4,000
Debtors	28,460
Creditors	25,000
Balance at bank	11,660

	£
Factory machinery (cost £56,000)	46,000
Office fixtures (cost £4,000)	2,400
Stock 1st April, 19x8	
Raw materials	4,200
Work in progress	2,700
Finished goods	7,780
Factory—Direct wages	36,000
Indirect wages	29,000
Office salaries	8,800
Salesmen's salaries	8,300
Discount allowed	960
Factory overhead expenses	6,200
Production royalties paid	1,400
Purchase raw materials	74,000
Office expenses	2,680
Bank charges	460
Carriage inwards	700
Carriage outwards	1,180
Factory power	2,740
Lighting and heating	1,500
Rent and rates	2,400
Insurance	840
Sales	200,000

You are required to prepare a manufacturing, trading, and profit and loss account for the year ended 31st March, 19x9, and a balance sheet as at that date after taking into account the following information:

(a) Stocks as at 31st March, 19x9   £

	£
Raw materials	4,800
Work in progress	3,000
Finished goods	8,000

(b) Lighting and heating, rent and rates, and insurance are to be apportioned 80% to the factory, 20% to offices.
(c) Depreciation is to be provided for
    Factory machinery   10% on cost
    Office fixtures   5% on cost

20.7
The information given below relates to production and sales of a manufacturer for three years. Calculate the gross profits made each year valuing closing stock on:
(1) Prime cost.
(2) Factory cost.
The business adopts the principle of first in, first out for all sales.

	Year 1	Year 2	Year 3
	£	£	£
Prime costs	2,500	5,000	4,000
Factory overheads	3,000	3,400	3,000

275

	Units	Units	Units
Sales (£12 per unit)	300	800	1,200
Production	500	1,000	800

There is no work in progress at the beginning or end of each year.

21 Joint Venture Accounts

On certain occasions it may be to the benefit of two or more persons or businesses to act together for a particular undertaking. This undertaking is known as a joint venture and its working is similar to a partnership. The main difference is that each business retains its identity instead of combining into one firm. The joint venture ceases when the particular operation that brought it into being has been achieved. There is nothing to stop the same individuals or businesses entering into a series of joint ventures, but each will be treated as a separate venture.

A joint venture might occur where one business has an opportunity of acquiring certain goods which are not in its usual line of purchases. In order to sell the goods it may enter into a joint venture with another person who has business or social contacts and through him find customers. An agreement must be reached beforehand as to how any profits are to be divided and the rights and duties of each venturer.

Unless the joint venture is of such a size or so complicated as to warrant a separate bank account and books of account, the entries relating to the venture are incorporated in the books of each venturer. Each party to the venture will pay certain sums into the undertaking and will also receive amounts from the proceeds of sale. At the conclusion of the venture an account will be drawn up to show the profit attributable to each venturer and the amounts to be paid among them to settle their indebtedness to each other.

There are two methods of incorporating the joint venture in the books. The first method consists of opening a single account termed the joint venture account and shows only the transactions relating to the person in whose books the account is opened. The second method involves two or more accounts, these being a joint venture account and personal accounts relating to the other venturers. In this second method all transactions relating to the venture are recorded in each venturer's books. Students should be careful to ensure that the correct method is given when answering examination questions.

Example

Sun and Moon entered into a joint venture to buy and sell sports equipment. They agree to share profits, Sun 60%, Moon 40%. Details of their transactions are

	£
Sun supplied equipment costing	800
Moon supplied equipment costing	400
Sun paid storage expenses	50
Sun paid advertising expenses	30
Moon paid selling expenses	120
Sun received cash from sales	900
Moon received cash from sales	1,100

Method One

Under this method it will be necessary to compile a memorandum joint venture account made up from particulars supplied by each venturer. Although it may be entered in the books of each venturer it does not form part of the double entry. Its purpose is to determine the profit made on the venture.

Memorandum Joint Venture Account

	£	£		£	£
Sports equipment			Cash sales		
Sun	800		Sun	900	
Moon	400		Moon	1,100	
		1,200			2,000
Expenses					
Sun—storage	50				
Sun—advertising	30				
Moon—selling expenses	120				
Profit divisible		200			
Sun 60%	360				
Moon 40%	240				
		600			
		£2,000			£2,000

Having calculated the profit it can be included in each venturer's books.

In Sun's Books

Joint Venture with Moon

	£		£
Cash—Sports equipment	800	Cash—sales	900
Storage	50	Balance	340
Advertising	30		
Transfer profit and loss account			
Profit on venture	360		
	£1,240		£1,240
Balance	340		

In Moon's Books

Joint Venture with Sun

	£		£
Cash—Sports equipment	400	Cash—sales	1,100
Selling expenses	120		
Transfer profit and loss account			
Profit on venture	240		
Balance	340		
	£1,100		£1,100
		Balance	340

It can be seen from the two accounts above that Moon owes Sun £340. To close off the venture Sun should pay Moon this amount. The entries are:
(a) in Sun's books debit cash, credit joint venture account,
(b) in Moon's books credit cash, debit joint venture account.

Method Two

In this method all transactions relevant to the joint venture are recorded in each venturer's books.

279

In Sun's Books

Joint Venture with Moon

	£	£		£
Cash—Sports equipment	800		Cash—sales	900
Storage	50		Transfer Moon personal a/c	
Advertising	30		Sales	1,100
Transfer Moon personal a/c		880		
Sports equipment	400			
Selling expenses	120			
Profit transferred		520		
Profit and loss a/c	360			
Moon personal a/c	240			
		600		
		£2,000		£2,000

Moon Personal Account

	£		£
Transfer joint venture a/c		Transfer joint venture a/c	
Sales	1,100	Sports equipment	400
		Selling expenses	120
		Profit	240
		Balance	340
	£1,100		£1,100

In Moon's Books

Joint Venture with Sun

	£	£		£
Cash—Sports equipment	400			
Selling expenses	120		Cash—sales	1,10
Transfer Sun personal a/c		520	Transfer Sun personal a/c	
Sports equipment	800		Sales	9(
Storage	50			
Advertising	30			
Profit transferred		880		
Profit and loss a/c	240			
Sun personal a/c	360			
		600		
		£2,000		£2,0(

Sun Personal Account

	£			£
Transfer joint venture a/c	900	Transfer joint venture a/c		
Balance	340	Sports equipment		800
		Storage		50
		Advertising		30
		Profit		360
	£1,240			£1,240
		Balance		340

The results in each method are identical. The amount due between venturers to settle the venture is shown in the joint venture account in method one, whereas it is brought down in the personal account in method two. To compensate for the additional entries necessary in method two the benefit is that all transactions are incorporated in the books of account. In practice the entries in the joint venture account would be in chronological order instead of the summarised form shown in the example.

Certain refinements may have to be made to the basic structure of joint venture accounting to deal with the following circumstances:

1. Cash paid by one venturer to another during the course of the joint venture.
2. Sales made by any of the venturers on a credit basis.
3. Stock taken out of the joint venture by one of the parties for his own use.
4. Where the period of the venture extends beyond the accounting year of any of the venturers.

The recording of the first three circumstances is dealt with in the following illustration.

Example

Jones and Casey enter into a joint venture to buy and sell paintings. They agree to share profits equally. A summary of their transactions is:

	£
Jones bought paintings	300
Casey bought paintings	400
Jones paid renovation expenses	150
Jones paid cash to Casey on account	100
Casey paid selling expenses	50

281

	£
Jones received cash from sales	800
Casey sold paintings on credit	500
Casey received cash from debtors	300
Jones retained a painting for his own use valued at	100

Using Method 1

Memorandum Joint Venture Account

	£	£		£	£
Paintings			Sales		
Jones	300		Jones	800	
Casey	400		Casey	500	
	—	700		—	1,300
Expenses			Painting acquired		
Jones	150		by Jones		100
Casey	50				
	—	200			
Profit					
Jones	250				
Casey	250				
	—	500			
		£1,400			£1,400

There is no need to enter the cash transfer between Jones and Casey.

In Jones' Books

Joint Venture Account with Casey

	£		£
Cash—Paintings	300	Cash—sales	800
Renovation expenses	150	Transfer drawings	100
Cash to Casey	100	(painting acquired for	
Transfer profit and loss a/c	250	own use)	
Balance	100		
	£900		£900
		Balance	100

Note

In the above account the painting acquired for own use has been transferred to drawings account. In other circumstances it would be transferred to purchases if it was the type of goods sold in the normal course of the venturers' business, or transferred to fixed asset account if relevant.

In Casey's Books

Joint Venture with Jones

	£		£
Cash—Paintings	400	Credit sales	500
Selling expenses	50	Cash received from Jones	100
Transfer profit and loss a/c	250	Balance	100
	£700		£700
Balance	100		

Joint Venture Debtors

	£		£
Credit sales	500	Cash received	300
		Balance	200
	£500		£500
Balance	200		

Note

Although the debtors have been shown in a total account, in fact separate accounts should be opened for each debtor. Thus, Casey is owed £100 by his co-venturer, and £200 by debtors. It may be advisable to wait until all cash has been received from the debtors before calculating the profit in case any bad debts are suffered.

Using Method 2

In Jones' Books

Joint Venture with Casey

	£	£		£
Cash—Paintings	300		Cash—sales	800
Renovation			Transfer Casey	
expenses	150		credit sales	500
Transfer—Casey		450	Transfer drawings	
Paintings	400		painting taken over	100
Selling expenses	50			
Profit transferred		450		
Profit and loss a/c	250			
Casey	250			
		500		
		£1,400		£1,400

283

Casey Personal Account

	£		£
Transfer joint venture a/c		Transfer joint venture a/c	
credit sales	500	Paintings	400
Cash paid to Casey	100	Selling expenses	50
Balance	100	Profit	250
	£700		£700
		Balance	100

Note
The £100 paid by Jones to Casey is debited directly to Casey's personal account.

In Casey's Books

Joint Venture with Jones

	£	£		£	£
Cash—Paintings	400		Debtors—credit sales		500
Selling expenses	50		Transfer Jones		
Transfer Jones		450	Cash sales	800	
Paintings	300		Painting taken over	100	
Renovation					900
expenses	150				
Profit transferred		450			
Profit and loss a/c	250				
Jones	250				
		500			
		£1,400			£1,400

Jones' Personal Account

	£		£
Transfer joint venture a/c		Transfer joint venture a/c	
Cash sales	800	Paintings	300
Painting taken over	100	Renovation expenses	150
		Profit	250
		Cash received from	
		Jones	100
		Balance	100
	£900		£900
Balance	100		

284

Joint Venture Debtors

	£		£
Credit sales	500	Cash received	300
		Balance	200
	£500		£500
Balance	200		

Where the venture extends beyond the financial year-end an interim statement should be prepared showing the profit earned at that stage. The balance of unsold stock should be brought down on the joint venture account to continue the undertaking in the following period. The profit earned should be credited to the profit and loss account and any balances entered on the venturer's own balance sheet under current assets or current liabilities.

When the venture is of such magnitude as to warrant a separate bank account, the venturers will each pay in an agreed amount. All dealings are then paid from or into this bank account. Books of account are opened and when the venture is completed final accounts will be drawn up. The balance in the bank will be distributed to the venturers according to their entitlements which should then close all the remaining balances in the joint venture ledger.

The entries required in the venturer's own books will be:

Joint Venture with xxxxxxx

	£		£
Cash paid into joint venture bank account	xxx	Cash received from joint venture bank account	xxx
Transfer: Profit and loss account profit on venture	xxx		
	£xxx		£xxx

EXERCISES

21.1

Blue and Gold enter into a joint venture to buy and sell bicycles. They agree to share profits 2:1 respectively. The following is a list of their transactions.

			£
Mar.	1	Blue bought bicycles at an auction for	420
	1	Blue paid storage charges of	35
	6	Gold paid for repairing and renovating bicycles	125

285

		£
12	Blue paid advertising and sundry charges	48
22	Gold bought bicycles costing	150
25	Gold paid selling expenses amounting to	56
31	Blue received for sale of bicycles	600
31	Gold received for sale of bicycles	570

You are required to write up in each venturer's books the accounts necessary to show all the transactions of the joint venture including the final cash settlement between the venturers.

21.2

Jones and Robinson enter into a joint venture to buy and sell second-hand furniture. They agree to share profits Jones 60%, Robinson 40%.

The following is a list of their transactions:

		£
Jan. 1	Jones bought furniture costing	327
	Jones paid carriage charges	72
5	Robinson bought furniture costing	136
15	Jones paid for repairs	204
22	Robinson paid advertising charges	25
	Robinson paid insurance	15
28	Jones received cash for sales	600
	Robinson received cash for sales	363
	Robinson retained furniture for his own use valued at	136

You are required to prepare a memorandum joint venture account and to show the entries in each of the venturer's books necessary to record only their respective transactions regarding the joint venture.

21.3

Adams and Lever enter into a joint venture to buy and sell diamond rings. They agree to share profits equally after each venturer received a commission of 10% on the sales made by him.

The following is a list of their transactions:

		£
June 1	Adams bought goods for	1,250
8	Lever bought goods for	850
8	Adams paid insurance charges of	120
9	Adams paid for packing material	80
15	Adams sent a cheque to Lever for	300
28	Lever paid sales expenses of	140
30	Adams received cash from sales	2,400
30	Lever received cash from sales	1,400

You are required to write up in each venturer's books the accounts necessary to show all the transactions of the joint venture including the final cash settlement between the venturers.

286

21.4

Old and Young enter into a joint venture to buy and sell second-hand motor vehicles. They agree to share profits in the ratio 3:2 respectively.

On 1st September, 19x3, Old purchases two vehicles for £1,500. On 3rd September he spent £200 on new parts and repairs, and £50 on tax and insurance. He sold the vehicles on 15th September, 19x3, for £2,200.

On 22nd September, 19x3, Young purchases four vehicles for £2,750. He sold three of these vehicles for £3,200 on 25th September.

The remaining vehicle which was unsold was taken over by Young for use of his business at a valuation of £700.

It was agreed that before the profits are calculated expenses of £150 are allowed for Old, and £100 for Young to compensate for the time and effort put into the venture by each.

You are required to prepare the memorandum joint venture account and the entries in each venturer's books to record their respective transactions.

21.5

Rough and Smooth enter into a joint venture to buy and sell antiques. They agree to share profits equally.

On 2nd October they attended an auction and Rough acquired antiques paying £1,600 by cheque. Expenses of £50 were incurred of which Rough paid £35 and Smooth £15.

On October 15th Rough sold antiques for £650, and on the 20th October Smooth sold the remainder for £2,500. All these sales being on a credit basis. Selling expenses amounted to £120 of which £75 was paid by Rough and £45 by Smooth.

On 31st October Rough had received £500 from debtors and Smooth £2,000. At this date the joint venture was wound up. It was agreed that Smooth would be responsible for the collection of all the outstanding debts of the venture.

You are required to write up the transactions in the books of Smooth necessary to record all the transactions of the joint venture.

21.6

Wilson, Heath and West enter into a joint venture to buy and sell electrical goods. They agree to share profits 4:3:3 respectively.

The transactions were as follows:

			£
Apr.	1	Wilson bought radios paying by cheque	310
	1	Heath paid insurance charges	90
	3	Wilson bought record players paying by cheque	210
	6	Heath paid selling expenses	35
	7	Wilson bought records for resale costing	70
	12	Wilson bought plugs, connectors etc. for	55
	18	West bought radios paying by cheque	140

		£
25	West paid incidental expenses	26
26	Heath bought packing materials	14
30	West received cash from sales	1,250
	Wilson took over the unsold stock for use in his	
	own business, valued at	100

You are required to show the accounts necessary to record all the above transactions in the books of West, showing the cash adjustment necessary to close the joint venture.

22 Consignment Accounts

When a business wishes to sell goods in different parts of the country or abroad it may be advisable to appoint an agent to find customers for those goods, rather than set up a branch office. There are many advantages to be obtained by doing this. The volume of trade may not warrant the expense of establishing an office, or the sales may be so spasmodic that there is not sufficient work available to employ a permanent staff. The agent will have business contacts in his locality and, therefore, easier access to the market for these goods. Costs will also be saved, for the agent will only receive the expenses he has incurred in selling the goods plus a commission based on the sales he has made which will be far less than the costs of running a branch office.

The important thing to remember with consignments is that the goods never belong to the agent. If he is unable to sell them, the goods are returned to the principal. Whilst goods are in the hands of the agent he is responsible for them and must indemnify the principal if any are lost. The agent is also responsible for the collection of monies from the persons to whom he has sold the goods and must remit these receipts less any expenses and commission to the principal.

There are specialised terms used in consignment accounting which must be understood. A number of these terms and their meanings are given below.

Consignor. This refers to the principal in the transaction, that is, the person who owns the goods and sends them to his agent.

Consignee. This is the agent in the transaction who received the goods and sells them on behalf of the consignor.

Del Credere Commission. This commission represents an additional payment to the agent over and above his normal commission. It is given when the consignee indemnifies the consignor against any bad debts that might arise as the result of the sales made by him. Some consignors insist on this guarantee otherwise the consignee might, in order to dispose of all the goods he has received, sell them to known bad payers or to other customers without investigating their credit worthiness.

Pro Forma Invoice. This document is sent to the consignee giving details of the goods sent to him. It is used for information only as the goods are still the property of the consignor. The details it contains are usually the number or weight of the goods, a description of them, and the minimum selling price. No entry is required in the books of account of either the consignor or consignee in respect of this invoice.

Account Sales. This is a document sent by the consignee to the consignor giving details of the sales he has made, the expenses he has suffered and the commission to which he is entitled. The net amount is the sum due to the principal. In some instances the agent's commission is not calculated on sales but on cash collected from debtors.

The entries required in the respective books of consignor and consignee vary considerably. The consignor has not only to keep a record of the consignee's indebtedness, but also as the unsold goods are still his he must incorporate a system of stock control. The consignee need only keep a record of the sales and expenses relative to the consignment. For this reason the accounting entries are dealt with in two sections.

Consignor's records

Four basic accounts are required.

1. *Goods Sent on Consignments Account.* This account is a comprehensive account and includes all goods consigned during the trading period to all agents. The initial entry is to credit this account with the cost price of goods consigned. At the end of the trading period the total of this account is transferred to the credit of the trading account.

2. *Individual Consignment Outwards Accounts.* These are opened for each agent and are debited with the cost of the goods consigned plus any expenses incurred on the consignment. The latter will include not only expenses originally paid by the consignor, but also expenses incurred by, and commission due to, the consignee. Credit items will be in respect of sales made by the consignee together with any goods returned by him. The purpose of this account is to calculate profits on consignments and keep a record of stocks.

3. *Individual Consignees Personal Accounts.* An account must be opened for each agent which shows the amount due from the agent.

The account is debited with sales made, and credited with the agent's expenses and commission.

4. *Profit and Loss on Consignments Account.* This account is also a comprehensive account and contains profits made on all consignments carried out during the trading period. The total of this account is transferred to the credit of profit and loss account at the year end.

The method outlined above may seem unnecessarily complicated. Unfortunately it is essential, for the initial consigning of the goods does not represent a sale, it is a mere transfer of stock from one locality to another. Profit can only be taken when the goods have been sold by the agent. In the meantime records must be kept to show the value of the goods in the consignor's books.

Example

G. Lamb consigned 300 cases of goods to B. Cook in Otago on 1st February, 19x3. B. Cook is entitled to a commission of 5% on sales and an additional del credere commission of 2% on sales.

The goods cost G. Lamb £8 a case and he paid £280 in freight charges and insurance premiums of £100.

B. Cook received the cases on 28th February, 19x3, and on 31st March, 19x3, he sent an account sales to G. Lamb showing he had sold all the cases for £15 each, and had incurred landing charges of £580 and selling expenses of £120.

You are required to show the account sales sent by B. Cook and to record the transactions in the books of G. Lamb, whose year end is 31st December.

ACCOUNT SALES

B. Cook.
Otago,
New Zealand.

Consignment of goods sold on behalf of G. Lamb, England.

	£	£
Sales: 300 cases at £15 each		4,500
Payments.		
Landing charges	580	
Selling expenses	120	
		700
		3,800
Commission at 5% on £4,500	225	
Del credere commission at 2% on £4,500	90	
		315
		£3,485

Goods sent on Consignments

	£		£
Dec. 31. Transfer trading a/c	—	Feb. 1. Consignment to B. Cook	2,400

Consignment outwards to B. Cook, Otago

	£		£
Feb. 1. Goods sent on consignment	2,400	Mar. 31. Transfer B. Cook.	4,500
Cash freight charges	280		
Cash insurance premiums	100		
Mar. 31. Transfer B. Cook			
Landing charges	580		
Selling expenses	120		
Commission	225		
Del credere commission	90		
Profit and loss on consignments	705		
	£4,500		£4,500

B. Cook, Otago

	£		£
Mar. 31. Consignment—sales	4,500	Mar. 31. Consignment	
		Landing charges	580
		Selling expenses	120
		Commission	225
		Del credere commission	90
		Balance	3,485
	£4,500		£4,500
Balance	3,485		

Profit and Loss on Consignments

	£		£
Dec. 31. Transfer profit and loss account	—	Mar. 31. Consignment B. Cook	705

292

The effect of transferring the balance on goods sent on consignment account to the credit of the trading account is that the total amount of purchases is reduced. This means that the amount for purchases, i.e. the debit for total purchases less the credit for goods sent on consignment represents the cost of goods sold direct by G. Lamb. For this reason the goods on consignment are sometimes posted straight to the purchases account. The main objection to this is that if this is done the final accounts do not show what proportion of goods have been sold through agents.

The balance on B. Cook's account will be shown in the balance sheet as a debtor, though in practice the amount is usually remitted with the account sales or a bill of exchange is accepted by the agent (see next chapter).

Consignee's Records

As previously stated, the records in the agent's books are less involved. He does not have to keep a record of stock except by way of memorandum. The reason for this is that goods do not belong to him, he is merely holding them on behalf of the consignor, therefore there is no need to record the fact that the goods have been received. Only those transactions which affect the consignee, i.e. sales of goods for which he must account to the consignor, expenses incurred for the consignment, and commission received, are entered. The accounts involved are:

1. *The Consignor's Personal Account* (also known as Consignment Inwards). In this account are debited all expenses relating to the consignment. Sales of the specific goods are credited, the reason being that they cannot be credited to the sales account as they are not in respect of the agent's own goods. Commission due is debited to this account; the balance represents monies owing to the consignor.

2. *Commissions Received Account.* The commission debited in (1) is credited to this account which acts as a collection centre. At the end of the agent's trading period the total of this account is transferred to the credit of the profit and loss account.

3. *Debtors Account.* These are in respect of credit sales and it is the agent's duty to collect the money owing. Even if he is not receiving a del credere commission he should take all reasonable steps to obtain payment.

To illustrate the entries in the consignee's books the facts given in the previous example have been taken with the additional information that all sales were on a credit basis and that £3,800 has been received from debtors. The agent's financial year end is 31st December.

CONSIGNMENT INWARDS FROM G. LAMB

	£		£
Mar. 31 Cash—Landing charges	580	Mar. 31 Debtors—credit sales	4,500
Selling expenses	120		
Transfer commission received.			
Commission (5%)	225		
Del credere commission (2%)	90		
Balance	3,485		
	£4,500		£4,500
		Mar. 31 Balance	3,485

Commissions Received

	£		£	£
Dec. 31 Transfer profit and loss account	—	Mar. 31 G. Lamb commission	225	
		del credere	90	315

Debtors Accounts

	£		£
Mar. 31 Goods	4,500	Mar. 31 Cash received	3,800
		Balance	700
	£4,500		£4,500
Mar. 31 Balance	700		

The example shown illustrates the book-keeping entries when the consignment is commenced and brought to a conclusion within a specific trading period. It is inevitable that where a principal conducts a large part of his business through consignments, certain of these will be uncompleted at his year end.

This raises two problems in the consignor's books. The first is that of valuing the unsold stock for balance sheet purposes. The second problem is the calculation of the profit earned to the date of the balance sheet for inclusion in the profit and loss account. The amount of profit depends on the value placed on stock so the two problems are inter-related.

In Chapter 10 it was stated that stock should be valued at the lower of cost or market value. Cost represented the amount expended in bringing the goods to a saleable condition. In the case of goods on consignment this means that the goods will be valued at their original cost to the consignor plus a proportion of the expenses involved in getting them to their new destination. This will include carriage, insurance, landing duties, but excluding any selling expenses and agent's commission. Should this valuation exceed the value at which the goods can be sold then the latter value should be taken.

The amount of stock so calculated is entered as a credit in the consignment account. The account is balanced, the difference being the profit made up to date which is transferred to the profit and loss on consignments account for incorporation in the main profit and loss account. The stock figure is brought down as a debit and as such is entered as a current asset in the balance sheet, the description being "stock of goods on consignment'. Any further expenses are entered in the consignment account together with the remaining sales and the account is closed in the normal manner.

Example

Foster consigned goods to Bell on 1st April and it was agreed that Bell should receive a commission of 5% on the sales plus a further 2% del credere commission.

The consignment consisted of 120 articles valued at £50 each. Foster paid carriage charges of £200 and insurance premium of £160.

On 30th June Bell submitted an account sales showing 84 articles had been sold for £5,800. Bell had paid landing charges and duty of £180, and £125 in selling expenses. He sent Foster a remittance of £4,500 which represented cash he had received from debtors in respect of sales.

On 30th September articles had realised £2,600 and Bell had incurred further selling expenses of £120. The amount due to Foster was remitted on 7th October.

Foster makes up his accounts to 30th June.

You are required to write up the necessary accounts in Foster's books to record these transactions.

GOODS SENT ON CONSIGNMENT

	£			£
June 30 Transfer Trading a/c	6,000	Apr. 1 Consignment to Bell		6,000

Consignment Outwards to Bell

		Units	£			Units	£
Apr. 1	Goods sent on			June 30	Tfr. Bell		
	consignment	120	6,000		sales	84	5,800
	Cash—Carriage		200		Stock	36	1,962
	Insurance		160				
June 30	Transfer Bell						
	Landing charges		180				
	Selling expenses		125				
	Commission		290				
	Del credere						
	commission		116				
	Profit and loss on						
	consignments		691				
		120	£7,762			120	£7,762
July 1	Stock	36	1,962	Sept. 30	Tfr. Bell		
Sept. 30	Transfer Bell				sales	36	2,600
	Selling expenses		120				
	Commission		130				
	Del credere						
	commission		52				
	Profit and loss on						
	consignments		336				
		36	£2,600			36	£2,600

Note

The stock at 30 June is calculated

	£
Original cost	6,000
Carriage	200
Insurance	160
Landing charges	180
Total value of 120 articles	£6,540

Value of 36 articles $\frac{36}{120} \times 6,540 = 1,962$.

BELL

	£			£
June 30. Consignment sales	5,800	June 30	Consignment	
			Landing	
			charges	180
			Selling expenses	125
			Commission	290
			Del credere	
			commission	116
			Cash	4,500
			Balance	589
	£5,800			£5,800
July 1 Balance	589	Sept. 30	Consignment	
Sept. 30 Consignment sales	2,600		Selling expenses	120
			Commission	130
			Del credere	
			commission	52
		Oct. 7	Cash	2,887
	£3,189			£3,189

Profit and Loss on Consignments

	£			£
June 30 Transfer profit and				
loss account	691	June 30	Consignment Bell	691
		Sept. 30	Consignment Bell	£336

On the 30th June the balance of £1,962 on the consignment to Bell account will appear on Foster's balance sheet as stock on consignment. The balance of £589 on Bell's personal account will appear as a debtor.

In the consignee's books, assuming that his year end is 31st December, the accounts will comprise:

CONSIGNMENT INWARDS FROM FOSTER

		£			£
June 30	Cash—Landing charges	180	June 30	Debtors—sales	5,800
	Selling expenses	125			
	Transfer commission				
	received	290			
	Del credere commission	116			
	Cash—payment on				
	account	4,500			
	Balance	589			
		£5,800			£5,800
Sept. 30	Cash—Selling expenses	120	July 1	Balance	589
	Transfer commission		Sept. 30	Debtors—sales	2,600
	received	130			
	Del credere commission	52			
Oct. 7	Cash	2,887			
		£3,189			£3,189

Commission Received

		£			£
Dec. 31	Transfer profit and		June 30	Commission	290
	loss account	588		Del credere commission	116
			Sept. 30	Commission	130
				Del credere commission	52
		£588			£588

Debtors Accounts

		£			£
June 30	Goods	5,800	June 30	Cash	4,500
				Balance	1,300
		£5,800			£5,800
July 1	Balance	1,300	Oct. 7	Cash	3,900
Sept. 30	Goods	2,600			
		£3,900			£3,900

The sales would be entered in the books as and when they arise. The commissions would be calculated each month and transferred to commissions received account. Thus, no problem would arise should the consignment transactions cover more than one accounting period.

22.1

On 1st July, 19x8, B. Ryan consigned 100 cases of goods to W. Thompson in Ottawa. The goods cost £20 a case and Ryan paid £100 carriage and £40 in respect of insurance premiums.

Ryan received an account sales from his agent showing that up to 31st August, 19x8, 75 cases had been sold for £28 a case and that landing charges of £80 and selling expenses of £40 had been incurred.

The agent was entitled to a commission of 5% on sales and an additional del credere commission of 2% on sales. Money received from the agent amounting to £1,700 at 31st August.

Prepare the necessary accounts in Ryan's ledger to record the above mentioned transactions and to determine the profit at 31st August, 19x8.

22.2

On 1st March, 19x3 Torrence of Manchester consigned 200 cases of cutlery to Turner in Jamaica. The cost of the goods was £30 per case. Torrence paid carriage, freight, and insurance amounting to £150.

On arrival in Jamaica Turner paid landing and customs charges of £60. Turner was entitled to a commission of 5% on sales and a del credere commission of 1% on sales.

Turner sold 100 cases at £45 per case and 20 cases at £40 per case, and in doing so incurred selling expenses of £80. Details of these transactions were given in an account sales which was received on 30th June, 19x3 together with a remittance of £3,000.

Both Torrence and Turner make up their accounts to 30th June.

You are required:

(a) to draw up the account sales,
(b) show the entries in the consignor's books, and
(c) show the consignor's account in the consignee's books.

22.3

On 1st July Perry of London consigned to his agent Naylor in Hong Kong 100 cases of goods which were invoiced at £10 per case. He paid insurance and freight charges amounting to £75. Perry closed his books on 30th September at which date he had received an account sales from Naylor showing:

(1) 60 cases had been sold for £20 per case.
(2) Unloading and warehouse charges had been paid amounting to £50.
(3) Sales expenses had amounted to £35.
(4) Naylor had deducted his agreed commission of 4% plus 1% del credere commission, and had forwarded a cheque for the balance due.

You are required to record the above transaction in the books of the consignor showing the profit in respect of that part of the consignment that had been sold, and the value of the unsold portion.

299

22.4

On 12th January Rowland in France consigned 200 machines to Morley in Cardiff. On 31st March, Morley forwarded an account sales with a remittance for the balance, showing the following transaction:

(1) 150 machines sold at £30 each and 5 at £20.
(2) Port and duty charges—£675.
(3) Storage and carriage charges £400.
(4) Commission on sales 5% plus 1% del credere.

You are required to:

(a) prepare the account sales, and
(b) show the consignment inwards account in the books of Morley.

22.5

On 1st September Sullivan consigned to their agents Williams 200 articles valued at £25 each on which they paid freight, insurance etc. £250. Ten articles were lost in transit, and a claim for £262.50 had been admitted by the insurance company.

On 30th November Williams forwarded an account sales showing that 120 articles have been sold for £30 each and that £3,250 had been collected by the consignee in cash. The consignee's selling expenses amounted to £45, and commission had been agreed at 5%. On receipt of the account sales the consignment account was balanced off.

On 31st December a further account sales was received showing the remainder of the consignment had been sold for £2,750. All debtors had settled their account less a discount allowed amounting to £175. Selling expenses were £35.

Write up the consignment account and the consignee's account in the books of the consignor, assuming that the consignee remitted the balance due with each account sales.

22.6

On 3rd February Vickory consigned 100 cases of goods to Taylor in Sweden. The goods cost £40 per case and Vickory had paid carriage freight etc. amounting to £100. Four cases were lost in transit and a cheque was received for £164 in settlement.

On 31st March Taylor submitted an account sales showing that 56 cases had been sold for £60 each. Landing charges and import duty was £384, and selling expenses £40 had been paid. Commission at 5% on sales plus 2½% del credere was charged.

On 30th April a final account sales showed that the remainder of goods had been sold for £62 per case. Selling expenses amounted to £64 and commission was deducted at the same rate as previously.

Taylor had remitted £2,500 on 31st March and the balance on 30th April.

Vickory makes up his accounts to 31st March.

You are required to show the accounts necessary to record the above in the consignor's books.

23 Bills of Exchange

One of the problems that beset businessmen is that of liquidity, i.e. ensuring that there is a sufficient amount of cash available to pay running expenses and to replenish stock which has been sold. Because most business is conducted on a credit basis a trader has to wait for a certain length of time before he collects monies for goods he has sold. He must, therefore, have enough capital available to last him throughout this period. If the seller is short of capital, he must economise on his expenses or curtail his purchases of goods for resale; both these actions may adversely affect his business. The buyer of goods may also be short of money and therefore order less from the supplier, and so two businesses are affected.

To attempt to overcome this problem bills of exchange are sometimes used, particularly when the credit period is lengthy. This document is defined in the Bills of Exchange Act 1882 as:

"An unconditional order in writing addressed by one person to another, signed by the person giving it, requiring the person to whom it is addressed to pay on demand, or at a fixed or determinable future time, a sum certain in money to, or to the order of, a specified person or to bearer."

The meaning of the preceding paragraph is that the seller of goods, with the approval of the buyer, will make out a document requiring the buyer to pay, on demand or at a pre-determined date, a specific amount either to the seller himself or to a person of his (the seller's) choice, viz.:

Manchester
1st April, 19x3

Four months after date pay to me or my order the sum of three hundred and fifty pounds for value received.

£350   Signed   B. Ledger

To: S. Mutch, London

In the example above B. Ledger is the seller of the goods and it is he who makes out the bill. He is now known as the "drawer" of the bill. The person to whom the money is to be paid is known as the "payee". In this case the payee is also B. Ledger.

The buyer of the goods, S. Mutch, is the "drawee" of the bill. When he receives the bill he will write on the front of it the word "accepted" and sign it. From now on he is known as the "acceptor" of the bill. He will then return the bill of exchange to the drawer.

By accepting the bill of exchange the debtor acknowledges the amount owing and thereafter is not able to dispute the debt. To the holder of the bill it is known as a bill receivable and will be classified as a current asset in his balance sheet. To the acceptor of a bill it is known as a bill payable and will appear as a current liability in his balance sheet.

In the example given payment of the bill is due on 1st August, 19x3, but in practice three extra "days of grace" are allowed which would extend the date of payment to the 4th August, 19x3. If the last day of grace falls on a Sunday, Christmas Day, or Good Friday it is payable on the preceding business day. If it falls due for payment on a Bank Holiday other than those mentioned, it becomes payable on the succeeding business day.

The drawer of an accepted bill of exchange becomes the "holder" and he is able to take one of the following courses, each of which requires a different treatment in his books:

1. Hold the bill until it matures.
2. Discount it with a bank.
3. Negotiate it to another person.

Bills Held until Maturity

This course of action means that the drawer retains the bill until payment of it is due. The implication is that he is not in urgent need of cash and can, therefore, wait until that date. Apart from the debtors and cash account the only additional account is one for bills receivable. The entries required are to credit the debtor with the amount of the bill and debit bills receivable account, when payment is made bank or cash is debited and bills receivable credited.

Example

B. Ledger sells goods to the value of £350 to S. Mutch on 1st April, 19x3. A bill of exchange is drawn by Ledger and accepted by Mutch on that date, the date of maturity being 1st August, 19x3.

S. MUTCH

19x3		£	19x3		£
1st Apr.	Goods	350	1st Apr.	Bill receivable	350

Bills Receivable

19x3		£	19x3		£
1st Apr.	S. Mutch	350	1st Aug.	Bank	350

Bank

19x3		£	19x3		£
1st Aug.	Bills receivable	350	19x3		

Discounting Bills with the Bank

If the holder of a bill of exchange finds himself short of money, he may discount it at his bank. This means that the bank will treat the bill as a deposit, thereby increasing the holder's bank balance or reducing his overdraft. The bank will make a charge for providing this service which is known as a "Discounting Charge" which will be borne by the holder. The result is that the holder receives money in advance of the date when it should be paid, but in doing so receives a smaller net amount, i.e. the amount shown by the bill less the discounting charge. At maturity the bank, who is now the holder of the bill, will present it for payment to the acceptor and obtain the full amount.

The accounts in the drawer's books are similar to those used in the preceding course of action with the addition of an account for discounting charges. The latter account is debited with the charges made by the bank at the end of the year transferred to the profit and loss account.

Example

Using the same information as in the previous example, except that the bill is discounted with the bank on 1st May, 19x3, and the discount charged being £3.

S. MUTCH

19x3		£	19x3		£
1st Apr.	Goods	350	1st Apr.	Bills receivable	350

Bills Receivable

19x3		£	19x3		£
1st Apr.	S. Mutch	350	1st May	Bank	350

Bank

19x3		£			£
1st May	Bills receivable	350	1st May	Discounting charges	3

Discounting Charges

19x3		£		
1st May	Bank	3		Transfer profit and loss account

Negotiating the Bill to Another Person

A bill of exchange is a negotiable instrument which means that the value of the bill can be transferred by handing it over to another person. The drawer of a bill can, therefore, use it in settling one of his own debts, provided his creditor will accept the bill. In order to effect the transfer the holder must endorse the bill, i.e. write his signature on the back. There is no limit to the number of times a bill can be negotiated until the time for repayment is reached. If the drawer specifically names his creditor as payee, then there is no need for endorsement, unless, of course, the payee wishes to negotiate the bill.

If this course of action is followed, the accounts involved are the debtors, bills receivable, and the creditors account. On the bill being negotiated the bills receivable account is credited and the creditors account is debited.

Example

Using the facts given in the first example in this chapter except that instead of holding the bill until maturity it is negotiated to J. Grant, a creditor, in part payment of a debt for £450 on 1st May, 19x3.

S. MUTCH

19x3		£	19x3		£
1st Apr.	Goods	350	1st Apr.	Bills receivable	350

Bills Receivable

19x3		£	19x3		£
1st Apr.	S. Mutch	350	1st May	J. Grant	350

J. Grant

19x3		£	19x3		£
1st May	Bills receivable	350	1st May	Goods	450

The person who holds the bill when it matures is known as the " holder in due course ". The latter will present the bill to the acceptor for payment. If the acceptor is unable to pay, the bill is said to be dishonoured and the holder will be able to go to the last endorser for payment. That endorser will claim off the previous endorser until it reaches the drawer. For this reason a bill that has been discounted or negotiated is regarded as a contingent liability until it has finally been settled. Although a contingent liability is not recorded in the books of account, a note is attached to the balance sheet drawing attention to the fact that a possible liability exists.

In the acceptor's books the entries are the same no matter what course of action the drawer takes. The accounts involved consist of the creditor's account, the bank account, and an additional account for bills payable. When the bill is accepted a debit entry is made in the creditor's account and a credit entry in the bills payable account. When the bill is paid a debit entry is made in the bank account and a credit entry in the bills payable account.

Example

Using the information contained in the previous examples, the entries in the books of S. Mutch would be

B. LEDGER

19x3		£	19x3		£
1st Apr.	Bill payable	350	1st Apr.	Goods	350

Bills Payable

19x3		£			£
1st Apr.	Bank	350	1st Apr.	B. Ledger	350

305

Bank Account

			19x3		£
			1st Apr.	Bills payable	350

Treatment of Dishonoured Bills

If the acceptor of the bill fails to pay, the amount due at the time stipulated it is said to be dishonoured, and liability for settlement will fall on the drawer whether he has retained the bill, discounted it, or negotiated it to a third party. This means that some of the accounting entries must be reversed and the original debt revived. It is usual to obtain further evidence of the dishonour and to obtain this the bill is handed to a solicitor who acts as a Notary Public. The Notary Public will re-present the bill to the acceptor and when it is again refused will attach to the bill a slip bearing his name, the reason for the dishonour, and the fee for his services. This act is known as "noting" the bill and the noting charges will be claimed from the acceptor in addition to the original amount due. This treatment differs from discounting charges which are an expense of the holder.

The entries reflecting the dishonour are shown below.

Example

F. Smith sells goods to A. Jones for £500 on 1st January, 19x3. On the same day A. Jones accepts a bill for that amount, the date of maturity being 1st April, 19x3.

The bill when presented for payment is dishonoured and on 9th April, 19x3, is noted at a fee of £5.

1. When the bill is retained by drawer.

A. JONES

19x3			£	19x3			£
1st Jan.	Goods	A	500	1st Jan.	Bill receivable	A	500
1st Apr.	Bill receivable dishonoured		500				
9th Apr.	Bank noting charge		5				

Bills Receivable

19x3			£	19x3		£
1st Jan.	A. Jones A		500	1st Apr.	A. Jones Bill dishonoured	500

306

Bank

19x3		£
9th Apr.	Noting charge	
	A. Jones	5

Note

The letter A against entries shows the original transactions and applies to all the examples in this section.

2. When the bill is discounted for a charge of £3 on 5th January.

A. JONES

19x3			£	19x3			£
1st Jan.	Goods	A	500	1st Jan.	Bill receivable	A	500
1st Apr.	Bank bill						
	dishonoured		500				
9th Apr.	Bank noting charge		5				

Bills Receivable

19x3			£	19x3			£
1st Jan.	A. Jones	A	500	5th Jan.	Bank	A	500

Bank

19x3			£	19x3			£
5th Jan.	Bills receivable	A	500	5th Jan.	Discounting		
					charges	A	3
				1st Apr.	A. Jones		
					bill dishonoured		500
				9th Apr.	Noting charge		
					A. Jones		5

Discounting Charges

19x3			£
5th Jan.	Bank	A	3

3. When the bill is negotiated to a creditor in settlement of a debt.

A. JONES

19x3			£	19x3			£
1st Jan.	Goods	A	500	1st Jan.	Bill receivable	A	500
1st Apr.	Creditor—bill						
	dishonoured		500				
9th Apr.	Bank noting charge		5				

Bills Receivable

19x3		£	19x3		£
1st Jan.	A. Jones	A 500	5th Jan.	Creditor	A 500

Creditor

19x3		£	19x3		£
5th Jan.	Bill receivable	A 500	5th Jan.	Goods	A 500
1st Apr.	Bank	500	1st Apr.	A. Jones bill dishonoured	500

Bank

			19x3		£
			1st Apr.	Creditor	500
			9th Apr.	Noting charge A. Jones	5

In this case F. Smith would have to pay £500 to his creditor. He would then recover this amount from A. Jones together with the costs of noting the dishonoured bill.

The entries in the books of the acceptor would be the same no matter what course of action was adopted by the drawer.

F. SMITH

19x3		£	19x3		£
1st Jan.	Bill payable	A 500	1st Jan.	Goods	A 500
			1st Apr.	Bill payable dishonoured	500
			9th Apr.	Noting charges	5

Bills Payable

19x3		£	19x3		£
1st Apr.	F. Smith bill dishonoured	500	1st Jan.	F. Smith	A 500

Noting Charges

19x3		£
9th Apr.	F. Smith	5

The balance on noting charges account would be transferred to the profit and loss account at the end of the trading year.

The concept of using bills of exchange is that the seller can obtain money for goods in advance of the due date of payment and the buyer has time to sell the goods before he has to pay for them. If the buyer is unable to honour the bill on the due date, the original bill may be renewed. In fact the old bill is cancelled and a new bill accepted. The new bill will, of course, extend the credit period. In view of this a sum representing interest is added to the original value.

The entries involved in dealing with this are to treat the original bill as being dishonoured and the new bill is recorded in the usual manner. The entries for the additional interest are a debit to the debtors account and a credit to an interest account. The latter is transferred to the profit and loss account at the end of the trading year.

Although the term of a bill is fixed by the wording thereon, it sometimes happens that the acceptor is willing to repay a bill before it matures. Usually, if the holder is agreeable, a sum lower than the face value of the bill is paid. The difference between the payment and the face value of the bill represents interest or discount allowed to the debtor. This settlement is termed "retiring" a bill of exchange.

The entries involved in dealing with this interest are shown in the following example.

Example

G. Long sold goods to F. Short on 1st January, 19x5, for £200. On that date F. Short accepted a bill of exchange payable on 1st April, 19x5.

Both parties agreed to settle the bill on 1st February for £197.

In the Drawer's Book

F. SHORT

19x5		£	19x5		£
1st Jan.	Goods	200	1st Jan.	Bill receivable	200

Bills Receivable

19x5		£	19x5		£
1st Jan.	F. Short	200	1st Feb.	Bank	197
				Discount account	3

Bank

19x5		£
1st Feb.	Bills receivable—F. Short	197

Discount (or Interest) Account

19x5		£		
1st Feb.	Bills receivable—F. Short	3	Transfer profit and loss account	

Converse entries would be made in the books of the acceptor.

Where dealings in bills of exchange are numerous, subsidiary books of accounts are opened. These correspond with the day books already described in Chapter 6. Each bill is entered separately and posted to the individual debtors or creditors accounts. Totals are made at determined intervals and entered in the bills receivable or bills payable account.

The rulings in the day books will give more detailed information than can be obtained from the ledger itself. Thus, in addition to the date, name of debtor, and amount of the bill, additional columns can be added to show the name of the drawer, payee, or acceptor, the date of the bill, the term and due date, and how the bill has been discharged.

Promissory Notes

These are written notes promising to pay a certain amount to a particular person. They are defined by the Bills of Exchange Act, 1882 as

an unconditional promise in writing made by one person to another, signed by the maker, engaging to pay on demand, or at a fixed or determinable future time, a certain sum in money to or to the order of a specified person or to bearer ".

The main difference between promissory notes and bills of exchange is that the former are made out by the debtor, therefore do not require acceptance. The accounting entries follow the same lines as for bills of exchange.

EXERCISES

23.1

On 1st January, 19x7, the following balances appeared in the books of J. Cone.

Debits	S. Brady	£300
	T. Hope	£500
Credits	F. Glynn	£350
	W. Ellis	£150

The following transactions took place in the three months ended 31st March, 19x7.

Jan. 1   Received a bill for two months from T. Hope for £500 duly accepted.

      8   Accepted a bill drawn by F. Glynn for £350 due at one month.

23   S. Brady forwarded a draft duly accepted at two months for £300.
Feb. 1   Accepted a bill drawn by W. Ellis for three months for £150.
11   Bill due to F. Glynn duly honoured.
15   Discounted T. Hope's bill, discount charges £7.
Mar. 26   Proceeds of S. Brady's bill paid into bank.

You are required to write up the above transactions in the ledger of J. Cone, and to bring down any balances.

23.2

On 1st March M. Fox sold goods to J. Crooke for £450, the latter accepting a bill of exchange for three months for this amount.

On 18th March M. Fox negotiated this bill to P. Flint in settlement of a debt owed to the latter.

On 4th June P. Flint notified M. Fox that the bill had been dishonoured. M. Fox paid the amount due and noted the bill at a cost of £4.

On 8th June M. Fox agreed to accept a further bill from J. Crooke for one month for the amount owing plus £6 interest. On 11th July the new bill was paid.

You are required to enter the above transactions in the books of M. Fox.

23.3

On 1st September B. Taylor sold goods to J. Nicklin for £600 and purchased goods from P. Roche for £850. On the same date Taylor drew a bill on J. Nicklin for three months, which was accepted, for £500.

On 15th September J. Nicklin drew a bill for £100 on H. Oliver which was accepted, the term being three months.

On 18th September J. Nicklin endorsed the bill over to M. Taylor and on the same date B. Taylor endorsed the bill to P. Roche, at the same time paying the balance due in cash.

On 4th December the bill for £500 was paid.

On 18th December P. Roche informed B. Taylor that H. Oliver's acceptance had been dishonoured and that noting charges amounted to £4. B. Taylor paid the amount due.

You are required to enter the above transaction in the books of B. Taylor.

23.4

On the 30th June, 19x2, Allan owes Butters £200, Butters owes Clegg £600, and Clegg owes Duncan £300.

On 1st July, 19x2, Allan accepted a bill for three months in favour of Butters for £200.

On 1st August, 19x2, Clegg drew a bill (which was accepted) on Butters for £400, term two months and for the balance took the bill drawn on Allan.

On 4th August, 19x2, Clegg negotiated the bill for £200 to Duncan and paid the balance due in cash. On the same day he discounted the bill for £400 with his bank incurring charges of £8.

Both the bills were dishonoured on their due dates.

Show the entries necessary to record the above in Clegg's books.

311

23.5

The following transactions relate to the business owned by H. Hunter during the year ended 30th June, 19x7.

19x6

July 15   Received a bill from F. Farmer for £600. This bill was paid on the due date.

Oct. 22   Received a bill from S. Shepherd for £300 and discounted it on the same day incurring a charge of £4.

Nov. 8   Received a bill from J. Smith for £700.

19x7

Feb. 11   Smith's bill was dishonoured and a new one was accepted to include interest of £7.

Note All bills are of a three month tenure.

Other transactions were:

19x7

June 30		
Sales on credit for year	£96,814
Cash received from debtors during year	£86,468
Discounts allowed for year	£4,320
Returns by customers	£981
Bad debts written off	£427
Accounts settled by contra with purchase ledger	£368

Balances at 1st July, 19x6, on the debtors account were debits £18,462, credits £148. There were no credit balances at 30th June, 19x7.

You are to write up:
(a) the bills receivable account, and
(b) the debtors control account for the year ended 30th June, 19x7.

23.6

On 8th May, 19x2, Paul buys goods for £750 from Anthony and accepts a bill at three months. Some of the goods which were not up to standard valued at £80 were returned by Paul and Anthony issued a credit note. Anthony negotiated the bill to Patrick on 10th June in settlement of a debt.

On maturity the bill was dishonoured and Anthony paid Patrick the amount due plus noting charges of £8.

Paul accepts a new bill at one month for the amount due plus interest of £5.

Show the ledger accounts in:

(a) Paul's ledger, and
(b) Anthony's ledger to record the above.

24 Departmental Accounts

Where a business uses several distinct departments in its operations or where the goods it sells can be classified into a number of groups, it would be of the utmost benefit if the owner knew how much profit was being earned by the separate departments or groups as well as the aggregate profits.

To some extent this information can be achieved by preparing analysed or departmental final accounts. In order to do this it is necessary to provide sufficient detail in the books of account. The day books can be easily adapted by adding a number of columns, each column containing sales or purchases referring to individual departments. As departmental accounts do not extend to balance sheets the cash book might be analysed as to (a) on the debit side, a column for receipts from debtors, a column for each department's cash sales, and a column for miscellaneous items, and (b) on the credit side a column for payments to creditors, a column for each department's expenses, and a miscellaneous column. Petty cash and expense day books can be similarly analysed.

The ledger itself can be so designed that each account is broken down to give the relevant information as, for example, the sales account can be entered in columnar form, each column referring to a separate department. On the other hand, if the number of departments is few, a separate account may be opened for each, and there would be in fact several sales accounts.

Although the number of book-keeping entries is increased the benefits to be gained by providing the additional information must be weighed against the cost of achieving it. Generally it will be worthwhile for the owner will be able to discover which departments or lines contribute most profit to the business, and by concentrating his efforts upon these, and allowing the less profitable ones to fade out, the aggregate profit will increase.

Unfortunately, not all expenses can be directly allocated to a specific department and these will have to be apportioned in a pre-determined ratio, for example:

(1) *Rent and Rates.* As these are payable in one amount for the whole property the total should be split on the basis of floor area.

(2) *Heating and Lighting.* Unless there are separate meters available for each department the total amount should be allocated on the number of electrical points in each department or on volume occupied.

(3) *Office Wages and Expenses.* These are perhaps more difficult to allocate and are usually spread on an arbitrary basis, e.g. on sales achieved by each department, or spread equally over all departments.

Once these matters have been decided the departmental trading and profit and loss accounts can be prepared. The presentation is usually in vertical or narrative style and in no way differs from the preparation of other final accounts so far described except that extra columns are used.

Example

D. Fowler operates a garage comprising (a) petrol sales, (b) repairs and servicing, and (c) second-hand car dealing. The trial balance extracted from his books at 31st March, 19x5, showed the following:

	£	£
Capital account		12,000
Drawings	2,400	
Freehold premises at cost	22,000	
Servicing tools and equipment at cost	5,000	
Servicing tools and equipment depreciation provision		1,500
Stocks 1st April, 19x4		
Petrol	500	
Spares	250	
Second-hand cars	3,500	
Debtors	2,100	
Bank		5,000
Cash in hand	100	
Creditors		1,500
Sales—Petrol		30,000
Servicing and repairs		40,000
Cars		80,000
Purchases—Petrol	24,000	
Spares	20,000	
Second-hand cars	60,000	

	£	£
Wages—Forecourt attendants	3,200	
Mechanics	15,000	
Car salesmen	4,300	
Office personnel	3,000	
Rates	1,500	
Heating and lighting	300	
Advertising	600	
Office expenses	1,800	
Bank interest	450	
	£170,000	£170,000

(1) Stocks at 31st March, 19x5, comprised:

	£
Petrol	600
Spares	300
Second-hand cars	5,000

(2) Expenses are to apportioned: *Petrol   Repairs   Second-hand cars*

	Petrol		Repairs		Second-hand cars
Rates	1	:	2	:	2
Heating and lighting	1	:	2	:	2

All others in proportion to sales.

(3) Depreciation on tools and equipment is to be provided at 5% on cost

You are required to prepare departmental trading and profit and loss account for the year ended 31st March, 19x5, and a balance sheet as at that date.

Note

Include all wages in the profit and loss account.

D. FOWLER
Trading and Profit and loss Accounts
Year ended 31st March, 19x5

	Petrol sales	Repairs and servicing	Second-hand cars	Total
	£	£	£	£
Sales	30,000	40,000	80,000	150,000
Opening stock	500	250	3,500	4,250
Purchases	24,000	20,000	60,000	104,000
	24,500	20,250	63,500	108,250
Less Closing stock	600	300	5,000	5,900
Cost of goods sold	23,900	19,950	58,500	102,350
Gross profit	6,100	20,050	21,500	47,650

	£	£	£	£
Wages—direct	3,200	15,000	4,300	22,500
Office wages	600	800	1,600	3,000
Rates	300	600	600	1,500
Heating and lighting	60	120	120	300
Advertising	120	160	320	600
Office expenses	360	480	960	1,800
Bank interest	90	120	240	450
Depreciation—tools and equipment		250		250
	4,730	17,530	8,140	30,400
Net profit	£1,370	£2,520	£13,360	£17,250

Balance Sheet as at 31st March, 19x5

	£	£		£	£
Capital account			Fixed assets		
Balance 1.4.19x4		12,000	Freehold premises at cost		22,000
Profit for year		17,250	Tools and equipment at		
		29,250	cost	£5,000	
Less Drawings		2,400	Less Provision		
		26,850	depreciation	1,750	
					3,250
Current liabilities					25,250
Creditors	£1,500		Current assets		
Bank overdraft	5,000		Stock—Petrol	600	
		6,500	Spares	300	
			Second-hand cars	5,000	
			Debtors	2,100	
			Cash in hand	100	
					8,100
		£33,350			£33,350

In practice the wages of mechanics would be entered in the trading account.

It is not essential to complete the total column. Where this is omitted the individual profits (and losses) are summarised and the aggregate figure shown beneath the profit and loss account.

Because of the difficulty in apportioning certain expenses, in particular those relating to administration, shortened versions of the full departmental accounts are used. It is argued that because some of the expenses charged to departmental profit and loss accounts are mere estimates the relative net profit cannot be regarded as true.

316

The gross profit will be sufficient to give an indication of each departments' contribution to the firm's overheads. This information is enough to help management to formulate policies which will increase the overall net profit. Furthermore, the recording of entries is simplified and the time taken to make the entries is shortened, thus saving costs in clerical staff.

Under this method departmental trading accounts are prepared. The gross profits are credited to a general profit and loss account in which all expenses are entered in total.

A refinement of the above method is to show not the gross profit made by each department but the contribution made by each to the administration and other overheads of the business. It is recognised that some expenses will have to be paid whether a department operates or closes down. For example, rent and rates will have to be paid no matter what department is being operated or indeed if all the premises are being used. Only direct expenses are controlled by the department itself and these are the only expenses which should be taken into account. The difference between these expenses and the revenue produced by each department represents the contribution made by each to the fixed expenses of the business.

Example

Taking the information in the previous example as a basis

D. FOWLER
Trading and Profit and loss Accounts
Year ended 31st March, 19x5

	Petrol sales £	Repairs and servicing £	Second-hand cars £
Sales	30,000	40,000	80,000
Opening stock	500	250	3,500
Purchases	24,000	20,000	60,000
	25,500	20,250	63,500
Less Closing stock	600	300	5,000
Cost of goods sold	23,900	19,950	58,500
Wages—direct	3,200	15,000	4,300
Depreciation—tools and equipment		250	
	27,100	35,200	62,800
Contributions	£ 2,900	£ 4,800	£17,200

317

	All departments £
Contributions	24,900
Office wages	3,000
Rates	1,500
Heating and lighting	300
Advertising	600
Office expenses	1,800
Bank interest	450
Total fixed expenses	7,650
Net profit	£17,250

It can be seen from the results obtained that the most profitable department is that selling second-hand cars, whilst the least profitable is petrol sales. At first sight it would seem to be in the best interests of the firm to close the latter department down and concentrate on the former. Unfortunately, this might not necessarily result in increased profits. To some extent the departments may be dependent on each other. Persons calling in for petrol may see a car they wish to purchase, whereas if there were no petrol sales the number of cars sold might drop. In the same way, if the repairs and services department was closed this might affect the revenues produced by the other two departments.

In the manner used by some super-markets to sell loss-leaders (i.e. sell goods at a very small profit) as an inducement to tempt customers into the shop so they might purchase other goods, a business must be aware that even if a particular department is making a lower contribution to the overheads, the overall contribution would fall if that department was closed down. Though the department or function is making no direct contribution, it may be worthwhile for it to continue. To take an extreme case, it may be of considerable benefit to the business if valuable land was used to provide parking facilities for its customers. Although the parking space provides no revenue (in fact rates and maintenance charges will have to be paid thereon) the contributions provided by other departments might increase with additional customer spending.

Where departments are inter-dependent on one another, and the closing down of one will affect the revenue of the others, it is important that the siting of each department is considered. Revenue might be lost to competitors if certain departments are difficult to find or awkward to get to. In large departmental stores it is recognised that departments selling the small consumable household supplies are situated in a more convenient place than those departments selling the more expensive household durable goods. It is considered that the customer, having easy access to his day-to-day purchases, would be more tempted to use that particular firm than one that has the same type of goods in an inconvenient part of its premises. The effect of this is two-fold. Customers who have entered the stores to purchase a small item may stay to look round the other departments or, conversely, if they intend buying a durable item they will have to pass through the departments selling the daily needs of the individual.

Where departments are not inter-dependent on one another it is up to the management to ensure that the highest contributions possible are gained from all available space. This means that certain departments will be closed down and more profitable ones opened or extended. Care must be taken, if established departments are extended, in case the market for the goods is restricted, thereby resulting in larger stocks being carried and expenses increased without a corresponding increase in revenue.

Departmental accounts do not furnish the complete answer to managerial policies. They form a working base which, taken into account with other factors, should lead management to effect policies which will increase profits.

EXERCISES

24.1

The following particulars are taken from the trial balance of B. Kidd as at 31st December, 19x6. The business has three departments—gardening, household, and car maintenance.

	£		£
Stocks 1st Jan., 19x6		Purchases	
Gardening	3,000	Gardening	6,000
Household	6,000	Household	30,000
Car maintenance	4,000	Car maintenance	22,000
Sales		Wages	
Gardening	20,000	Gardening	10,000
Household	56,000	Household	12,000
Car maintenance	36,000	Car maintenance	5,600
Rent and rates	7,000	Office wages	4,000
Administration expenses	10,000	Heating and lighting	4,000
General expenses	2,000		

The stocks at 31st December, 19x6, comprised: gardening £5,000, household £8,000, and car maintenance £6,000.

You are required to prepare:

(a) A departmental trading account and a general profit and loss account.
(b) A calculation of the contribution made by each department to the general overheads.

24.2
From the following information prepare a departmental trading account and a general profit and loss account.

	£		£
Opening stocks		Closing stocks	
Wines and spirits	8,000	Wines and spirits	3,000
Tobacco and cigarettes	6,000	Tobacco and cigarettes	4,000
Purchases		Returns inwards	
Wines and spirits	53,000	Wines and spirits	750
Tobacco and cigarettes	28,000	Tobacco and cigarettes	500
Sales		Returns outwards	
Wines and spirits	84,000	Wines and spirits	500
Tobacco and cigarettes	58,000	Tobacco and cigarettes	800
Wages		Office salaries	23,000
Wines and spirits	6,000	Heating and lighting	1,000
Tobacco and cigarettes	4,000	Sundry expenses	1,500

24.3
The following particulars relate to a business having three departments and are in respect of the year ended 31st December, 19x4.

	£		£
Sales		Opening stock	
Groceries	60,000	Groceries	11,000
Fruit and vegetables	48,000	Fruit and vegetables	8,500
Meat	36,000	Meat	7,000
Purchases		Closing stock	
Groceries	40,000	Groceries	9,000
Fruit and vegetables	32,000	Fruit and vegetables	6,000
Meat	26,000	Meat	7,500
Wages		Discounts received	1,440
Groceries	6,000	Office salaries	2,400
Fruit and vegetables	5,000	Advertising	1,200
Meat	4,000	Insurance	600
Rent and rates	3,600	Delivery expenses	1,800
General expenses	6,000		

The following expenses are to be apportioned in relation to sales:
discounts received, advertising, and delivery expenses
All other expenses are to be apportioned equally.

You are required to prepare departmental trading and profit and loss accounts for the year ended 31st December, 19x4.

24.4

P. Jones carries on a newsagents business selling (1) papers and books and (2) sweets and chocolates. The following is his trial balance for the year ended 31st December, 19x9.

	£	£
Capital account		11,500
Drawings	2,220	
Fixtures and fittings at cost	1,200	
Freehold shop at cost	4,800	
Depreciation provision fixtures		400
Debtors	500	
Creditors		1,200
Stocks—1st January, 19x9		
Papers	2,400	
Sweets	3,600	
Sales		
Papers		13,000
Sweets		15,000
Purchases		
Papers	9,600	
Sweets	10,800	
Wages		
Papers	1,000	
Sweets	2,400	
Office wages	1,200	
General expenses	360	
Rates	180	
Insurance	90	
Balance at bank	750	
	£41,100	£41,100

(1) Closing stocks were—papers £3,000, sweets £4,200
(2) Administration expenses are to be apportioned equally.
(3) Depreciation on fixtures is to be calculated at 5% on cost.

You are required to prepare departmental trading and profit and loss accounts for the year ended 31st December, 19x9, and a balance sheet as at that date.

24.5

The following is the trial balance of G. Bond, who deals in radios and bicycles at 31st December, 19x2.

	£	£
Capital		20,000
Drawings	3,750	
Debtors	3,600	

	£	£
Creditors		1,800
Premises	13,000	
Fixtures and fittings	2,500	
Motor vans	4,000	
Cash at bank	60	
Cash in hand	8,000	
Sales—Radios		50,320
Bicycles		60,480
Purchases—Radios	28,600	
Bicycles	35,800	
Stock 1st January, 19x2		
Radios	8,000	
Bicycles	4,000	
Returns inwards—Radios	320	
Bicycles	480	
Returns outwards—Radios		600
Bicycles		800
Salaries—Radios	5,000	
Bicycles	4,000	
Office	7,000	
Rates and insurance	2,000	
Van expenses	2,860	
Repairs to equipment	564	
Lighting and heating	520	
Discount allowed	396	
Discount received		450
	£134,450	£134,450

(1) Closing stock amounted to: radios £8,000, bicycles £3,500.
(2) Van expenses and discount allowed are to be allocated net sales, discount received on net purchases, all other expenses are to be shared equally.

You are required to prepare a departmental trading and profit and loss account for the year ended 31st December, 19x2 (do not show a total column) and a balance as at that date.

24.6
From the following information relating to the firm of Vehicle Services you are required to prepare trading and profit and loss accounts to show gross and net profits of the sales department and servicing departments. A balance sheet is not required.

Trial Balance at 30th June, 19x6

	£	£
Capital		10,000
Drawings	2,500	
Debtors	1,760	
Creditors		300

	£	£
Furniture and fittings	2,600	
Servicing equipment at 1st July, 19x5	1,700	
Bank balance	1,500	
Stock 1st July, 19x5		
Sales departments	3,000	
Servicing department	600	
Sales—Sales department		11,240
Income from servicing		7,940
Purchases		
Sales department	7,980	
Servicing department	1,200	
Testing machine for use in		
servicing department	700	
Wages—Service manager	2,400	
Sales staff	1,300	
Rent, rates and insurance	1,300	
Office expenses	760	
Provision for bad debts		60
Carriage on goods sold	40	
Advertising	200	
	£29,540	£29,540

(1) Stock at 30th June, 19x6 were: sales department £2,400, servicing department £500.
(2) Servicing equipment is to be depreciated at 10% on written down value. Furniture and fittings are to be depreciated at 5% on written down value.
(3) Expenses, except where otherwise indicated, are to be apportioned 40% to sales department and 60% to the servicing department.

25 Limited Companies— Shares and Debentures

There are a number of disadvantages in setting up a business as a sole trader or in partnership with other people. In particular the main drawbacks are that:

1. On the death of the owner(s) the business comes to an end.
2. The amount of capital available to the business depends on the financial resources of a few persons.
3. If the business gets into difficulties the creditors have a claim on the personal assets of the owners.

The third point mentioned above is perhaps the most important as it deters a great many persons from putting their money into businesses. This did not matter quite so much when businesses were small and the owners could themselves supply the capital necessary to satisfy its operations. When businesses became much larger and the costs involved in their formation increased, it became impossible for promoters to supply all the money which was required. Although many persons had money available they were not willing to invest a particular amount if the rest of their capital was at risk.

In 1855 an act was passed in parliament, the first "Joint Stock Companies Act" which allowed a new business unit to be formed with limited liability for its members. The first act led to a succession of further acts culminating in the two Companies Acts of 1948 and 1967 which govern company procedures at the present day.

The capital of limited companies is divided into shares which may be of any pre-determined denomination, e.g. £5, £1, 50p, or 25p. The members or shareholders, who now own the company, agree to purchase a certain number of shares and their liability is restricted to the nominal, or face, value of the shares they have agreed to buy.

In addition to the members having limited liability another important feature of limited or joint stock companies is that they have a separate legal entity or "being" independent of the members. This means they can sue or be sued, or enter into contracts in their own names. Being a

324

separate entity they also have continuity of existence which means that the company continues its life even though the membership changes.

There are two types of limited liability companies—the Private Company and the Public Company.

The private company is the most common of the two types as the number of members may be as low as two and as high as fifty. It is ideally suited to small and medium sized businesses as it retains many of the benefits of a partnership with the additional advantage of limited liability. The disadvantages of a private company are that it:

1. Restricts the right to transfer its shares.
2. Limits the number of its members to fifty, excluding employees and ex-employees of the company.
3. Prohibits any invitation to the public to subscribe for any shares or debentures of the company.

A public company is one which must have at least seven members. The maximum number of members is restricted only by the number of shares it can issue. It can offer its shares and debentures to the general public by advertisement and is, therefore, favoured by the larger businesses who require large amounts of capital. If a person is a shareholder in a public company, he can sell his shares to a third person without obtaining the company's consent, whereas transfers of shares in a private company must have the approval of the other members. If the company is recognised by a stock exchange, there is an available market for the purchase or sale of the shares.

In order to form a company certain documents have to be filed with the Registrar of Companies. If these documents are approved a Certificate of Incorporation is then issued which brings the company into existence. The documents involved are:

The Memorandum of Association which gives details of the name of the company, the address of its registered office, the objects of the company, the fact that its members' liability is limited, and the amount of its share capital divided into classes of shares. The memorandum defines the situation of the company and its relationship with the outside world. Any breach of the sections contained in the memorandum constitutes an "ultra vires" act which is illegal.

The Articles of Association defines the internal rights and duties of the members. It contains such matters as the appointment of directors, the voting rights of the members, matters affecting dividends and meetings.

The other documents are not as comprehensive as the memorandum and articles. They are:

1. A statutory declaration that the requirements of the Acts have been complied with.
2. A statement of the nominal capital of the company.
3. In the case of a public company the written consent of each person to act as a director, together with an undertaking to pay for any qualification shares.

The members of a company do not necessarily take an active part in the day-to-day running of the business. Instead they appoint a board of directors to manage the business activity. Normally each director is required to purchase a minimum number of shares (known as qualification shares) as a condition of his appointment. In such a case the directors are not only part owners, but are also employed by the company. The directors may be removed by the members by a majority vote at a properly convened meeting. There must be at least one members' meeting each year.

The members are not allowed to withdraw any monies from the business on account of profits, nor to demand repayment of their capital. If the company makes a profit, they may receive a dividend which is based as a percentage of the nominal value of the shares they possess. In certain cases the dividend is fixed, in others it is variable according to the type of share held. The directors recommend a dividend and the shareholders approve or disapprove of it in general meeting.

As stated above there are various types of shares, the main ones being (a) ordinary shares, (b) preference shares, and (c) deferred shares.

Ordinary Shares

These are the most common type of share. They carry no fixed rate of dividend, but as they are entitled to participate in the profits remaining after payment of dividends on preference shares the maximum rate is restricted only to the profits available or the dividend policy of the directors. The ordinary shareholders are the greatest risk bearers in a company, and for this reason dividends are usually greater than on other shares.

Preference Shares

These shares can be of different varieties. All, however, carry a fixed rate of dividend, provided profits are available to pay it. They are preferred because their dividend must be met before any ordinary dividend is paid. In the event of the company closing down they may also be preferred in repayment of capital. In some instances several classes of preference shares may be issued and are usually described as first preference or second preference, the former taking prior rights to the second. The varieties of preference shares are:

1. *Non-cumulative Preference Shares.* These are preferred on a year to year basis. If there are sufficient profits to pay a preference dividend, the preference shareholders will benefit, but if there are insufficient profits the dividend is lost for that particular year.
2. *Cumulative Preference Shares.* In this type of share if a dividend is not paid in any year or years, the arrears of dividend must be made up before any dividend can be paid to the ordinary shareholders. If there is no mention that preference shares are non-cumulative, it is understood that they are cumulative in nature.
3. *Redeemable Preference Shares.* Generally a company cannot buy its own shares. However, in the case of redeemable preference shares the company is empowered to re-purchase them at a pre-determined date. The redemption must take place out of the proceeds of a new issue of shares or out of profits. In the latter case an equivalent amount must be put into a reserve account (see following chapter) before issue (and in the memorandum) the shares must be designated as redeemable.

Deferred Shares

This type of share is fairly uncommon and is occasionally issued to founders or directors of the company. They rank last as regards dividend or repayment of capital.

The term "capital" may be capable of several different meanings for, although the nominal capital is stated in the memorandum of association, the company may not sell all the shares. Furthermore, even if the company sells a number of shares it may not require the purchaser to pay the total amount due immediately. The term capital must, therefore, be qualified, viz.:

Authorised Capital

This is the total amount of shares which the company is empowered to issue. The company will have to pay stamp duty on this amount even if the shares are not issued.

Issued Capital

The issued capital represents the amount of shares which has been issued by the company whether they have been fully paid or not.

Called-up Capital

This is the amount due to the company in respect of shares issued. It may not be the amount actually received.

Paid-up Capital

This represents the amount actually paid by members in respect of their shares. If this is less than the called-up capital, the difference represents "calls in arrear".

The Issue of Shares

When a public company wishes to issue shares a prospectus is published which invites the public to subscribe for shares. An application form is usually attached to the prospectus which is completed and returned to the company together with application monies. The sum payable on application is determined by the company, but must not be less than 5% of the nominal value of the shares. The prospectus gives the minimum amount of shares (known as the minimum subscription) that must be applied for before any issue can take place. The company must open a special bank account to deal with this money.

If the applications are sufficient to comply with the minimum subscription, the directors allot the shares to be issued. Once this has been done the amount in the special bank account can be transferred to the general account. If the applications exceed the number of shares to be issued, the excess monies must be returned to the unsuccessful applicants or, if shares are issued on a pro-rata basis, the excess monies may be carried forward against future calls. On allotment a further amount is due from the applicant. This amount can be the balance due or only part thereof.

If the amount due on application is not the total amount outstanding, further calls will be made until the shares are fully paid.

The entries necessary to record these entries are as follows

1. On receipt of application monies:
     Debit   Special bank account
     Credit   Application and allotment account.
2. On allotment of shares:
     Debit   Application and allotment account
     Credit   Special bank account
        (This is only applicable when monies are returned to un-successful applicants.)
     Debit   Application and allotment account with amount called
     Credit   Share capital
        (This last entry refers to the amount actually due to date on the allotment of the shares. Once this has been done the amount in the special bank account can be transferred to the general bank account.)
     Debit   Bank account with amount received
     Credit   Application and allotment account.
3. If the total amount is not payable on allotment, when calls are due:
     Debit   Call account with amount due.
     Credit   Capital account.
     Debit   Cash account with money received.
     Credit   Call account.

Example

The Updown Trading Company, Ltd., has an authorised capital of 25,000 £1 shares. On 1st January, 19x3, it offered to the public 20,000 shares payable

> 25p per share on application
> 50p per share on allotment
> 25p per share on 31st March, 19x3

The public applied for 28,000 shares. On 15th January application monies for 3,000 shares were returned to applicants and shares were allotted on the basis of 4 shares for every 5 applied for.

The balance of monies due on allotment was received in full on 31st January, 19x3. All the holders of shares paid the final call on 31st March with the exception of one person owning 1,000 shares who paid on 15th April, 19x3.

Show the ledger accounts necessary to record the above transactions and the balance sheet extracts on the 31st January, 31st March, and 15th April, 19x3.

Application and Allotment Account

19x3			£	19x3				£
Jan. 15	Cash	(B)	750	Jan. 1	Cash		(A)	7,000
	Capital account		15,000	31	Cash		(C)	8,750
			£15,750					£15,750

Ordinary Share Capital Account

19x3			£	19x3				£
Mar. 31	Balance	C/D	20,000	Jan. 15	Application and allotment a/c	(D)	15,000
				Mar. 31	Call account	(E)	5,000
			£20,000				£20,000
				Mar. 31	Balance	B/D	£20,000

Call Account

19x3		£	19x3			£
Mar. 31	Share capital a/c	5,000	Mar. 31	Cash	(F)	4,750
				Balance		250
		5,000				5,000
Mar. 31	Balance	£250	Apr. 15	Cash		£250

Notes
(A) Cash received: $28,000 \times £0.25 = £7,000$.
(B) Cash returned: $3,000 \times £0.25 = £750$.
(C) Cash received: $20,000 \times £0.50 = £10,000$ less excess already received on application $£(5,000 \times 0.25) = £1,250$.
(D) Amount due on allotment: $20,000 \times £(0.25+0.50) = £15,000$.
(E) Amount due on call: $20,000 \times £0.25 = £5,000$.
(F) Cash received: $19,000 \times £0.25 = £4,750$.

Balance Sheet as at 31st January, 19x3

	£
Authorised share capital	
25,000 ordinary shares of £1 each	25,000
Issued share capital	
20,000 ordinary shares of £1 each (£0·75 called)	15,000

Balance Sheet as at 31st March, 19x3

	£
Authorised share capital	
25,000 ordinary shares of £1 each	25,000
Issued share capital	
20,000 ordinary shares of £1 (fully called)	20,000
Less Calls in arrear	250
Paid up capital	£19,750

Balance Sheet as at 15th April, 19x3

	£
Authorised share capital	
25,000 ordinary shares of £1 each	25,000
Issued share capital	
20,000 ordinary shares of £1 each (fully paid)	20,000

The balance on the call account at 31st March can be transferred to a calls in arrear account which is then credited when cash is received on 15th April.

Shares may be offered to the public at prices different from their nominal or par value.

If shares are offered for less than their par value, they are said to be issued at a discount. This action is extremely rare and in order for it to be carried out

(a) the issue must be approved in general meeting by the members and sanctioned by the court,
(b) the company must have been trading for at least a year,
(c) the shares must be issued within one month of the court's sanction or within a period specified by the court,
(d) the maximum rate of discount must be specified by the members.

Where a company has been successful in the past the value of its existing issued shares on the stock exchange may be greater than the par value; when the company makes a further offer of shares it may ask

331

PRINCIPLES OF ACCOUNTS

a price greater than the par value. This is known as issuing shares at a premium. The premium itself is the difference between the nominal value of each share and the issue price.

When an issue is made at a premium, the total amount involved is not treated as capital. The amount attributable to the premium represents a capital profit and is credited to a separate share premium account. This profit is not merged with the revenue profit and cannot be used to pay dividends. It can be used as a means of issuing bonus (or free) shares to the members or in writing off certain fictitious assets such as preliminary expenses, discounts on shares, or debentures etc.

The accounting entries necessary to record the issue of shares at a premium are similar to those already described with the addition of one further entry. The terms of issue will determine when the premium is due, i.e. on application or allotment or at a specific call. When this time arrives the share premium account is credited and the allotment or call account debited.

Example

The Downham Packing Co., Ltd., issues 20,000 ordinary shares of £1 at a premium of 25p. The amount due on application was 25p, on allotment 25p, first call 50p which included the premium, and 25p on the final call.

The issue was fully subscribed and all monies paid on the due dates.

Show the ledger accounts necessary to record the above, and the balance sheet after all the entries have been recorded.

Ordinary Share Capital Account

	£
Application and allotment a/c	10,000
1st call account	5,000
Final call account	5,000
	£20,000

Application and Allotment Account

	£		£
Share capital account	10,000	Cash—Application monies	5,000
		Allotment monies	5,000
	£10,000		£10,000

332

1st Call Account

	£		£
Share capital account	5,000	Cash	10,000
Share premium account	5,000		
	£10,000		£10,000

Share Premium Account

	£
1st call account	5,000

Final Call Account

	£		£
Share capital account	5,000	Cash	5,000

Balance Sheet (after share issue)

		£		£
Issued share capital			Bank	25,000
20,000 ordinary shares of				
£1 each full paid	20,000			
Share premium account	5,000			
	£25,000			£25,000

Forfeiture of Shares

When amounts are due on shares, but the member is unable to pay, these shares may be taken from him and retained by the company. This is known as forfeiture of shares. The right to forfeit shares must be directly expressed in the articles of association together with the conditions attached thereto. It is usual for a period of time to elapse after the due date for payment before any action can be taken and for the directors to notify the defaulting member of their intention.

When forfeiture has taken place the shares are not cancelled but held by the company who may re-issue them to a third party. The defaulting member cannot claim any monies he has previously paid in respect of the shares and is still liable for the balance until, in the event of re-issue, the new member has paid the amount due. The shareholder ceases to become a member immediately on the forfeiture of his shares.

The accounting entries necessary to record the forfeiture are

(a) Debit share capital account with the amount called up to the date of forfeiture.

(b) Credit a forfeited shares account with the above amount.
Credit any call account (or calls in arrear) with sums owing.
Debit forfeited shares account.

The balance on forfeited shares account is shown in the balance sheet immediately below share capital. This account represents a capital profit in the same way as share premium.

Example

The House Supply Co., Ltd., issued 25,000 £1 shares at par. The terms of the issue were

25p on application	1st January
25p on allotment	15th January
25p on 1st call	31st March
25p on final call	30th June

A holder of 1,000 shares failed to pay the first call and the shares were forfeited by the directors on 30th April. Show the entries necessary to record the above, and the balance sheet as at 30th June.

Share Capital Account

		£				£
30 Apr.	Forfeited shares a/c (A)	750	15 Jan.	Application and allotment a/c		12,500
30 June	Balance	24,000	31 Mar.	1st Call a/c		6,250
			30 June	Final call a/c (B)		6,000
		£24,750				£24,750
			30 June	Balance		£24,000

Application and Allotment Account

		£			£
15 Jan.	Share capital account	12,500	1 Jan.	Cash application monies	6,250
			15 Jan.	Cash allotment monies	6,250
		£12,500			£12,500

1st Call Account

		£				£
31 Mar.	Share capital account	6,250	31 Mar.	Cash (C)		6,000
			30 Apr.	Forfeited shares a/c		250
		£6,250				£6,250

334

Forfeited Shares Account

		£			£
30 Apr.	1st call account	250	30 Apr.	Share capital account	750
	Balance	500			
		£750			£750
			30 Apr.	Balance (D)	£500

Final Call Account

		£			£
30 June	Share capital account	6,000	30 June	Cash	6,000

Notes

(A) This represents the amount called on the shares up to 30th April, i.e. $1,000 \times 75p$.

(B) This is made up of the number of shares still in existence, i.e. 24,000 at 25p.

(C) This represents the cash received on 24,000 shares at 25p.

(D) The balance represents the amount actually paid on the shares forfeited, i.e. $1,000 \times (25+25)p$.

Balance Sheet as at 30th June

	£		£
Issued share capital		Bank	24,500
25,000 ordinary shares			
of £1 each full called	25,000		
Less 1,000 shares forfeited	1,000		
	24,000		
Forfeited shares account	500		
	£24,500		£24,500

The issued share capital is described as fully called and not fully paid as the balance due on the shares forfeited is still unpaid.

Reissue of Forfeited Shares

The directors may re-issue the forfeited shares at a price which will ensure that the balance owing on them is made up. In the example shown above the shares must be issued at 50p minimum. If the amount asked is greater than this, the excess is classified as share premium.

335

The accounting entries necessary to record the transaction involve opening a further account—a forfeited shares reissued account, viz.:

1. Credit Share capital account with total amount called.
   Debit Forfeited shares re-issued account.
2. Debit Forfeited shares account with balance outstanding.
   Credit Forfeited shares re-issued account.
3. Debit Cash account with amount received.
   Credit Forfeited shares re-issued account.
4. Debit Forfeited shares re-issued account with amount necessary to close off the account.
   Credit Share premium account.

Example

Using the facts in the previous example, show the entries necessary to show the re-issue of the shares on 31st July at a price of 75p per share, cash being received the same day.

Share Capital Account

		£
	30 June Balance	24,000
	31 July Forfeited shares reissues a/c (A)	1,000
		£25,000

Forfeited Shares Account

	£		£
31 July Tfr. forfeited shares reissued a/c	500	30 June Balance	500
			——

Forfeited Shares Reissued Account

	£		£
31 July Capital account	1,000	31 July Forfeited shares	500
Tfr. share premium a/c	250	Cash	750
	£1,250		£1,250

Share Premium Account

		£
	31 July Forfeited shares reissued a/c (B)	250

336

Notes

(A) As the existing shares have been fully called at the date of re-issue the full nominal value must be transferred.

(B) The share premium is made up of £500 paid by the original applicant plus £750 paid by the new holder less the nominal value of £1,000.

At 31st July the balance sheet would show:

	£		£
Issued share capital		Cash	25,250
25,000 ordinary shares			
of £1 fully paid	25,000		
Share premium account	250		
	£25,250		£25,250

Occasionally members may pay in advance for calls on their shares. Where this happens an account for calls in advance must be opened. Amounts would be transferred from this account to the respective call accounts on the due date. This account would be shown in the balance sheet as follows:

Balance Sheet (Extract)

	£
Issued share capital	
50,000 ordinary shares of	
£1 each 75p called	37,500
Less Calls in arrear	250
	37,250
Add Calls in advance	500
Paid-up capital	£37,750

Debenture

If a company wishes to borrow money for a medium- or long-term period it is customary to issue debentures. The debenture itself is an acknowledgement of a debt due by the company. The holder of a debenture is entitled to a fixed rate of interest per annum as agreed in the debenture deed. The holder is not a member of the company, merely a creditor. As security for the loan an asset can be mortgaged to the debenture holders in which case the debentures are said to be secured or mortgaged. In some cases, to ensure preferential treatment in repayment of the debt, the debentures may have a floating charge on all the assets of the company.

Generally, the debentures are repayable on a fixed future date which is defined in the debenture deed and are known as redeemable debentures. In rare circumstances debenture holders are repaid only when the company closes down, in which case they are known as irredeemable debentures.

If a company becomes insolvent before repayment is due, the debenture holders will be repaid out of the proceeds of the sale of a specific asset, if they are secured on that asset. If they are unsecured, they will rank before the shareholders.

Because debentures are not part of the share capital of the company they can be offered to the public at par or at a premium or at a discount. The latter is where a nominal loan of, for example, £100 is recognised, but the cash actually received is less than this amount. The purpose of issuing debentures at a discount is to encourage lenders, for the latter will not only receive interest on the nominal value of the debenture but also will be repaid the full amount.

Generally, the amount payable for each debenture is received in one transaction, i.e. the total amount is not spread over a number of calls. The entries necessary to record the issue are

1. At par:
   - Debit   Cash
   - Credit   Debentures account (with nominal value)
2. At a premium:
   - Debit   Cash
   - Credit   Premium on debentures account (with amount of premium)
   - Credit   Debentures account (with nominal value)
3. At a discount:
   - Debit   Cash
   - Debit   Debenture discount account (with amount of discount)
   - Credit   Debentures account (with nominal value)

The debentures are shown in the balance sheet as a liability under the heading of long-term loans. The premium is shown as a reserve similar to share premium account. The discount, being a debit, is shown as a fictitious asset immediately below the current assets or working capital. This debit is usually written off over a period of years to the profit and loss appropriation account.

Example

A company issued 200 10% debentures of £100 each on 1st January, 19x8, at a discount of 5%. All were taken up and cash was received on 3rd January, 19x8. Show (a) the entries necessary to record the above and (b) a balance sheet extract at 3rd January.

Cash Account

19x8		£
Jan. 3 10% debentures		19,000

Debenture Discount Account

19x8		£
Jan. 3 10% debentures		1,000

10% Debenture Account

	19x8		£
	Jan. 3 Issue 200 £100		
	debentures		20,000

Balance Sheet as at 3rd January, 19x8

	£		£
Long-term loans		Current assets	
10% debentures	20,000	Cash	19,000
		Fictitious assets	
		Debenture discount	1,000
	£20,000		£20,000

EXERCISES

25.1

The Gossamer Shoe Co., Ltd., invited the public to subscribe for 200,000 ordinary shares of 50p each, at a premium of 10p, payable as follows:

On application	1st January, 19x3	15p
On allotment	31st January, 19x3	15p
1st call	30th April, 19x3	20p (including premium)
Final call	31st July, 19x3	10p

All the shares were subscribed for and monies received on the due dates.

Show the ledger entries necessary to record the above and a balance sheet extract on 31st July, 19x3.

25.2

Smith & Co., Ltd., offered 100,000 ordinary shares of £1 each to the general public at a price of £1·25, payable as follows:

On application	1st March	25p
On allotment	31st March	50p (including premium)
1st call	30th June	25p
Final call	30th September	25p

Applications were received for 140,000 shares. It was decided to return application monies to applicants for 15,000 shares and to allot the 100,000 shares pro-rata amongst the remaining applicants.

Show the entries necessary to record the above in the ledger of Smith & Co., Ltd., and the balance sheet on 30th September.

25.3

The Obelisk Manufacturing Co., Ltd., offered 50,000 ordinary shares of 50p each at a premium of 25p, payable as follows:

On application	1st June	15p
On allotment	30th June	30p (including premium)
1st call	30th September	15p
Final call	31st December	15p

Applications were received for 200,000 shares and it was decided to allot shares on the basis of one for every four applied for. No monies were returned.

You are required to show the ledger entries recording the above, and a balance sheet as at 31st December.

25.4

Slapdash & Co., Ltd., offered 100,000 ordinary shares of £1 each at par, payable as follows:

On application	25p	1st January
On allotment	25p	31st January
1st call	25p	31st March
Final call	25p	30th June

Applications were received for 120,000 shares and it was decided to return cash in respect of 20,000 shares. A holder of 2,000 shares defaulted on the 1st call. These shares were forfeited on 30th April and re-issued on 30th June at a price of 75p each.

Show the ledger accounts necessary to record the above, and a balance sheet as at 30th June.

25.5

Jones & Co., Ltd., offered 200,000 ordinary shares of 50p each at a premium of 10p payable:

| On application | 20p | 1st January |
| On allotment | 20p | 31st January (including premium) |

| 1st call | 10p | 31st March |
| Final call | 10p | 30th June |

Applications were received for 250,000 shares and it was decided to allot them on the basis of four for every five applied for. All monies were received on the due date except for one shareholder who had applied for 2,000 shares and defaulted on the first call. The shares were forfeited on 15th April and reissued for 45p each on 1st July.

Show (a) the ledger accounts necessary to record the above in the ledger of the company, and (b) the balance sheet at 1st July.

25.6

F. Read & Co., Ltd., offered 100 £200 10% debentures to the general public. They are fully applied for and cash was received on 15th March, 19x7.

Show the journal entries necessary to record the above if the debentures were issued at

  (a) par,
  (b) a premium of 5%,
  (c) a discount of 10%.

26   Limited Companies— Final Accounts

The final accounts of limited companies are completed in two stages. The first stage is for internal purposes and the accounts are built up in the conventional manner with the trading and profit and loss accounts containing all relevant items. The second stage comprises the final accounts as they will be presented to the members. The contents of the latter are governed by the Companies Acts of 1948 and 1967, and show only the minimum information required by those Acts. The appropriation account and balance sheet are similar for both purposes.

The reason for not disclosing all the information showing how the net profit is calculated, is that, as the accounts have to be published and distributed to the members of the company, it would be relatively easy for a competitor to obtain a copy. If all figures and details were given, the competitor would be able to learn the company's secrets and thereby gain a considerable advantage. On the other hand, as the members are the owners of the company they are entitled to have such information that will enable them to ensure themselves that the directors are running the company in an able manner and not abusing their positions of trust. For example, the published accounts must show amounts of directors' remuneration and the depreciation which is considered necessary to provide for the declining value of the fixed assets. The directors may provide more than the minimum information if they wish.

The contents of this chapter deal with the compilation of accounts for internal use and a brief description of the entries in each section is given.

Manufacturing and Trading Accounts

The entries in these two accounts are identical to those outlined for sole traders and partnerships. Where a director has been appointed to take charge of the factory or manufacturing side of the company's activities his salary must be included in the factory overheads.

Profit and Loss Account

The entries in this account are consistent with items in a sole traders' or partnership profit and loss account together with additional items which are peculiar to companies. The latter comprise the balance of directors' emoluments which have not been included in the manufacturing account, debenture interest, and taxation.

Because the directors are actively engaged in running the affairs of the company any monies they receive in respect of their employment (including pensions for past services) constitute a business expense. Dividends they receive on their shares are not in respect of services and will be entered in the appropriation account.

As the company is a separate entity any taxation due is the liability of the company itself and not the liability of the members. The amount of tax due on the yearly profits must be shown as a debit, thereby reducing the amount available for the shareholders, and shown as a liability in the balance sheet.

Debenture interest is in the same category as any loan interest and, therefore, is a charge against profits. The interest must be paid whether the company makes a profit or not, thus differing from dividends which can only be paid to shareholders if the company has sufficient profits available.

In order to emphasize the various profits made, company accounts are usually presented in vertical form, viz.:

	£	£
Net trading profit		xxx
Add income from investments		
Quoted	xxx	
Unquoted	xxx	
		xxx
Profit before taxation		xxx
Less Corporation tax		xxx
Profit after taxation		£xxx

The presentation outlined above gives a break-down of how the year's profit available to the shareholders has been reached. The net trading profit is the total profit made from the company's main business activities. To this is added the extra income gained by holding shares in other companies. This figure is usually split between quoted (those investments quoted on stock exchanges—shares in public companies) and unquoted (shares held in private companies). The total now represents the overall profit from which must be deducted the company's liability to tax. The resultant figure represents the year's profits which are available to the shareholders.

Appropriation Account

This account shows what has happened to the profits available for the members. The amount will be reduced by dividends, transfers to reserves, and writing off certain assets (but excluding depreciation).

Dividends are debited to the appropriation account as they represent a distribution of profits to the members. Some dividends may have already been paid during the year (interim dividends) whilst others may be proposed final dividends. As the latter will not have been paid at the balance sheet date they must be included as a current liability. Dividends on the various classes of shares must be shown separately.

Other debits will be transfers to reserves if required. Reserves are amounts set aside out of profits which the directors consider should not be considered as available for distribution. These reserves are known as revenue reserves and may be general or specific. Examples of the latter are debenture redemption reserve and fixed asset replacement reserve. These reserves may be brought back to the appropriation account in later years and used to pay dividends. Reserves must be distinguished from provisions, the latter being charges against profits which provide for some anticipated loss, the amount of which cannot be accurately determined.

The third type of debit is when some asset is being written off, for example goodwill or a fictitious asset such as preliminary expenses or debenture discount.

The balance remaining after the above entries have been made is known as the unappropriated profit for the year. To this figure is added any unappropriated profits from previous years and the total carried forward to the balance sheet as a revenue reserve.

Balance Sheet

The form and content of the balance sheet are presented in the same manner as for sole traders and partnerships, except that the shareholders' stake in the business is presented in aggregate. More detail and some notes are necessary and these are outlined below.

344

Fixed Assets. Tangible fixed assets should be shown at cost or, if a revaluation of any of these assets has taken place, the revalued price. If the revaluation has taken place in the current year, the date and the person responsible for the revaluation of the asset should be added as a note. The aggregate depreciation for each type of asset should also be shown together with the written down value. In the case of intangible fixed assets such as goodwill, patents, and trade marks the net value only need be shown.

Investments in Other Companies. Although these should be shown in the balance sheet at cost or possibly at revalued amounts where necessary, the market value of the quoted investments at the balance sheet date should be added as a note. In the case of unquoted investments the directors' valuation of the securities should be noted.

Current Assets. These are generally identical with the current assets in sole traders or partnerships, but where loans have been made to officers of the company, e.g. directors or the company secretary, these must be shown as a separate item, unless it is the company's business to lend money in its normal trading activities and these loans were made in the normal course of business.

Current Liabilities. These again conform to the normal current liabilities plus those items peculiar to companies, i.e. proposed dividends and current corporation tax.

Long-term Liabilities. These generally relate to debentures. The amount of debentures issued should be shown together with a note giving details of the terms of redemption and, if the debentures are secured, the nature of the security must be disclosed. In a number of cases two years' taxation may be owing by a company. In this event the taxation on the current year's profit may be classed as a long-term liability, whilst the tax in respect of the previous year will be a current liability.

Fictitious Assets. These consist of debit balances which are not trading expenses nor, in fact, true assets. Examples of these are preliminary expenses, i.e. formation expenses paid before the company receives its certificate of incorporation, expenses relating to the issue of share capital, and discount arising on the issue of debentures. These items are shown on a company's balance sheet immediately under current assets or working capital.

Share Capital. Full particulars of the various classes of shares must be shown. The authorised capital must be noted, but is not included in the total of liabilities. The issued capital must then be shown and a note made of the amount called on each class of share. Adjustments for calls in arrear and calls in advance are made so that the resultant amount represents the paid-up capital. If redeemable preference shares have been issued, a note giving details of the date and terms of redemption should be added.

Reserves. Under the 1948 Companies Act capital and revenue reserves had to be distinguished. The 1967 Companies Act made this no longer compulsory, but it is still regarded as prudent to separate the two types. Capital reserves are not available for the payment of dividends whereas revenue reserves can be brought back to the appropriation account. Both types of reserves can be used to issue bonus shares to the existing members. Examples of capital reserves are: share premium account, capital redemption reserve fund, profits arising prior to incorporation, and profits arising on revelation of fixed assets. Each reserve is listed separately and the aggregate totals added to the paid-up capital to give the total shareholders' funds.

Notes

In addition to the figures contained in the books of a company other details must be added as notes to the accounts.

Contingent liabilities must be shown as these may arise in the future. Examples of these are discounted bills of exchange, guarantees given by the company, possible damages to be paid in court actions.

Details must be added of any contracts entered into which are of a capital nature. Although no amounts may be due at the balance sheet date because contracts have not been signed, the company will be committed to paying the price at some future date. The nature of the contract and the amount involved must be shown.

Where the directors have powers to spend up to a certain sum in respect of capital items, this must also be stated. The difference between this item and the preceding one is that in this instance the contract has not been signed.

Example

The following balances were extracted from the books of John Brown and Company, Limited, at 31st December, 19x4. You are required to prepare trading, profit and loss, and appropriation accounts for the year ended 31st December, 19x4, and a balance sheet at that date for the directors.

	£	£
Preference share capital £1 each fully paid		40,000
Ordinary share capital £1 each 75p called		180,000
Share premium account		20,000
Buildings (cost £200,000)	150,000	
Motor vehicles (cost £15,000)	10,000	
Equipment (cost £30,000)	20,000	
Sundry debtors	109,000	
Sundry creditors		50,000
Sales		723,000
Purchases	558,000	
Returns inwards	2,500	
Returns outwards		2,000
Salaries	43,500	
Directors' remuneration	17,500	
Motor vehicle expenses	12,500	
Office expenses	14,000	
Carriage inwards	3,000	
Carriage outwards	2,000	
Stock at 1st January, 19x4	34,000	
Investments—Quoted, at cost	12,000	
Unquoted, at cost	4,000	
Profit and loss account, 1st January, 19x4		27,000
Income from investments—Quoted		1,000
Unquoted		500
Cash at bank	11,000	
6% Debentures		40,000
Debenture interest (half year to 30th June, 19x4)	1,200	
Preference share dividend (half year)	1,400	
Bad debts	5,500	
Provision for doubtful debts		7,000
Freehold land at cost	100,000	
General reserve		22,000
Preliminary expenses	1,400	
	£1,112,500	£1,112,500

Notes

1. The authorised share capital consists of:
   40,000 7% preference shares of £1 each,
   250,000 ordinary shares of £1 each.
2. Stock at 31st December, 19x4, was valued at £43,000.
3. Provision for doubtful debts is to be adjusted to 5% of debtors.
4. Depreciation is to be provided for:
   Buildings 5% on original cost.
   Motor vehicles 25% on written down value.
   Equipment 10% on written down value.

347

5. The directors wish to provide for the following:
   A dividend of 10% on the ordinary shares.
   A transfer of £20,000 to the general reserve.
6. The market value of the quoted investments was £15,000, the directors' valuation of the unquoted securities was £3,500.
7. The debentures are redeemable at par in 19x8 and are secured on the freehold land.
8. Discounted bills of exchange amount to £12,000.
9. A contract has been signed for the extension to the buildings amounting to £50,000.
10. Corporation tax on the year's profits is estimated at £20,000.

JOHN BROWN AND COMPANY LIMITED
Trading and Profit and Loss Account
Year ended 31st December, 19x4

	£	£	£
Sales			723,000
Less returns			2,500
			720,500
Opening stock		34,000	
Purchases	558,000		
Less Returns	2,000		
		556,000	
		590,000	
Less Closing stock		43,000	
		547,000	
Carriage inwards		3,000	
Cost of goods sold			550,000
			170,500
Salaries		43,500	
Directors' remuneration		17,500	
Office expenses		14,000	
Motor vehicle expenses		12,500	
Carriage outwards		2,000	
Debenture interest (A)		2,400	
Bad debts		5,500	

	£	£	£
Depreciation			
Buildings	10,000		
Motor vehicles	2,500		
Equipment	2,000		
		14,500	
			111,900
			58,600
Reduction. Provision doubtful debts			1,550
Net trading profit			60,150
Income from investments—Quoted		1,000	
Unquoted		500	
			1,500
Profit before tax			61,650
Less Corporation tax			20,000
Profit after tax			£41,650

Appropriation Account

		£	£
Profit for year (after taxation)			41,650
Less Transfer general reserve		20,000	
Preference dividend paid $3\frac{1}{2}\%$		1,400	
Preference dividend proposed $3\frac{1}{2}\%$	(B)	1,400	
Ordinary dividend proposed 10%	(C)	18,000	
			40,800
Unappropriated profit for year			850
Balance brought forward			27,000
Balance carried forward			£27,850

Balance Sheet as at 31st December, 19x4

	Cost £	Depreciation £	Net £
Fixed assets			
Freehold land	100,000		100,000
Buildings	200,000	60,000	140,000
Equipment	30,000	12,000	18,000
Motor vehicles	15,000	7,500	7,500
	345,000	79,500	265,500
Investments			
Quoted (market value £15,000) at cost		12,000	
Unquoted (directors' valuation			
£3,500) at cost		4,000	
			16,000
Current assets			
Stock		43,000	
Debtors	109,000		
Less Provision doubtful debts	5,450		
		103,550	
Cash at bank		11,000	
		157,550	
Current liabilities			
Creditors	50,000		
Accrued debenture interest	1,200		
Corporation tax	20,000		
Proposed preference dividend	1,400		
Proposed ordinary dividend	18,000		
		90,600	
Working capital			66,950
Fictitious assets			
Preliminary expenses			1,400
			349,850
Long-term liabilities			
6% Debentures (secured on freehold			
property)			40,000
			309,850
Authorised share capital			
40,000 7% Preference shares of £1 each			40,000
250,000 Ordinary shares of £1 each (D)			250,000
			£290,000

Issued share capital	£	£
40,000 7% Preference shares of £1 each		
(fully paid)		40,000
240,000 Ordinary shares of £1 each		
(75p called)		180,000
		220,000
Capital reserve		
Share premium account		20,000
Revenue reserves		
General reserve	42,000	
Profit and loss account	27,850	
		69,850
		£309,850

Notes to Accounts
1. The debentures are redeemable at par in 19x8.
2. There is a contingent liability amounting to £12,000 in respect of bills of exchange discounted.
3. A contract valued at £50,000 has been entered into for extension to existing buildings.

Notes to Workings
(A) As debenture interest is an expense the balance owing must be brought into the accounts as an accrual.
(B) As the directors have proposed a dividend on the ordinary shares the balance due to the preference shareholders must be taken into account.
(C) The amount of the ordinary dividend is based on the paid-up capital.
(D) The number of shares issued is calculated by taking the amount in the trial balance multiplied by the nominal value and divided by the amount called, i.e.

$$180,000 \times \frac{1 \cdot 00}{0 \cdot 75} = 240,000$$

Although the answer to the problem has been presented in vertical form the horizontal lay-out is equally acceptable. The presentation of the balance sheet in this latter case would be:

Share capital	Fixed assets
Reserves	Investments
Long-term liabilities	Current assets
Current liabilities	Fictitious assets

351

PRINCIPLES OF ACCOUNTS

EXERCISES

26.1

The following items relate to Wilson Enterprises Ltd.

	£
Authorised share capital	
60,000 8% Preference shares of £1 each	60,000
160,000 Ordinary shares of £1 each	160,000
Issued share capital	
60,000 Preference shares fully paid	60,000
100,000 Ordinary shares 75p called	75,000
Share premium account	12,000
Provision for doubtful debts	500
Debenture interest accrued	700
Proposed ordinary dividend	7,000
Proposed preference dividend	2,400
Unpaid directors' fees	3,000
Calls in arrear	5,000
Profit and loss account	16,000
Goodwill	6,000
Buildings at cost	50,000
Debtors	15,000
Stock	35,000
Fixtures (cost £28,000)	20,000
Balance at bank	5,600
Plant and machinery (cost £93,000)	60,000
£20,000 7% Debentures	20,000

You are required to prepare a balance sheet in good style.

26.2

Anglo Products Ltd. has an authorised capital of £150,000 divided into 30,000 preference shares of £1 each, and £120,000 ordinary shares of £1 each. The preference shares issued have been fully paid, but only 75p has been called on the ordinary shares.

The following balances have been extracted from the books at 31st March, 19x6.

	£	£
Preference share capital		20,000
Ordinary share capital		75,000
Profit and loss account 1st April, 19x5		12,000
Share premium		15,000
General reserve		11,200
Freehold land at cost	50,000	
Buildings (cost £150,000)	75,000	
Motor vehicles (cost £25,000)	15,000	

6% Debentures		20,000
Sundry debtors	54,920	
Sundry creditors		25,170
Stock 31st March, 19x5	17,120	
Sales		371,320
Purchases	279,220	
Returns inwards	1,300	
Returns outwards		1,040
Warehouse wages	8,760	
Salaries	17,800	
Directors' remuneration	6,000	
Office expenses	5,100	
Motor vehicle expenses	6,300	
Repairs to warehouse premises	700	
Warehouse expenses	5,600	
Carriage inwards	750	
Carriage outwards	970	
Cash at bank	5,330	
Cash in hand	160	
Provision doubtful debts		3,400
Preference dividend (half year)	700	
Debenture interest (half year)	600	
Bad debts	2,800	
	£554,130	£554,130

Notes

(1) Stock at 31st March, 19x6, was valued at £25,000.

(2) Provision for doubtful debts to be adjusted to 5% of debtors.

(3) Depreciation is to be provided:
Motor vehicles 20% on written down value.
Buildings 10% on original cost.

(4) The directors wish to provide for an ordinary dividend of 10% and to transfer £10,000 to general reserve.

Prepare trading, profit and loss, and appropriation accounts for the year ended 31st March, 19x6, and a balance sheet as at that date.

26.3

The Upalong Novelty Co., Ltd., has an authorised share capital of 200,000 £1 ordinary shares. All these shares have been issued, but only 75p per share has been called. In addition to the capital account the following balances appeared in the books at 31st December, 19x3.

	£
Profit and loss account 1st January, 19x3	30,000
8% Debentures (issued 1st July, 19x3)	37,500
Stocks at 1st January, 19x3	
Raw materials	17,925
Finished goods	15,000

353

Purchases raw materials	321,180
Sales	400,600
Office expenses	9,135
Carriage inwards	630
Carriage outwards	910
Returns inwards	1,075
Returns outwards	2,345
Discount allowed	2,325
Discount received	1,210
Insurance and rates	3,250
Salaries	10,100
Directors' remuneration	7,000
Factory wages	11,050
Factory overheads	4,875
Provision doubtful debts	1,150
Debtors	30,200
Creditors	13,640
Plant and machinery (cost £28,000)	15,000
Premises—leasehold (cost £200,000)	187,500
Balance at bank (O/D)	1,210
Cash in hand	500

Notes

(1) Stocks at 31st December, 19x3, were:

Raw materials	£16,400
Finished goods	£20,000

(2) Provision for doubtful debts to be adjusted to 5% of debtors.
(3) Depreciation to be provided:
Plant and machinery 10% on written down value.
Leasehold premises 2% on cost.

(4) 80% of insurance and rates and depreciation on leasehold premises to be charged to the factory.
(5) No debenture interest has been paid.
(6) The directors propose a final dividend of 15%.

You are required to prepare manufacturing, trading, profit and loss, and appropriation accounts for the year ended 31st December, 19x3, and a balance sheet as at that date.

26.4
The balances remaining in the books of the Sale Surplus Co., Ltd., after the calculation of the net trading profit for the year ended 30th September, 19x9, were:

	£
Net trading profit year ended 30.9.19x9	20,000
Income from investments	
Quoted	1,000
Unquoted	880

Profit and loss account 1st October, 19x8	2,000
Ordinary share capital (fully paid)	120,000
Preference share capital (fully paid)	40,000
Share premium account	16,500
General reserve	20,000
8% Debentures	12,000
Land and buildings at cost	64,000
Plant and machinery (cost £50,000)	36,000
Provision for bad debts	4,000
Motor vehicles (cost £7,000)	4,600
Stock	35,000
Debtors	37,000
Creditors	3,600
Balance at bank	14,500
Cash in hand	180
Quoted investments (market value £40,000) at cost	36,000
Unquoted investments (directors' valuation £10,000) at cost	12,700

The authorised share capital of the company is £250,000 divided into 50,000 8% preference shares of £1 each and 200,000 ordinary shares of £1 each.

The directors propose an ordinary dividend of 8% and to transfer £5,000 to general reserve. No preference dividend has been paid.

You are required to prepare an appropriation account and a balance sheet.

26.5
The following balances were extracted from the books of the Avavan Hire Co., Ltd., at 30th June, 19x7.

	£	£
Share capital—authorised and issued		
200,000 ordinary shares of £1 each		200,000
8% Debentures		50,000
Profit and loss account 1st July, 19x6		20,000
Land and buildings at cost	230,000	
Fixtures and equipment (cost £25,000)	16,000	
Debtors	33,000	
Creditors		20,000
Provision doubtful debts		500
Bank overdraft		1,250
Purchases	301,000	
Sales		377,000
Wages and salaries	29,000	
Directors' fees	9,000	
Rent and rates	3,750	
General expenses	8,000	
Bad debts	2,500	

	£	£
Debenture interest (half year)	2,000	
Preliminary expenses	3,500	
Stock 1st July, 19x6	31,000	
	£668,750	£668,750

Notes
(1) Stock in trade at 30th June, 19x7, amounted to £35,000.
(2) The provision for doubtful debts is to be adjusted to 2% of debtors.
(3) Prepaid rates amounted to £250.
(4) Depreciation is to be provided on furniture and equipment at 10% on the written down value.
(5) The directors propose to write off 20% of the preliminary expenses and to pay a dividend of 10%.

You are required to prepare trading, profit and loss, and appropriation accounts for the year ended 30th June, 19x7, and a balance sheet as at that date.

26.6
The following trial balance was extracted from the books of Garden Supplies Limited at 31st December, 19x5.

	£	£
Bank balance	10,910	
Creditors		12,250
7% Debentures		12,000
Debtors	21,000	
Directors' salaries	9,400	
Debenture discount	480	
Furniture and fittings	17,800	
Goodwill	10,000	
Gross profit on trading		59,900
Motor vehicles at cost	45,000	
Motor vehicle disposals		700
Provision depreciation of vehicles		14,600
Preliminary expenses	870	
Profit and loss accounts 1st Jan., 19x5		16,780
Rent, salaries and expenses	33,490	
Share capital (authorised and issued)		
50,000 Ordinary shares of £1 each		50,000
10,000 6% Preference shares of £1 each		10,000
Share premium account		12,000
Stock in trade 31st December, 19x5	39,280	
	£188,230	£188,230

Notes
(1) The debentures were issued on 1st January, 19x5, but no interest has been paid.

356

(2) A provision for doubtful debts amounting to 5% of debtors should be created.

(3) A motor vehicle costing £3,000 with a written down value of £800 was sold for £700. The only entries made were to debit cash and credit disposals account with the proceeds of sale. Depreciation should be provided on the remaining vehicles at 10% on cost.

(4) Corporation tax on the current year's profit is estimated at £8,000.

(5) The directors propose that a dividend of 5% should be paid on the ordinary shares and that £3,000 be transferred to a general reserve.

You are required to prepare the profit and loss and appropriation accounts for the year ended 31st December, 19x5, and a balance sheet as at that date.

26.7

The draft final accounts for Robin Enterprises Limited are shown below. The accounts are badly presented and you are required to present them in a conventional manner after providing for a dividend of 8%, taxation of £4,000, and a transfer to general reserve of £3,000.

Profit and Loss Account
Year ended 31st March, 19x2

	£		£
Purchases	108,000	Investment income	500
Opening stock	50,000	Closing stock	30,000
Office salaries	11,000	Sales	162,500
Office expenses	5,350		
Directors' remuneration	5,750		
Provision doubtful debts	700		
Debenture interest	750		
Net profit	11,450		
	£193,000		£193,000

Balance Sheet as at 31st March, 19x2

	£		£
Authorised share capital		Bank	1,000
50,000 Ordinary shares		Debtors	25,000
£1 each	50,000	Calls in arrear	1,000
Less Shares not issued	10,000	Freehold property at cost	16,500
		Quoted investments at cost	9,000
	40,000	Plant and machinery	
7½% Debentures	10,000	(cost £60,000)	24,000
Trade creditors	16,000	Stocks	30,000
Share premium	10,000	Goodwill	8,000
Profit and loss account	37,500		
Provision doubtful debts	1,000		
	£114,500		£114,500

Answers to Exercises

1.1
Debits—(i) cash, (ii) fixtures, (iii) rent, (iv) purchases, (v) cash, (vi) wages, (vii) drawings, (viii) E. Smith, (ix) motor vehicles, (x) stationery.
Credits—(i) capital, (ii) cash, (iii) cash, (iv) W. Jones, (v) sales, (vi) cash, (vii) cash, (viii) sales, (ix) capital, (x) cash.

1.2
Totals. Cash £1,285 dr., £645 cr.; capital £750 cr.; purchases £500 dr.; B. Sykes £400 dr., £400 cr.; stationery £10 dr.; sales £625 cr.; A. Fagin £200 dr., £200 cr.; wages £80 dr.; drawings £30 dr.; rent £25 dr.; A. Dodger £90 dr.

1.3
Totals. Cash £740 dr., £265 cr.; capital £1,300 cr.; motor vehicle £1,000 dr.; advertising £20 dr.; motor expenses £120 dr.; sales £440 cr.; E. Steptow £75 cr.; fixtures £140 dr.; stationery £10 dr.; wages £50 dr.

1.4
Debits (1), (3), (4), (6), (8), (11), (12).
Credits (2), (5), (7), (9), (10).

1.5
Totals. Bank £805 dr., £442 cr.; cash £295 dr., £280 cr.; capital £675 cr.; purchases £350 dr.; packing materials £12 dr.; sales £375 cr.; rent £25 dr.; shop fitting £80 dr.; wages £60 dr.; drawings £50 dr.; F. Jones £80 dr.; advertising £15 dr.

2.1
(a) Debits— Cash £640, purchases £500, stationery £10, wages £80, drawings £30, rent £25, A. Dodger £90.
   Credits—Capital £750, sales £625. Totals £1,375.
(b) Debits—Cash £475, motor vehicle £1,000, advertising £20, motor expenses £120, fixtures £140, stationery £10, wages £50.
   Credits—Capital £1,300, sales £440, E. Steptow £75. Totals £1,815.
(c) Debits—Bank £363, cash £15, purchases £350, packing materials £12, rent £25, shop fittings £80, wages £60, drawings £50, F. Jones £80, advertising £15.
   Credits—capital £675, sales £375. Totals £1,050.

2.2
Debits—Cash £60, rent £80, purchases £850, W. Williams £120, motor van £600, wages £200, motor expenses £50, sundry expenses £23, advertising £12, drawings £80.
Credits—Bank £150, capital £1,075, C. Charles £175, sales £675. Totals £2,075.

2.3
Debits—Bank £2,848, purchases £830, cash £20, L. Lark £50, sundry expenses £44, rent £25, wages £110, advertising £18. S. Sparrow £210.
Credits—Capital £3,000, R. Robin £500, sales £655. Totals £4,155.

2.4
Gross profit £3,800, net profit £830.

2.5
Gross profit £12,800, net profit £5,100.

2.6
Gross profit £18,125, net profit £8,800.

3.1
Gross profit £10,250, net profit £5,000. Balance sheet totals £11,000, viz.: capital £10,000, current liabilities £1,000, fixed assets £5,500, current assets £5,500.

3.2
Gross profit £14,900, net profit £6,650. Balance sheet totals £11,000, viz.: capital £8,000, current liabilities £3,000, fixed assets £1,500, current assets £9,500.

3.3
Gross profit £4,320, net loss £2,865. Balance sheet totals £13,150, viz.: capital £9,410, long-term loans £2,000, current liabilities £1,740, fixed assets £3,150, current assets £10,000.

3.4
Gross profit £19,090, net profit £820. Balance sheet totals £27,500 viz.: capital £17,500, long-term loans £4,000, current liabilities £6,000, fixed assets £12,500, current assets £15,000.

3.5
Capital (a), (b), (f), (g), (h). Revenue (c), (d), (e), (i), (j). Some apportionment of (e) and (h) may be necessary.

3.6
Balance sheet totals £10,512, viz.: capital £3,439, long-term loans £5,000, current liabilities £2,073, fixed assets £4,270, current assets £6,242.

359

3.7

Balance sheet totals £14,860, viz.: capital £8,720 (introduced £6,000, profit £4,010 less drawings £1,290), long-term loans £3,000, current liabilities £3,140, fixed assets £9,075, current assets £5,785.

4.1

Totals. Bank £1,170, cash £250. Balances, bank £473 (dr.), cash £40 (dr.).

4.2

Totals. Bank £1,280, cash £290. Balances, bank £762 (dr.), cash £55 (dr.).

4.3

Totals. Discount allowed £104, discount received £21, bank £1,616, cash £400. Balances, bank £357 (dr.), cash £100 (dr.). Ledger accounts, discount allowed £104 (dr.), discount received £21 (cr.).

4.4

Totals. Discount allowed £150, discount received £54, bank £2,126, cash £216. Balances, bank £1,445 (dr.), cash £109 (dr.). Ledger accounts, discount allowed £150 (dr.), discount received £54 (cr.).

4.5

Totals. Discounts allowed £49, discount received £26, bank £933, cash £294. Balances, bank £312 (cr.), cash £99 (dr.). Ledger accounts, discount allowed £49 (dr.), discount received £26 (cr.).

4.6

Totals. Receipts £50, payments totals £45, postage and stationery £10, travelling expenses £11, motor expenses £13, sundries £11. Closing balance £5.

4.7

Totals. Receipts £110, payments total £97, postages and stationery £18, travelling expenses £26, cleaning £21, sundries £14, ledger £18. Closing balance £13. Imprest cheque required £47.

4.8

Totals 6th July. Receipts £50. Total payments £33, postages and stationery £9, travelling expenses £8, motor expenses £6, office expenses £10. Closing balance £17.

Totals 13th July. Receipts £50 (including £33 imprest cheque). Total payments £39, postages and stationery £9, motor expenses £3, office expenses £11, travelling expenses £16. Closing balance £11. Amount required to make up imprest £39.

5.1

Corrected cash book balance £724 + £45 − £15 = £754. Bank statement £914 − £280 + £120 = £754.

5.2
Corrected cash book balance £550 + £35 − £5 − £12 − £18 = £550. Bank statement £438 + £225 − £113.

5.3
Corrected cash book balance £247 + £50 + £90 + £90 − £27 − £83 = £367. Bank statement £367 − £546 + £79 = £100 overdrawn.

5.4
Bank statement £270 + £500 − £94 = £676. Cash book original balance £676 + £8 + £22 = £706.

5.5
Corrected cash book balance £3,642 + £85 − £45 − £125 − £25 = £3,532. Bank statement £3,532 + £3,240 − £2,200 = £4,572.

5.6
Bank statement £950 + £360 − £750 = £560. Cash book original balance £560 + £120 + £18 − £140 − £60 − £14 = £484.

5.7
Corrected cash book balance £270 + £18 − £9 = £279. Bank statement £288 + £71 − £14 − £37 − £29 = £279.

6.1
Credit balances J. Lynch £442, F. Hurst £247, J. Wilson £111, D. Barnett £132, B. Baxter £58, D. Mortimer £108. Debit balance purchases £1,098.

6.2
Debit balances J. Edwards £541, L. Vale £188, R. Stuart £323, K. Hill £102, S. Webb £254, B. Charles £181. Credit balance sales £1,589.

6.3
Day book totals. Sales £620, purchases £710, returns outwards £182, returns inwards £98. Debit balances B. Long £207, S. Ward £133, C. Stone £121, G. Tombs £61, purchases £710, returns inwards £98. Credit balances F. Riley £82, T. Short £176, L. Lewis £147, B. Read £123, sales £620, returns outwards £182.

6.4
Day book totals. Sales £1,230, purchases £825, returns outwards £126, returns inwards £128. Debit balances J. Swaine £419, E. Short £328, N. Sands £277, L. Scott £78, purchases £825, returns inwards £128. Credit balances O. Reece £253, D. Poole £301, S. Pearce £103, E. Moore £42, sales £1,230, returns outwards £126.

6.5
Ledger balances debit—bank £566, cash £95, stationery £15, purchases £520, W. Tapper £130, wages £160, J. Webb £120, returns inwards £57, drawings

361

£50, stock £175. Credit balances—capital £800, C. Monk £116, sales £555, returns outwards £77, B. Lee £165. Gross profit £230, net profit £55. Balance sheet totals £1,086—capital £805, creditors £281, current assets £1,086.

6.6
Ledger balances debit—bank £9, cash £10, purchases £821, shop fittings £560, rent £36, W. Spence £84, P. Barrow £262, V. Strong £201, returns inwards £82, sundries £15, wages £125, stock £200, drawings £60. Credit balances—capital £750, J. Wild £298, sales £1,014, returns outwards £37, A. Knott £166. Gross profit £348, net profit £172. Balance sheet totals £1,326—capital £862, current liabilities £464, fixed assets £560, current assets £766.

7.1
Profit and loss cr. £3,960. Rent received account £4,320. Balances £150 dr., £180 cr.

7.2
Profit and loss dr. rent £2,000, rates £950. Rent and rates account, totals £3,920. Balance £610 dr.

7.3
Profit and loss dr. £807, lighting and heating account, totals £902. Balances £52 dr., £92 cr.

7.4
Profit and loss account, gross profit £5,926, net profit £3,376. Balance sheet totals £5,646, capital £5,160, current liabilities £486, fixed assets £480, current assets £5,166.

7.5
Profit and loss account, gross profit £32,590, net profit £16,849. Balance sheet totals £44,756, capital £32,649, current liabilities £12,107, fixed assets £10,150, current assets £34,606.

7.6
Profit and loss account, net profit £4,311. Balance sheet totals £13,242, capital £10,541, current liabilities £2,701, fixed assets £6,580, current assets £6,662.

8.1
Machinery account balances: 19x1 £1,600, 19x2 £4,800, 19x3 £4,800, 19x4 £4,200. Depreciation account balances: (a) 19x1 £160, 19x2 £640, 19x3 £1,120, 19x4 £1,340. (b) 19x1 £320, 19x2 £1,216, 19x3 £1,932, 19x4 £2,098. Disposals (a) loss £100, (b) profit £60.

8.2
Machinery account totals £34,600, balance dr. £22,000. Depreciation account

totals £7,680, balance cr. £5,160, transfer to profit and loss account £3,680. Disposals account totals £12,600, loss £2,780.

8.3
Yearly transfer profit and loss account £1,448. Balances cr. sinking fund, dr. sinking fund investment account Year 1 £1,448, Year 2 £2,968, Year 3 £4,564, Year 4 £6,240, Year 5 £8,000.

8.4
Machinery account totals £104,000, balance dr. £92,000. Machinery depreciation account totals £43,800, balance £37,800 cr., transfer profit and loss £9,200. Loss on disposal £1,000. Motor vehicles account totals £19,800, balance £15,800 dr. Motor vehicle depreciation account totals £10,228, balance £7,915, transfer profit and loss account £2,628. Profit on disposal £13.

8.5
Vehicle register written down values: (1) £675, (3) £675, (4) £675, (5) £675, (6) £1,125, (7) £1,125. Revised values (1) £760, (3) £760, (4) £800, (5) £800, (6) £1,240, (7) £1,240. Motor vehicles account: 19x4 £4,800, 19x5 £5,600, 19x6 £8,600. Depreciation account: 19x4 £1,200, 19x5 £2,000, 19x6 £3,650. Loss on disposals £100. Adjustment necessary on 1st January, 19x7, £650 depreciation written back.

8.6
(1) Year 1 £375, Year 2 £750, Year 3 £1,125, Year 4 £1,500.
(2) Year 1 £800, Year 2 £1,200, Year 3 £1,400, Year 4 £1,500 (rate 50%).
(3) Year 1 £348, Year 2 £715, Year 3 £1,099, Year 4 £1,500 (profit and loss account debit £348).

8.7
Original depreciation machinery: 19x1 £400, 19x2 £400, 19x3 £400; motor vehicles: 19x1 £3,000, 19x2 £3,000, 19x3 £3,000. Revised depreciation machinery: 19x1 £640, 19x2 £560, 19x3 £490; motor vehicles: 19x1 £6,400, 19x2 £4,800, 19x3 £3,600. Revised profits; 19x1 £2,280, 19x2 £4,350, 19x3 £5,684.

9.1
Provision doubtful debts balances: 19x2 £600, 19x3 £500, 19x4 £700. Discount allowed totals: 19x2 £2,948, 19x3 £3,240, 19x4 £4,516.

	19x3	19x4	19x5
Profit and loss account entries	£	£	£
Discounts	2,948 dr.	3,012 dr.	4,326 dr.
Bad debts	600 dr.	700 dr.	300 dr.
Provision doubtful debts	600 dr.	100 cr.	200 dr.

9.2
Provision doubtful debts totals £804, balance £674 cr., transfer profit and loss

363

account £130. Balance sheet debtors £12,074 less provision £674, net amount £11,400.

9.3
Gross profit £25,440, net profit £13,178. Balance sheet totals £41,758, capital £31,338, current liabilities £10,420, fixed assets £17,100, current assets £24,658.

9.4
Adjusted profit £6,980. Balance sheet totals £35,980, capital £26,980, current liabilities £9,000, fixed assets £16,630, current assets £19,350.

9.5
Provision doubtful debts balances: 19x5 £420, 19x6 £560, 19x7 £500, 19x8 £600. Transfers profit and loss account bad debts: 19x5 £3,200, 19x6 £1,600, 19x7 £2,200, 19x8 £1,800. Provision doubtful debts: 19x5 £420, 19x6 £140, 19x7 £60 cr., 19x8 £100.

9.6
Gross profit £26,000, net profit £6,945. Balance sheet totals £45,975, capital £33,745, loan £2,400, current liabilities £9,830, fixed assets £16,300, current assets £29,675.

10.1
Lowest £6,610. Highest £6,900.

10.2
(a) £9,600, £13,600. (b) £6,400, £10,400. (c) £8,800, £12,800.

10.3
(a) £137·50, £275. (b) £125, £262·50. (c) £137·50, £275.

10.4
(a) £11,000 reduced to £9,000. (b) £9,000. (c) £10,500 reduced to £9,000.

10.5
Leasehold premises £4,300, depreciation £1,720, motor vehicle £625, depreciation £500, stock £2,760, debtors £4,040, provision doubtful debts £240, provision discounts £38. Total £9,227.

10.6
Adjusted profit £6,000 less £600, £125, £500, £150, £50, £155, £30, plus £100 equals £4,490. Balance sheet capital £12,490, current liabilities £3,230, fixed assets £7,775, current assets £7,945. Totals £15,720.

11.1
Debit realisation account £8,300. Credit office fittings £2,000, motor vehicles £1,500, stock £3,000, debtors £1,800. Debit cash £10,000. Credit realisation

account £10,000. Debit realisation account £1,700, credit capital £1,700. Debit capital £9,700, creditors £1,000, credit cash £10,700.
Debit office fittings £2,000, motor vehicles £1,500, stock £3,000, debtors £1,800, goodwill £1,700, credit cash £10,000. Debit cash £10,000, credit capital £10,000.

11.2
Profit on realisation £1,300, cash paid to V. Blank £6,500. Balance sheet J. Dash. Capital £8,000, creditors £800, goodwill £1,560, office fittings £1,150, motor vehicles £900, stock £1,750, debtors £1,500, less provision £60, cash £2,000.

11.3
Debits: Rates in advance £300, repairs £8, suspense £100, creditors £50, discount received £30, suspense £150. Credits: Suspense £300, purchases £8, purchases £100, returns outwards £50, creditors £30, rents received £75, rents paid £75. Suspense account: debits £50, £100, £150; credit £300, rates.

11.4
Adjusted profit £2,500 plus £130, minus £400, £35, equals £2,195. Credit side larger by £405.

11.5
Adjusted profit £6,152 plus £34, £80, £87, £87, £120, £120, £370, minus £43, £120, equals £6,887. Debit side greater by £775.

11.6
Debits: Purchases £1,750, suspense account £572, debtors £45, creditors £260, suspense account £1,880. Credits: Creditors £1,750, bank £572, bad debts £45, purchases £260, returns inwards £940, returns outwards £940.

11.7
Debits: debtors £250, returns inwards £240, stock £160, suspense account £130, sales £175, debtors £27, loss on sale £10, depreciation £45. Credits: suspense £250, debtors £240, profit and loss stock £160, accrued electricity £65, prepaid electricity £65, debtors £175, suspense account £27, fixtures £55. Adjusted profit £2,235. Balance sheet: capital £2,735, current liabilities £2,704, fixed assets £1,069, current assets £4,370. Totals £5,439.

12.1
Totals £36,145, balances debit £40, credit £6,100.

12.2
Totals £175,550, balances debit £16,610, credit £90.

12.3
Debtors: control totals £77,660, balances debit £6,080, credit £100.
Creditors: control totals £58,375, balances debit £75, credit £9,555.

12.4

Debtors: control totals £118,950, balances debit £6,330, credit £20.
Creditors: control totals £92,820, balances debit £40, credit £4,720.

12.5

Creditors: control totals £9,127 balance credit £8,627, adjusted balances £8,420 plus £120, £150 less £45, £18, equals £8,627.

12.6

Debtors: control original totals £103,500, debit balance £8,400. Adjusted balance £8,260. List of balances £7,990 plus £90, £120, £100 less £40, equals £8,260.

12.7

Debtors control totals £12,490, balance debit £11,510. Total sales ledger balances £11,510. Creditors control total £7,810, balance credit £7,310. Total purchase ledger balances £6,992 plus £300, £18 equals £7,310.

13.1

Gross profit £16,344, net profit £4,276. Balance sheet capital £25,956, current liabilities £4,016, fixed assets £18,520, current assets £11,452.

13.2

Gross profit £4,052, net profit £1,970. Balance sheet capital £16,430, current liabilities £1,126, fixed assets £11,500, current assets £6,056.

13.3

Gross profit £41,530, net profit £9,365. Balance sheet capital £56,925, current liabilities £25,275, fixed assets £34,000, current assets £48,200.

13.4

Opening balance £1,000, add profits £9,200, loan £1,500, less office fittings £2,000, working capital £5,200, drawings £3,000. Closing balance £1,500.

13.5

Opening balance £2,000 cr., add furniture £2,000, working capital £2,500, drawings £3,000, less profits £6,600, cash from disposal £400. Closing balance £2,500 cr.

13.6

Opening balance £2,000, add loan £2,000, cash from disposal £250, working capital £2,000, less loss £2,750, drawings £2,500. Closing balance £1,000.

13.7

Opening balance £9,920 cr., add loan £5,000, drawings £3,000 less profit £8,400, sale property £7,500, working capital £6,660. Closing balance £4,640.

14.1

Appropriation account debits: salaries Clarke £1,500, Hughes £1,000, interest on capital Clarke £1,000, Charlton £1,200, Hughes £800. Balance: Charlton £1,500, Clarke £1,000, Hughes £500. Current account balances: Charlton £300 dr., Clarke £750 cr., Hughes £100 cr.

14.2

Appropriation account debits: salaries Percy £2,000, George £1,000; interest on capital Ronald £500, Percy £300, George £200. Balances: Ronald £2,400, Percy £2,400, George £1,200. Current account balances: Ronald £2,600, Percy £4,400, George £3,000.

14.3

Appropriation account debits: salary Bird £1,000; interest on capital: Fish £475, Fowl £475, Bird £250; balance: Fish £1,070, Fowl £1,070, Bird £535. Credits—interest on drawings: Fish £30, Fowl £25, Bird £20. Current account balances: Fish £85 dr., Fowl £120 cr., Bird £365 cr. Capital accounts: Fish £9,000, Fowl £10,000, Bird £6,000.

14.4

Appropriation account debits—interest on capitals: High £480, Wide £230. Short £115; salary Short £134. Balances: High £603, Wide £402, Short £201. Current account balances: High £1,083, Wide £632, Short £450.

14.5

Gross profit £24,014, net profit £2,670. Balance sheet totals £28,618. Capital accounts: Smith £16,000, Jones £12,000; current accounts Smith £418, Jones £200; fixed assets £15,880; current assets £12,738.

14.6

Gross profit £50,668, net profit £16,002. Balance sheet totals £124,002. Capital accounts: Spence £34,000, Marks £26,000; current accounts: Spence £10,101, Marks £6,401; loan Spence £8,000; current liabilities £39,500; fixed assets £53,100; current assets £70,902.

14.7

Current account balances 31st December, 19x1: Charles £3,700 cr., George £1,300 cr., Henry £100 dr. Adjustment: Charles £200 dr., Henry £200 cr. Balances 31st December, 19x2: Charles £1,800 cr., George £100 dr., Henry £1,000 dr.

15.1

(a) Clark £8,400, Davies £4,200, Eccles £5,000.
(b) Clark £5,400, Davies £2,700, Eccles £3,500.
(The amount due to Brunt remains unchanged at £8,400.)

15.2

Cash to be introduced Greer £1,400, Hatton £4,900, Ince £4,200.

15.3
(a) King £2,000, Knox Nil.
(b) King £8,000, Knox £4,000.

15.4
(a) £34,200, (b) £27,750, (c) £22,500.

15.5
(a) Capital account: Blaze £5,200, Flare £4,400, Flicker £2,700; creditors £5,600, goodwill £5,000, fittings £1,000, motor vehicle £800, stock £4,000, debtors £5,400, cash £1,700.
(b) Capital accounts: Blaze £3,200, Flare £2,400, Flicker £1,700. All other items as in (a) except for elimination of goodwill.

15.6
(a) Chadwick: debit goodwill £6,000, cash £3,000, credit balance £10,000, goodwill £8,000. Cowan: debit goodwill £6,000, credit balance £6,000, goodwill £8,000, cash £1,000. Cross: debit goodwill £6,000, credit balance £8,000, goodwill £4,000, cash £3,000. Doolan: debit goodwill £2,000, credit cash £5,000.
(b) Capital accounts: Chadwick, Cowan and Cross £9,000 each, Doolan £3,000, creditors £3,000, assets £22,000, cash £11,000.

16.1
Realisation account totals £9,000, loss £850. Cash account totals £10,800. Creditors account totals £5,500. Capital accounts totals: Torr £4,000, Vase £3,000. Cash paid to Torr £2,690, to Vase £2,660.

16.2
Realisation account totals £53,810, profit £3,150. Cash account totals £48,760. Creditors account totals £20,000. Capital accounts totals: Taylor £24,100, Turner £15,050. Cash paid to Taylor £14,100, to Turner £15,050.

16.3
Realisation account totals £43,035, profit £25. Cash account totals £35,825. Creditors account totals £4,500, loan account totals £6,000. Capital accounts totals: Lee £14,010, Mee £11,005, Ray £29,275. Cash paid: Lee £14,010, Mee £11,005, overdraft taken over by Ray £19,665.

16.4
E's loss £540 (£600 −£60) transferred A £180, B £120, C £120, D £120. B's loss £84 (£120 −£36) transferred A £36, C £24, D £24. Cash paid A £3,784, C £4,856, D £3,056. Total £11,696 (£11,600 + £60 + £36).

16.5
Realisation account totals £10,800, loss £2,400. Cash account totals £8,900. Creditors account totals £2,000. Capital accounts: Roberts balance £300

transferred Radford £200, Richards £100. Cash paid: Radford £4,550, Richards £2,050.

16.6
Realisation accounts profits: £800 Paton and Prescott, £770 Price. Balance sheet—capital account Paton £5,400, Prescott £3,400, Price £3,370, current liabilities £900, fixed assets £8,200, current assets £4,870.

16.7
Realisation accounts profits: £4,100 Slight and Slater, £2,400 Ryan and Rowley. Capital accounts old firms: Slight £5,050, Slater £5,050, Ryan £4,600, Rowley £2,300. Balance sheet new firm—property £5,000, fixtures £1,600, stock £3,900, debtors £1,600, bank £400. Capital accounts: Slight £2,950, Slater £2,950, Ryan £3,200, Rowley £900, creditors £2,500.

17.1
19x3 profit £2,465. 19x4 loss £455, 19x5 profit £5,480.

17.2
Profits: 19x7 £7,550, 19x8 £1,400, 19x9 £11,150. Capital account balances: A £8,030, B £6,130, C £3,120, D £1,620.

17.3
Profit £665. Capital account £1,747, i.e. £2,282 + £665 − £1,200.

17.4
Gross profit £7,410, net profit £5,000. Balance sheet—capital £11,780, current liabilities £2,160, fixed assets £3,600, current assets £10,340. Totals £13,940.

17.5
Gross profit £25,560, net profit £8,820. Balance sheet capitals: Parke £4,000, Scott £4,000; current accounts: Parke £690, Scott £710; current liabilities £20,306; fixed assets £4,366; current assets £25,340. Totals £29,706.

17.6
Gross profit £17,920, net profit £10,654. Balance sheet: capital £9,878, current liabilities £3,892, fixed assets £2,000, current assets £11,770. Totals £13,770.

17.7
(a) £1,240.
(b) Gross profit £7,040, net profit £2,740. Balance sheet: capital £8,180, current liabilities £860, fixed assets £3,500, current assets £5,540. Totals £9,040.

17.8
Gross profit/sales 1/7th. Insurance claim £5,422.

17.9
(a) Claim £4,405 stock, £725 cash, total £5,130.
(b) Gross profit £5,379, net profit £1,179. Balance sheet: capital £10,329,

current liabilities £3,295, fixed assets £1,200, current assets £12,424. Totals £13,624.

17.10

(a) Claim £450 stock, £316 cash. Total £766.
(b) Gross profit £5,420, net profit £1,650. Balance sheet: capital £5,310, current liabilities £6,736, fixed assets £800, current assets £11,246. Totals £12,046.

18.1

Surplus £92. Balance sheet reserve £1,573, current liabilities £117, fixed assets £1,350, current assets £340. Totals £1,690.

18.2

Bar profit £16,898, surplus £3,496. Balance sheet: reserve £13,646, current liabilities £4,538, fixed assets £13,550, current assets £4,634. Totals £18,184.

18.3

Bar profit £1,700, surplus £446. Balance sheet: reserve £1,945, current liabilities £688, fixed assets £1,200, current assets £1,433. Totals £2,633.

18.4

Bar profit £700, deficit £345. Balance sheet: reserve £670, current liabilities £295, fixed assets £560, current assets £405. Totals £965.

18.5

Bar profit £2,500, deficit £148. Balance sheet: reserve £11,449, current liabilities £1,465, fixed assets £10,800, current assets £2,114. Totals £12,914.

18.6

Receipts and payments account totals £17,616, balance £828 dr. Income and expenditure deficit £151. Balance sheet: long-term loans £7,000, current liabilities £894, fixed assets £6,600, current assets £1,143, reserve £151 dr. Totals £7,894.

19.1

(a) (1) £36,000, (2) £48,000, (3) 5x, (4) 25%.
(b) Sales £60,000, opening stock £7,850, purchases £57,300, closing stock £10,150, gross profit £15,000.

19.2

(a) Gross profit £10,000, net profit £1,000.
(b) Increase of £1,000.

19.3

(a) Gross profit £25,000, net profit £7,500.
(b) Gross profit £33,000, net profit £11,000.

19.4

Increase from 12x to 16x.

19.5

(1) 33⅓, (2) 20%, (3) 60%, (4) 2·4, (5) 1·4.

19.6

Stronger "A" proprietorship ratio, working capital, acid test, gross profit percentage.
Stronger "B" returns on capital, return on assets, net profit percentage.

19.7

Sales £165,000, purchases £135,000, closing stock £15,000, gross profit £45,000, expenses £30,000, net profit £15,000.
Balance sheet: capital account £60,000, long-term loan £20,000, creditors £30,000, fixed assets £50,000, stock £15,000, debtors £33,000, cash £12,000. Totals £110,000.

20.1

Prime cost £112,500, factory cost £132,300, cost of finished goods £129,300. Gross profit £28,700, net profit £6,900.

20.2

Prime cost £576,000, factory cost £661,500, cost of finished goods £658,500. Gross profit £174,000, net profit £86,600.

20.3

Prime cost £110,500, factory cost £142,900, factory profit £31,600. Gross profit £36,000, net profit £27,700.

20.4

Prime cost £96,650, factory cost £114,850, factory profit £15,950. Gross profit £26,100, net profit £26,050.

20.5

Prime cost £56,850, factory cost £71,525, cost of finished goods £71,675. Gross profit £27,725, net profit £12,200. Balance sheet: capital £69,050, current liabilities £13,200, fixed assets £44,500, current assets £37,750. Totals £82,250.

20.6

Prime cost £111,500, factory cost £158,832, cost of finished goods £58,532. Gross profit £41,688, net profit £18,160. Balance sheet: capital £73,520, current liabilities £25,000, fixed assets £42,600, current assets £55,920. Totals £98,520.

20.7

(1) Year 1 loss £900, Year 2 profit £2,200, Year 3 profit £5,400.
(2) Year 1 profit £300, Year 2 £2,360, Year 3 profit £4,040.

21.1
Joint venture account totals £1,170, profit £336 (in both books). In Blue's books Gold's account totals £570, in Gold's books Blue's account totals £727. Gold pays Blue £127.

21.2
Memorandum joint venture account totals £1,099, profit £320. In Jones' books—joint venture with Robinson totals £795, debit balance £195. In Robinson's books—joint venture with Jones totals £499, credit balance £195.

21.3
Joint venture account totals £3,800, profit £980 (in both books). In Adam's books Lever's account totals £1,700, in Lever's books Adam's account totals £2,480. Lever pays Adam £80.

21.4
Memorandum joint venture account totals £6,100, profit £1,350. In Old's books—joint venture with Young totals £2,710, debit balance £510. In Young's books—joint venture with Old totals £3,900, credit balance £510.

21.5
Joint venture account totals £3,150, profit £1,380. Rough's account totals £2,650, balance credit £1,900.

21.6
Joint venture account totals £1,350, profit £400. Wilson's account totals £805, Heath's account totals £259. West has to pay Wilson £705, Heath £259.

22.1
Consignment outwards Thompson: totals £2,655, profit £248, debit balance £555 stock, W. Thompson account totals £2,100, balance £133 dr.

22.2
(a) Account sales—sales £5,300, less expenses £140, less commission £318, net due £1,842.
(b) Consignment outwards Turner; totals £7,784, profit £1,176, debit balance stock £2,484, Turner's account totals £5,300, balance £1,842 dr.
(c) Consignment inwards Torrence: totals £5,300, balance £1,842 cr.

22.3
Consignment outwards Naylor: totals £1,650, profit £430, balance stock £450 dr., Naylor's account totals £1,200, cash remittance £1,055.

22.4
(a) Account sales—sales £4,600, expenses £1,075, commission £276, net due £3,249.
(b) Consignment inwards Rowland, totals £4,600.

22.5
Consignment outwards Williams: profits 30th November £225, 31st December £565, stock value 30th November, £1,837·50. Williams account: balance 30th November £125 dr., cash remittance 31st December £2,527·50.

22.6
Consignment outwards Taylor: profits 31st March £548, 30th September £430, stock at 31st March £1,800. Taylor's account: balance 31st March £184 dr., cash remittance 30th September £2,414.

23.1
S. Brady totals £300, T. Hope totals £500. Bills receivable £800, discounting charges £7 dr., F. Glynn totals £350, W. Ellis totals £150. Bills payable £150 cr.

23.2
J. Crooke totals £910, bills receivable balance £460 dr., P. Flint totals £900, interest received £6 cr.

23.3
J. Nicklin balance £104 dr. Bills receivable totals £600, P. Roche totals £954.

23.4
Butters balance £600 dr. Bills receivable totals £600, Duncan balance £200 cr., discount on bills £8 dr.

23.5
Bills receivable account totals £2,307, debtors control account totals £115,983, balance £20,964 dr.

23.6
Paul's ledger: Anthony totals £1,513, bills payable balance £683 cr., noting and interest charges £13 dr. Anthony's ledger: Paul totals £1,513, bills receivable balance £683 dr., interest received account £5.

24.1
(a) Gross profits: gardening £16,000, household £28,000, maintenance £16,000. Net profit £5,400.
(b) Contributions: gardening £6,000, household £16,000, maintenance £10,400.

24.2
Gross profits: wines and spirits £25,750, tobacco and cigarettes £28,300. Net profit £18,550.

24.3
Gross profits: groceries £18,000, fruit and vegetables £13,500, meat £10,500. Net profits: groceries £7,150, fruit and vegetables £3,780, meat £1,910.

373

24.4

Gross profits: papers £4,000, sweets £4,800. Net profits: papers £1,965, sweets £1,365. Balance sheet: capital £12,610, current liabilities £1,200, fixed assets £5,360, current assets £8,450. Totals £13,810.

24.5

Gross profits: radios £22,000, bicycles £24,500. Net profits: radios £10,678, bicycles £13,932. Balance sheet: capital £40,860, current liabilities £1,800, fixed assets £19,500, current assets £23,160. Totals £42,660.

24.6

Gross profits: sales £2,660, service £4,000. Net profits: sales £388, service £2,542.

25.1

Application and allotment account totals £60,000, capital account balance £100,000 cr., share premium account £20,000 cr. 1st call account totals £40,000, final call account totals £20,000. Balance sheet: share capital issued £100,000, share premium £20,000, cash £120,000.

25.2

Application and allotment account totals £78,750, capital account balance £100,000 cr., share premium account £25,000 cr. balance, 1st call account totals £25,000, final call account totals £25,000. Balance sheet: issued share capital £100,000, share premium account £25,000, cash £125,000.

25.3

Application and allotment account totals £30,000, capital account balance £25,000 cr., share premium account balance £12,500 cr., 1st call account totals £7,500, final call account totals £7,500. Balance sheet: issued share capital £25,000, share premium account £12,500, cash £37,500.

25.4

Application and allotment account totals £55,000, capital account balance £100,000 cr., totals £101,500, 1st call account totals £25,000, forfeited shares account totals £1,500, final call account totals £24,500, forfeited shares reissued account totals £2,500, share premium account balance £500 cr. Balance sheet: issued share capital £100,000, share premium £500, cash £100,500.

25.5

Application and allotment account totals £80,000, capital account totals £100,640, balance £100,000 cr., share premium account balance £20,400 cr., 1st call account totals £20,000, forfeited shares account totals £640, final call account £19,840 total, forfeited shares reissued account total £1,200. Balance sheet: issued share capital £100,000, share premium £20,400, cash £120,400.

25.6

(a) Debit cash £20,000, credit 10% debentures £20,000.

(b) Debit cash £21,000, credit 10% debentures £20,000, debenture premium £1,000.

(c) Debit cash £18,000, debenture discount £2,000, credit 10% debentures £20,000.

26.1

Authorised share capital £220,000, paid-up capital £130,000, capital reserves £12,000, revenue reserves £16,000, long-term liabilities £20,000, current liabilities £13,100, fixed assets £136,000, current assets £55,100.

26.2

Gross profit £83,910, net profit £26,394, unappropriated profit £19,494, authorised capital £150,000, paid-up capital £95,000, capital reserves £15,000, revenue reserves £40,694, long-term liabilities £20,000, current liabilities £33,970, fixed assets £122,000, current assets £82,664.

26.3

Gross profit £60,310, net profit £28,740, unappropriated profit £36,240, authorised capital £200,000, paid-up capital £150,000, revenue reserve £36,240, long-term liabilities £37,500, current liabilities £38,850, fixed assets £197,000, current assets £65,590.

26.4

Unappropriated profit £6,080. Authorised capital £250,000, paid-up capital £160,000, capital reserve £16,500, revenue reserve £31,080, long-term liabilities £12,000, current liabilities £16,400, fixed assets £104,600, investments £48,700, current assets £82,680.

26.5

Gross profit £80,000, net profit £22,240, unappropriated profit £21,540, authorised and issued capital £200,000, revenue reserves £21,540, long-term liabilities £50,000, current liabilities £43,250, fixed assets £247,200, current assets £67,590.

26.6

Net profit £2,820, unappropriated profit £13,500, authorised and issued capital £60,000, capital reserve £12,000, revenue reserves £16,500, long-term liabilities £12,000, current liabilities £24,190, fixed assets £53,200, current assets £70,140, fictitious assets £1,350.

26.7

Gross profit £34,500, net profit £10,950, unappropriated profit £27,380. Authorised capital £50,000, paid-up capital £39,000, capital reserve £10,000, revenue reserves £30,380, long-term liabilities £10,000, current liabilities £23,120, fixed assets £48,500, investments £9,000, current assets £55,000.

Additional Questions

1. "Accounting is a practical matter of recording financial transactions." Why, then, is it necessary to enforce certain concepts and conventions?

2. Cash and trade discounts are items allowed to purchasers of goods. Explain what each is, and their treatment in the accounts.

3. The trial balance does not prove that all entries are correct. What types of errors are not disclosed by the trial balance and what steps can be taken to discover these errors?

4. What is a balance sheet? Explain why assets and liabilities are grouped under several distinct headings.

5. Explain the purposes of preparing a trading and profit and loss account. Can it be stated that the profit and loss account ever shows the correct profit for a particular period?

6. The ledger is regarded as being the prime accounting book. Why is it therefore considered necessary to open additional books?

7. Define "depreciation" with regard to fixed assets. What factors must be considered when choosing a particular method to apply to a specific type of asset?

8. Explain briefly what you understand by (a) FIFO and (b) LIFO. What effect does each have on the revenue accounts and balance sheet of a business?

9. A manufacturing company may alter its profits considerably without contravening the accepted concepts. Explain how this can be done in the area of finished goods and work in progress valuations.

10. What benefits are achieved by presenting final accounts in vertical form?

11. Define a cash-flow statement. In what ways does a flow statement complement the final accounts?

12. In a great many businesses control accounting is regarded as a necessity. Outline the advantages to be gained by incorporating such a system within the accounting records.

13. In the absence of a partnership agreement, what rulings affect the partners in respect of the accounts?

14. It is dangerous to diagnose business ailments merely by reference to figures in the balance sheet. Although ratio analysis is accepted, what factors must be taken into account before reaching any conclusions?

15. Define the following terms and state the composition of each: (a) prime cost, (b) factory cost, (c) cost of finished goods.

16. Discuss the accounts necessary to record transactions in the books of (a) a consignor and (b) a consignee.

17. Define the following terms in the context of negotiable instruments: (a) bill of exchange, (b) a holder, (c) discounting a bill, (d) noting a bill.

18. What are the purposes of compiling departmental accounts? Does a loss in one department necessarily infer that the department should be closed down?

19. Compare the advantages and disadvantages of forming: (a) a sole traders business, (b) a partnership, (c) a limited company.

20. Detail the types of shares that can be issued by a limited company and discuss the rights and drawbacks of each.

Source of Answers for Additional Questions

1. Introduction, Chapters 7, 8, 9.
2. Chapter 4.
3. Chapters 3, 5, 6, 12, 19.
4. Chapters 3, 19.
5. Chapters 2, 7, 8, 9, 10.
6. Chapters 4, 7.
7. Chapter 8.
8. Chapter 10.
9. Introduction, Chapter 10.
10. Chapters 13, 19.
11. Chapter 13.
12. Chapter 12.
13. Chapter 14.
14. Chapter 19.
15. Chapter 20.
16. Chapter 22.
17. Chapter 23.
18. Chapter 24.
19. Chapters 14, 25, 26.
20. Chapter 25.

Index